Successful Homebuilding and Remodeling

Real-Life Advice for Getting the House You Want Without the Roof (or Sky) Falling In

Barbara B. Buchholz and Margaret Crane

Real Estate Education Company®
a division of Dearborn Financial Publishing, Inc.

Acquisitions Editors: Danielle Egan-Miller and Jean Iversen
Managing Editor: Jack Kiburz
Project Editor: Trey Thoelcke
Interior Design: Lucy Jenkins
Cover Design: DePinto Studios
Typesetting: Elizabeth Pitts

Published by Real Estate Education Company,® a division of Dearborn Financial Publishing, Inc.®

Library of Congress Cataloging-in-Publication Data

Buchholz, Barbara Ballinger.
    Successful homebuilding and remodeling : real-life advice for getting the house you want without the roof (or the sky) falling in / by Barbara B. Buchholz and Margaret Crane.
      p. cm.
    Includes bibliographical references and index.
    ISBN 0-7931-2883-8
    1. House construction—Amateurs' manuals. 2. Dwellings—Remodeling—Amateurs' manuals. 3. Building—Superintendence—Amateurs' manuals. 4. Contractors—Selection and appointment—Amateurs' manuals. I. Crane, Margaret. II. Title.
TH4812.B82   1999
690′.837—dc21   98-34007
                                               CIP

DEDICATION

To our families, whom we still love and live with despite our many remodelings and planned building projects

Contents

Preface

Write about what's right under your nose, an editor once told us. So, that's what we've done. This book is derived directly from our experiences remodeling several houses with our respective husbands, Ed Buchholz and Nolan Crane, and from the incident Barbara and Ed had while contemplating building a house.

We're far from alone in our desire to improve our surroundings. Owning and fixing up a house on your own land, no matter how small, remains firmly entrenched in the American dream. Some people want bigger closets, an updated eat-in kitchen, or a fourth bedroom, or they crave a house in a different school district or one that's closer to their workplace. Some even opt for intelligent homes, which are prewired for fully integrated home electronics control systems. These are and will continue to be the homes of the millennium.

More than 1.161 million people built a single family home in 1997, according to the National Association of Home Builders (NAHB) in Washington, D.C. About 745,000 of those houses were built by developers on speculation, which means that the houses were not built for specific buyers. The remaining 332,000 were built by homeowners who hired an architect, a builder or contractor, or a design-build group.

Of the 110 million housing units in this country, both rental and owner-occupied, 50 percent are remodeled every year with an average price tag of $2,200, according to Paul Deffenbaugh, editor of *Remodeling* magazine. More than $130 billion was spent on remodeling in 1997 in this country, up a staggering $5 billion from the year before, according to the latest figures from the National Association of the Remodeling Industry (NARI), the industry's largest trade association.

Those dollars were spent by diverse groups, each with its own goals: Generation Xers remodeled smaller, older homes; Baby Boomers sought convenience and comfort, sometimes sparing no expense to relax, entertain, or cook; and mature homeowners wanted their houses to be more efficient and comfortable, including universal design features for their safety.

Because a house is likely to be your largest lifetime investment, the route you take and all the decisions you make should be carefully deliberated. Neither task is for the faint of heart. Each demands detailed scrutiny and constant decision making, and the process can take a year—or more, as we discovered.

From our successes and disappointments, we gleaned a long litany of do's and don'ts, such as checking references thoroughly because incompetent work-staff and an owner's change orders can quickly derail a timetable, and bringing in additional experts when a design gets complicated or goes awry.

While putting together our newfound knowledge, we discovered the absence of an informative, fun-to-read book on remodeling and building that would have taken us through the process—from first deciding where to live to contemplating making a few changes, borrowing money to get the job done, moving, and settling in so that our houses go through what writer Sally Quinn Bradlee describes as the transformation from a house to a lived-in, loved home.

We are delighted to share our wealth of newfound information, based on our mistakes and achievements, as well as suggestions related by experts and individual homeowners. Our goal is to help you learn whom to contact for assistance so you can avoid pitfalls during what should be a laborious yet pleasurable experience.

You'll begin the process with a wish list of everything you want in your dream house. You'll then decide whether to build or remodel (each has pros and cons) and choose the right contractors. You'll also learn how to pick a lot (if you build), how to finance your plans (unless you have so much extra money sitting in your bank account that you can pay cash for the work) how to cut costs without cutting quality (because many bids come in over budget and costs escalate rather than decrease), and how to write a detailed contract (with the help of a real estate agent or attorney, depending on where you live).

You may feel a bit exhausted by now, but your work isn't finished yet. You must also become aware of common disasters you can avoid, learn to read a blue-print so you're not surprised by the end result, develop a realistic time frame with extra time built in for delays (which always occur due to snags with the manufacturer, the shipper or your change orders), and learn all about landscaping. Then you need to find out how to make your home safe, learn when to sign off on the punch list after that final walk-through and approval, move in with the least disruption, figure out how to decorate, and learn 100 ways to make your house the abode of your dreams.

Throughout the book, we've sprinkled some humorous comments from homeowners who've endured the processes. They're among the best sources of advice. We also offer constructive tips at the end of each chapter in the form of lists or quizzes that sum up the information in that chapter.

You'll find sample contracts that you can use as a guide (but ask a professional because no two situations are exactly the same), checklists of questions to ask workers before you hire them and questions to ask yourself if you are a do-it-yourselfer. The charts we included will help you decide what you can afford. There are also useful sketches and blueprints, recent statistics on which remodeling projects offer the largest percentage return on your investment, some wish lists for detailing your dreams, and the names of hundreds of major associations you can consult for advice or use to help you find professionals in your area.

We have tended to use the masculine pronoun (he) for simplicity, but we are fully aware that both women and men remodel and build houses. Even when couples tackle projects together, women often make many of the decisions and oversee the work.

Each of us and our spouses endured some tortuous moments that we equated with our worst nightmares. For Barbara, the experiences were akin to flying in a plane through terrible turbulence; for Margaret they were like racing down the Screaming Eagle. Yet, no matter how discouraged or frustrated we became, and no matter how many times we promised ourselves and our loved ones "never again," we have both lived long enough to know never say never.

Acknowledgments

The material for this book was a good many years in the making, although we did not realize it at the time. We never dreamed that our building and remodeling experiences, as well as our writing assignments on the topic, would lead to this end result. But we felt that a need existed. Many people who talked to us said, "Boy, could I use your book now" or "I wish I had had your book when I was building (remodeling)." Better late than never. We strove to write a fun-to-read, conversational guide filled with helpful tips and real-life advice.

In addition to our own expertise, many people contributed. Our acquisitions editor Danielle Egan-Miller had great faith in our idea. She understood our concept and approach. As a hands-on editor, she worked with us from the start. Every draft of every headline and chapter had the benefit of her scrutiny and suggestions. Even better, she shared our sense of humor as we telephoned and e-mailed regularly, and discussed where we should have our next lunch meeting.

The National Association of Home Builders was an invaluable resource for statistics and trends, and thanks go specifically to Gopal Ahluwalia, Brett Diggs, Allan Freedman, Andy Kochera, Dave Ledford, and Susan Ritter, who is with Smart House, Inc., a national network of home systems dealers and installers.

We regularly talked to a long list of other experts, and extend thanks to them: Joel Albizo with the American Nursery and Landscape Association; Patty Brown of the American Society of Civil Engineers; Paul Deffenbaugh of *Remodeling* magazine; Mike Doyle, with St. Louis County Department of Planning; Dan Dupree of the American Council for Construction Education; Kevin Enke of ISR, Inc.; Gary Garrity of the American Land Title Association; Michael Geary of the Home Builders Institute; Janice Hale of the Hobby Greenhouse Association; Esley Hamilton, historic preservation expert with the St. Louis Department of Parks and Recreation; Kim Horst of Commonwealth Land Title Insurance Company; John Kuzava with RESPA; Susan Maney of the National Remodeling Association; E. Stafford Manion of Gladys Manion, Inc., a St. Louis real estate agency; Keith Rich, president of ISR, Inc.; the St. Louis County Planning Board and Department of Public Works in St. Louis County; Phil Simon of the American Institute of Architects; and Bonnie Van Fleet with the Associated Landscape Contractors of America.

We owe many debts to other associations and institutions, such as the American Lighting Association, the American Society of Interior Designers, the Central Station Alarm Association, the National Burglar and Fire Alarm Association, and the many libraries (and many librarians) who helped us at the St. Louis County Library, the Washington University architecture library, and the Chicago Public Library.

In addition, we profited in a variety of ways from lengthy discussions with Chicago real estate agents Jennifer Ames and Elizabeth Ballis and St. Louis agents Faye Levey and Sherri Miller; St. Louis psychotherapists Barbara Bader, Michaeleen Cradock and John Yunker; insurance agents Jim Baxendale with Missouri General and Stephen Nechtow in Chicago with Baum/Nechtow Ltd.; bankers Rick Bechtel in Chicago and Mary Ellen Raymond in St. Louis; Chicago architects Richard and Nancy Becker, Paul Florian, H. Gary Frank, Allan J. Grant, Greg Maire; St. Louis architects Laurence Meyer, Charles Schragin, and Thomas Yanko; Dean Bordeaux of NewSpace in St. Louis; Dwane Boyer of Music for Pleasure and Charles Martin of Hi-Fi Fo-Fum both in St. Louis; landscape architects in Chicago, Scott Byron and Douglas Hoerr; Bob Cooney, owner of a Chicago waterproofing company; Mike Diehl of Hydro Dynamics in St. Louis; home office gurus and authors, Paul and Sarah Edwards; Louis O. Gropp, editor-in-chief of *House Beautiful* magazine; St. Louis locksmith Brian Hildebrand; Chicago real estate attorneys Steven Holler and Richard Nikchevich; Julie Kennedy of Taylor-Morley; Rob Kerr, St. Louis builder; Chicago builders Roger Mandekick and Orren Pickell; real estate attorney for St. Louis builder Taylor-Morley Bob Meier; decorators Keithley Miller of St. Louis, Marilyn Raines in Springfield, Missouri, Leslie Stern, Eva Quateman and John Robert Wiltgen in Chicago; Cal Nicholson who designs and builds wine cellars; Chicago engineer Jeff Palmer; St. Louis mortgage broker Kerry Rudin; Cliff Saxton of United Van Lines; and Software Plus.

We also wish to thank Marianne Sneider of Palm Springs and Ron Stein with Warner Bros. in Burbank, California, both of whom provided a pipeline to some celebrities whose homebuilding and remodeling stories are featured in the book, and to Deborah Taylor-Johnson, who offered many real estate sources.

Special thanks also go to members of our families. Margaret's immediate family members, son Tommy and husband Nolan who helped contribute ideas for the title and read portions of the book; and her post–college age and college age children Adam and Laura who added their input from afar; to Keith Rothberg, M.D., her brother, and Vinnie Rothberg, her sister, who shared some good anecdotes and helped her find others; to Beatrice Rothberg, Margaret's mother, who contributed ideas and sources; and her sister Mary Anne Rothberg Rowen who gave her help with sources and ideas when needed. To Barbara's husband Ed who lent his legal eye and sense of humor, her daughters Joanna and Lucy who contributed their remembrances of past remodelings, good and bad, and her mother Estelle Ballinger, whose words of advice are always with her: "Keep it low maintenance since you lead such a busy life."

Parts of the book are more accurate because of several people who graciously read early drafts: Elizabeth Ballis, Rick Bechtel, Allan J. Grant, Douglas Hoerr, Roger Mandekick, and Sandra Thomas.

It is also impossible to measure the benefits of conversations we've had with various people who have built or remodeled and shared their successes, horror stories, or lessons learned, which are interspersed in our anecdotes.

If we have forgotten to mention anyone, please excuse our negligence, and know that we truly appreciate your input.

Writers could scarcely ask for a better topic and more cooperative publisher, and we are deeply grateful to those who originally agreed to the need for this type of book and helped make it a reality. We know it will be of great value to anyone undertaking the most expensive and sometimes most frustrating endeavor of their lives—homebuilding and remodeling.

Barbara B. Buchholz and Margaret Crane

PART ONE

Early Decisions

CHAPTER 1

To Build or Not to Build?

George Bernard Shaw once remarked that the United States and Great Britain are two different nations separated by a common mother tongue. Today, he would say the opposite about homeowners and the professionals they hire to build or remodel their houses. Their objectives are the same—to execute and complete a project. But too often they do not speak the same language.

Horror stories abound about single-family home building and remodeling projects that have gone as haywire as 100-year-old plumbing. One reason is that often you spend more time buying a $25,000 automobile than you do a $250,000 house. Your purchase of a newly built speculation house, one constructed without a specific buyer in mind, or a lot on which you plan to build a custom home, a home constructed from scratch to your specifications, may be spurred by a puffed-up sales pitch from an aggressive or overenthusiastic real estate agent or developer.

Too many potential homeowners tend to think with their hearts rather than with their heads and wallets when making what is typically the biggest purchase of their lives. You don't really buy a home or build one, say experts. You buy Jimmy Stewart in the movie classic *It's a Wonderful Life* only to discover shortly thereafter that you've been duped. You might acquire a house built without any permits on a lot never approved by the right officials, or a garage converted to a house that was never sanctioned with the proper deed to be a residential abode.

These stories make great cocktail party gossip—for others. But pity those who find their headaches becoming migraines, their bank accounts drained, their marriages in shambles, and the chips on their shoulders as big as their houses.

Yet despite such potential problems, Americans continue their love affair with building and remodeling for one simple reason—just as many happy success stories exist. "Affluent Americans, those with incomes of $100,000 or more, spend $31 billion a year on home improvements," according to Yankelovich Partners, a research firm in Norwich, Connecticut. Kermit Baker, chief economist for The American Institute of Architects (AIA), estimates that about $34 billion is spent each year on additions to and major alterations of single-family homes.

What Do Most Women Want in Their Dream House?

A *USA Today* story reported on a *Traditional Home* magazine survey of 800 women who were asked what they wanted in their dream house. *USA Today* reported that the women want flexibility. "They want a house that is a living part of the family, changing as the family changes . . ." Highlights: "The rooms are all about the same size, so they can be either closed off or opened to create one large space; high-tech–capabilities are built into the walls for later use; and the kitchen is in the center of everything."

Why we build. Why the interest and escalation? Multiple reasons. There is nothing like building a new home or remodeling an existing one to turbocharge your life and help you better enjoy your surroundings. Another reason is that families can no longer be sliced into neat apple pie portions of mom, dad, two kids, and one dog with the same plan—a ranch or two-story house with living and dining rooms, eat-in kitchen, family room or den, three or four bedrooms, and an appropriate number of bathrooms. Stepchildren, stepparents, visiting grandparents, full- or part-time help create a need for different, flexible floor plans. Changing lifestyles and technological advancements have also fueled demand for rooms that relate better to nature, are more energy efficient, have computer capabilities, and can save time and money.

What better way to satisfy our dreams than to build or remodel? Statistics bear this out. The AIA reported that in recent years homeowners between 30 and 45 years old traded up to larger or better equipped houses while those a bit older, between 45 and 65, tackled extensive remodeling projects to get the homes they wanted.

Still another reason for the trend is that timing has never made it more propitious to build or remodel. Mortgage rates have stayed at low to moderate levels for several years, inflation is minimal if nonexistent, the economy remains robust, and housing prices remain relatively steady, climbing only a bit, not like the wild upticks of the eighties. This is good news for buyers and a bit upsetting for sellers.

Also, although two of the biggest remodeling markets, California and New England, witnessed economic downturns in 1996, remodeling projects overall were still up 3 percent and climbed back to double-digit growth by the end of 1997, according to Paul Deffenbaugh, editor of *Remodeling* magazine. When such statistics are analyzed and put into perspective for the future, the message emerges loud and clear that remodeling and building are more than passing fancies. They're here to stay.

But those most likely to endure the building and remodeling process, possibly multiple times, are those who understand a basic homeowner truth—you get out of your building or remodeling project what you put in, not dissimilar from an exercise regimen. Building takes work, time, and money. Unlike some endeavors that can be delegated, this one requires a full-time commitment to keep track of details and schedules.

RANDY EPSTEIN AUSTIN (Lennox, Massachusetts)

In trying to save money on a weekend home, Randy Epstein Austin, owner of The Gifted Child, and her former husband built in the Berkshires in Massachusetts. The couple had a budget of $100,000, but the home's design was really worth $200,000. "My ex thought we could save by using some contacts he had. We ordered all the siding and cabinets from a factory in Vancouver, Canada, where he knew some people. The cabinets came in damaged because they had been stacked atop the siding. A lot of the siding had to be discarded because it came in preformed lengths and had knots." The couple also hired an architect who was talented, but hadn't yet passed his architectural exams. He designed a six-foot fireplace on one plan, and made it 10 feet on another. Fortunately, when their contractor went to build the foundation, he discovered the discrepancy and corrected it. The architect also forgot to leave room for studs between rooms and closets, so in one place the laundry chute had to be placed sideways. "Everything cost us double." The moral of their story? "Don't cut corners to save money," Randy says. Fortunately, she adds, her ex wound up with the house in the divorce; she got their New York City apartment.

Everyone who has ever built or remodeled has war stories to share. You need to be prepared to circumvent your share of minefields. Among the most common problems is focusing too much on decorator-related decisions. "Your biggest concern becomes whether to install an opaque or clear shower door, what type of kitchen counters to pick or what color tile to use in your bathrooms," says Patty Brown, Technical Division, construction group, American Society of Civil Engineers in Reston, Virginia. You might neglect to find out what will lie under the tiles or even under the house or addition you build. In fact, a Yankelovich Partners survey of homeowners in the January 1997 *Builder's* magazine, a trade publication, reported that 77 percent of households that own a newly built home ranked the layout and selections of interior finishing materials as a prime reason to buy or build.

PEPPER SCHWARTZ (Seattle, Washington)

Pepper Schwartz, author of *The Great Sex Weekend* (Putnam), found that building was akin to chewing glass. "It was awful and painful, and there were a zillion places for mistakes. Even though my husband was trained as an architect and I'm a sociologist, we knew we'd have to have someone else do the design because we wanted to preserve the marriage. If something went wrong, we'd only have him to blame, we figured. But we didn't understand why every project costs 25 to 100 percent more than budgeted. It's as if you had an operation and the doctor said, 'Whoops. Sorry, it's going to be $50,000 rather than $10,000.' We love our house but it was a more painful exercise than we ever imagined. One day we came home to find the wrong roof on the house. It would have been too expensive to take it off, so the company paid us some money to accept it," she said.

Another common nightmare is finding your budget inching upward during the course of the work, often because the plans changed, while your bank account stays the same. Maybe, a bigger closet was added here, a fancier whirlpool tub there, or a finished basement with a bathroom. Before long, the increases add up to $10,000, $20,000 or much more.

Home building or remodeling may siphon off gallons of sweat and money, and cause intermittent disappointments, but if you have done your planning and research you will achieve long-lasting benefits.

You may even have an experience similar to the couple who built a 10,000-square-foot contemporary house with intricate design details. The ordeal brought them closer because they spent hours pouring over blueprints, jotting down ideas from magazines, going to the library together to do research, compiling a budget, and shopping for fixtures, appliances, and furniture. The husband was involved from the start, and the two made every decision together. The wife said only half-jokingly that she'd love to build another home. Her husband's reaction? He looked at her curiously and with a big grin on his face announced, "We'll see."

CHARLIE TROTTER (Chicago, Illinois)

Charlie Trotter, acclaimed chef of Chicago's Charlie Trotter's restaurant, says it's critical to stay focused on what you originally wanted to accomplish with your remodeling and not get caught up in the details of how to get it done. "Do not compromise because something may be difficult. There is always a creative solution to achieving your goal and it doesn't always have to cost more."

Each project may have its peccadillos, such as leaking sinks, cracked tiles, or wrong color cabinets. But if you stay involved, you have the ultimate control and can correct the problems. Just remember: Caveat Emptor—buyer beware—every single square foot of the way."

HOME IMPROVEMENT: REMODELING PROS AND CONS

Is remodeling or building the easier and cheaper route to getting the home you want? If you've outgrown your existing house, your choices are to remodel, move to a new house, build, or simply sit back and complain. Which will it be?

Often it depends on your mindset and circumstances when you undertake the particular project. You may want your younger child to finish high school in your neighborhood, so it might be easier to remodel the kitchen and bathrooms than to move.

Other times, however, it's how you feel deep-down about old versus new. Some people at a certain stage, or perhaps their entire lives, only want a brand-new house. These are often the same people who will only buy a new car instead of a used one, stay in a new hotel rather than an old B&B, and buy new furniture rather than antiques.

On the other hand, many believe that it's cheaper to remodel than to build. If you see new home buyers moving into bigger homes with bigger kitchens and you, too, want to expand your kitchen, it will definitely cost less to do so in your existing abode, according to the National Association of Home Builders (NAHB) in Washington, D.C., the main trade association of 195,000 builders. And you can take out a second mortgage or home equity loan to pay for the work.

Nationwide, remodeling seems to have an inside tract over building. Remodeling is 60 percent larger than new home construction, according to *Qualified Remodeler,* a trade magazine in Long Island, New York. *Remodeling* magazine has found that most houses purchased are existing homes, and that homeowners tend to remodel them within 18 months, allowing some time to decide what to keep and what to discard. At the top of homeowners' current list of favorite projects are kitchen and bathroom remodelings, other interior work, windows, room additions, and sunrooms.

JOHN CHALLENGER (Winnetka, Illinois)

"Throw out the old. Though you can't always do that, the problem with large additions is that you tend to live in them and forget about the old rooms," says John Challenger, executive vice president of Challenger, Gray & Christmas, an outplacement firm in Chicago. "Once we put our three-story addition on our house in Winnetka, everything else looked old and decrepit. Maybe, the only solution is to build a new house rather than add onto the old. Now we use our old rooms—the living room and dining room—mostly for storing things."

Room additions comprise the largest yearly segment of remodelings totaling 350,000; each pegged at more than $10,000. Additions fulfill consumer demand for 2,000 square feet of living space in older homes that are typically 1,500 square feet. Almost 250,000 kitchens are remodeled each year. Each kitchen costs in excess of $10,000 and often reaches $40,000 to $50,000, depending on the extent of the remodeling, and the choice of cabinetry, flooring, countertops, lighting and equipment. Almost 200,000 bathroom additions or remodelings are also done annually, priced conservatively at more than $5,000 apiece.

Structural remodelings. Remodeling doesn't have to be so extensive or expensive. Less attractive but vital structural remodelings sometimes are never seen by anyone except the work crew, but make a house more secure, livable, and sellable. Projects demanding immediate attention should be cracked foundations and walls, termite damage, uneven floors, loose bricks, bulging ceilings, flooded basements, and inefficient, old gutters and downspouts.

Some shrewd buyers simply remodel because it's considered a prudent investment. You buy a home and fix it up to sell. Remodeling enhances the value of a house, as long as it's not too quirky. Turning a third bedroom into a huge walk-in closet or replacing beige tiles with hot pink has a limited market value.

When *Remodeling* magazine surveyed more than 200 real estate agents regarding the investment potential of the 12 most popular remodeling projects for a mid-priced house in an established neighborhood, they agreed that remodeled homes generally sell faster, especially in highly competitive markets.

Few experts characterize remodeling, however, as a guaranteed cash cow. *Remodeling* editor Deffenbaugh says it's better to view remodeling in the context of return or cost versus value. "The motivating factor should be comfort, not economics. If you have a three-bedroom home with one bathroom and you add another, you are giving your house the amenities that are available on the new home market. If you are selling your home, new homes are the competition. If kitchens and baths are in demand, then remodeling them is generally a great investment. In the magazine's annual cost versus value report, such remodelings show a 95 to 100+ percent return on the investment."

But let's step back and play devil's advocate. Remodeling poses risks. You may think that as long as you're adding a new roof and heating system, you might as well reconfigure the master bedroom upstairs by adding a peaked roof and putting in a few skylights. As long as you're doing that, you might as well knock through a wall adjoining the bedroom and turn the guest room into a sitting area. And gee, as long as you're that far along in the construction game, you might as well finish the basement or attic, convert the garage into a family room, redesign the kitchen, and turn that extra bedroom into a home office. Wouldn't it be easier to build from scratch? Maybe yes, maybe no.

Remodeling can also be very messy. Bring out the jackhammers and it becomes demolition derby time. Walls that separated main rooms end up in the dumpster to make way for one big room or a different room configuration. And work crews will traipse through your home, often with muddy shoes, and mess up your bathrooms and closets.

ROZ AND ART SIEGEL (Brooklyn, New York)

In remodeling several homes and apartments through the years, the couple found that it is crucial to have a place that's habitable during the course of construction, if you're living there. "We're now working on a house," says Roz, "and the only way we have survived is that we've tackled it floor-by-floor so that there is always a place where there isn't any mess or construction debris. It makes it much more tolerable."

Talk with anyone who has been through remodeling. They'll tell you it takes the forbearance of an intensive care nurse to live in a house in the midst of construction chaos. Being without a bathroom for a month can be torture, even if work progresses in a timely fashion. And try living without a kitchen for six months, using a cooler as a refrigerator and a small bunsen burner in your living room for a stove. You like take-out food? You'll have plenty of time to frequent all the nearby establishments.

LISA AND HOWARD SKOLNIK (Chicago, Illinois)

Never do something unless your marriage can withstand it. Also organize a project step by step and take it in very small increments. "When our apartment flooded, it was so disruptive to get it back together that we found we had to do it on a small scale, such as turning a dog kennel into a guest room. We are very ordered people with four children, and it's very disconcerting to have anything out of order. Remodeling demands an incredible amount of effort, even if it seems simple," says Lisa, a design writer for *Metropolitan Home* magazine, the *Chicago Tribune,* and other publications.

In such cases, some move in with in-laws or parents, which can work wonders for family harmony. Others stay in a hotel, if pocketbooks permit. When family members are living on top of one another too long or involved in a protracted project, relationships change—fast. Just wait and see.

Remodeling can become a tricky business. Putting rooms back together with a logical layout that is also aesthetically pleasing—you'll want to match millwork and window styles—requires an overall plan. There are also limitations. You can't always increase insulation quality in existing walls or make an 8½ foot-high ceiling 10 feet when you're working with built space.

Remodeling requires twice the amount of management time and labor as building. St. Louis builder Rob Kerr of Premiere Homes, Inc., estimates that remodeling jobs are finished on schedule only 50 percent of the time, not because of lazy workers but because of owners' change orders, unexpected obstacles, and unforeseen problems that make experts halt to debate options.

It's impossible to know what a contractor will find when walls or ceilings are opened. That pillar you thought was decorative but unattractive may be a structural support that must stay. The wiring may not meet current codes and may have to be replaced. There may be termite damage.

When Kerr used to oversee remodelings, he'd add 10 to 15 percent more in costs to any remodeling job to cover these just-in-case scenarios, and if they didn't occur, he subtracted the amount. Some build-design groups will agree to tackle a remodeling or rehab, but will warn you, as St. Louis builder/developer

Edgar W. Ellermann does: "This is what it will cost and this is what it will cost us to do it (a fixed fee). We'll keep an open budget and show you the bill."

Remodeling can also prove to be a waste of money if not handled with care. You may tear out something of value, throw it away, and replace it with something that will not last as long.

On a cost-per-square foot basis, remodeling can be more costly than building new, but rarely does a remodeling project encompass as many square feet as a new house. So, on a total dollar basis, remodeling is cheaper.

Before you finalize your decision, weigh all the benefits and analyze the possible returns. Do you really need more space for the long term or just for a few years before the children go away to college when you can turn one of their bedrooms into a sitting room or home office? You may be able to improve some of your spaces to create the illusion of more room. A lighter wallpaper, better lighting, more mirrors, new closet systems, or a single new window might make your child's small bedroom look much larger.

If cosmetic changes won't work, a little remodeling job can still be less time consuming and costly than a large scale project. You don't have to make as many decisions all at once, and you can upgrade in stages as your budget, personality, and family needs demand.

How much should you spend? Unfortunately, there's no magic formula for pegging what's reasonable. If you're contemplating remodeling, you might consider spending 10 percent of the value of your home, based on a recent estimate from a real estate appraiser or agent. This approximates what it would cost to sell your home and move into a new place today, according to the American Homeowner Foundation, a nonprofit consumer group. Just think how much more space, light and style you can add to your current home for 10 percent of its value.

STARTING FROM SCRATCH: BUILDING FROM THE GROUND UP

In some cases remodeling is not an option. There may be no room to expand because your lot is too small, the setback restrictions won't allow it, or the expansion will be so expensive that you would never recoup the cost.

Sometimes when renovation is not cost efficient, or a house isn't worth salvaging but the land is, it may be smarter and cheaper to knock down the existing home and start from scratch. This seems to be a trend in established neighborhoods where buildable empty lots are at a premium or don't exist at all. Another advantage of building new is that you have all new materials and appliances that you won't have to worry about replacing for at least 15 or 20 years.

MARY ENGELBREIT (St. Louis, Missouri)

Mary Engelbreit, president of Mary Engelbreit Studios and editor-in-chief of *Mary Engelbreit's Home Companion* magazine, lived in an incredibly expansive home that had been built in 1913. The day she had to use the intercom to locate her children in the house was the day she realized it was simply too big. Her family built a smaller more urban-style townhouse in the same St. Louis suburb. She feels that scaling down is one way to cope with day-to-day stress. Having a new home where everything works makes life much easier. Also, she now knows where everybody is at all times.

There are various ways to start the building process. You can find an empty lot on which to build a custom single-family dream home—one that you build totally from scratch to meet your specifications. You can buy a spec home that's already built or partly built, and make adjustments in the design options or room reconfigurations or you can choose a professional, find the site together, and develop the plan to fit the topography, views, your wish list, and your budget.

BOB AND RANDY COSTAS (St. Louis, Missouri)

Sports announcer Bob Costas and his wife Randy built their home in suburban St. Louis ten years ago. Bob gave Randy carte blanche when designing the house because he said that this was the last time he was ever moving. "I would love to build another house. It's fun to think about and piddle around with stuff like that," says Randy. She admits that she has amassed a file of ideas just in case.

The march toward domestic bliss is much more predictable when building than remodeling. It's also usually faster. Many builders agree that they can build a home within six months to one year, if most of the decisions such as developing the lot, which takes about a month, have been made up-front. Production builders—those who build on volume and make most of the decisions before you buy, giving you little to no leeway to make custom choices—can often deliver their product within 120 days.

While new homes have been built in recent years with fewer rooms, many have greater visual richness through more architectural detailing and square footage, both demanding time and money. The median size home in 1996 was 2,000 square feet, up from 1,660 square feet 10 years ago, and 1,590 square feet 20 years ago. Today's new home typically includes 2½ bathrooms, three bedrooms, air conditioning, a two-car garage, and a fireplace. Lot size averages a quarter of an acre.

The Five Steps of Remodeling
(from the National Kitchen & Bath Association)

Step 1: Research

- Takes six months to two years.
- Homeowner researches products, designs, finance options, and construction professionals. Accomplishes this through visits to friends' homes, listening to friends, looking at design magazines, visiting home shows and showcase homes, and reading newspaper and magazine articles.

Step 2: Narrow the Field

- Homeowner narrows the list of professionals to contact, using referrals from friends and family, Yellow Pages, direct mail, newspapers, magazines, and home shows/showcase homes.

Step 3: Hire the Professionals

- Personality and listening skills are the two top attributes to consider when hiring a professional.
- Professionals must show respect for consumer's ideas and budget.

Step 4: Installation

- Considered by homeowners to be the worst part of the process.
- Poor service is the biggest problem. Homeowners can survive torn-out cabinets, but are aggravated when professionals will not return calls or answer questions.

Step 5: Completion

- Best part of the process.
- Homeowners view the end result as "their" space—their design, their ideas—with just a little help from the professionals.
- The happiest customers viewed the professional as their "best friend."

CONSTRUCTIVE TIPS

Diary of a Mad Homebuilder or Remodeler

Are you running in 1,001 different directions every day? If you wonder whether you have the time to devote to building or remodeling a house, take this simple test

1. Do you work part-time or full-time, at least 30 hours a week?

2. Are you involved in caring for an elderly parent, whom you call daily, visit at least once a week, occasionally take to the doctor, and grocery shop for?

3. Do you frequently travel for business or pleasure—at least twice a week and for several days?

4. Do you hate making home-related decisions, such as choosing door knobs, cabinet fronts, countertop surfaces, paint, and tile colors, electrical outlet locations, window frames and sashes, and doors?

5. Do you have young children, whom you must carpool each day and whose homework and other activities you supervise?

6. Do you have a dog you must walk or other pets you care for?

7. Are you overloaded with volunteer work—on at least three major committees or boards that take up at least ten hours a week of your time?

8. Do you make dinner or other meals from scratch, requiring daily preparation time?

CONSTRUCTIVE TIPS (continued)

9. Is your marriage a bit precarious where you and your spouse fight frequently about how to spend money for your home?

10. Are you thinking of staying in your new home for only five years, and then downsizing or relocating?

ANSWERS: If you answered "yes" to at least eight of these questions, think twice about building or doing a major remodeling. Instead, redecorate or do a small-scale remodeling. If you answered yes to five, you're borderline and should consider paring your activities if you want to proceed. If you answered yes to only three, you're a contender but be prepared for what lies ahead.

Individual rooms have not just been getting bigger but fancier. Kitchens, for instance, are better equipped, which is ironic because people are spending less time cooking. Other new house trends include double-glazed windows for better insulation, and fewer separate dining rooms giving way to an open kitchen–dining room arrangement. The living room is beginning to vanish, often replaced by a great room or hearth room, but not totally disappearing as once predicted. Basements are common in the Northeast and Midwest, but rare in the South and West where some homes have crawl spaces.

On the outside, the most common material used is vinyl siding, which covers 33 percent of homes built; 21 percent use brick; 23 percent wood; 16 percent stucco, stone, or other materials; and 7 percent aluminum siding.

To be on the safe side, do your research. Once you make the commitment to either build or remodel, fate begins to unfold.

✔ **CHECKLIST**

Managing Your Project

Pitfalls are avoidable if you manage your project like a business deal and adhere to the following chronological steps:

❏ Start the process with in-depth research.

❏ Develop a budget and building plan, both short-term and long-term, and stick to them. Decide what you can afford and consider maintenance costs (a swimming pool is nice but it's expensive to maintain). Map out what you really need and differentiate those necessities from your wants, which may have to go, depending on costs. You'll also need to factor into your budget where you will live during the construction—possibly a hotel or rental home—and the inconvenience; the extra professional costs you may incur such as hiring a painter, carpenter, decorator, moving company, and attorney; and the new furnishings you want when all's done. Playing it safe by adding more costs initially will produce a safer return. If you end up with extra funds, so much the better.

❏ Draft a mission statement so you, the rest of your family, and those you hire understand your collective objectives.

❏ Learn from the mistakes of others. This book will point out quite a few.

❏ Select the right partners or professionals.

❏ Manage the job from start to finish.

✓ TEST

20 Questions to Ask Yourself before You Get Started
(from the American Institute of Architects)

Before you start, especially if you are trying to decide between building and remodeling, ask yourself the following questions. Left unanswered, they could come back to hit you like a ton of bricks.

1. Describe your current home. What do you like about it, what's missing, and what don't you like?

2. Do you want to change the space you have?

3. Do you want to build a new home?

4. Why do you want to build a house or add to or renovate your current home? Do you need more room, are children grown and moving, is your lifestyle changing?

5. What is your lifestyle? Are you at home a great deal, do you work at home? Do you entertain often? How much time do you spend in the living areas, bedrooms, kitchen, den or office, and utility space?

6. How much time and energy are you willing to invest to maintain your home?

7. If you are thinking of adding on, what functions/activities will be housed in the new space?

8. What kind of spaces do you need?

9. How many of those spaces do you think you need?

10. What do you think the addition/renovation/new home should look like?

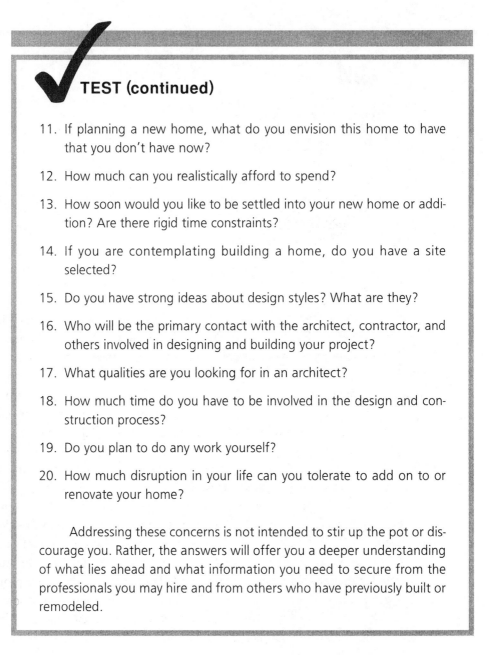

✔ TEST (continued)

11. If planning a new home, what do you envision this home to have that you don't have now?

12. How much can you realistically afford to spend?

13. How soon would you like to be settled into your new home or addition? Are there rigid time constraints?

14. If you are contemplating building a home, do you have a site selected?

15. Do you have strong ideas about design styles? What are they?

16. Who will be the primary contact with the architect, contractor, and others involved in designing and building your project?

17. What qualities are you looking for in an architect?

18. How much time do you have to be involved in the design and construction process?

19. Do you plan to do any work yourself?

20. How much disruption in your life can you tolerate to add on to or renovate your home?

Addressing these concerns is not intended to stir up the pot or discourage you. Rather, the answers will offer you a deeper understanding of what lies ahead and what information you need to secure from the professionals you may hire and from others who have previously built or remodeled.

2

Help!
Who Do I Call?

You've decided you want to build or remodel and have a ballpark idea of what you can afford. Not unlike the old television show *The Dating Game,* it's time to choose someone to do the work, unless you envision yourself as a modern Paul Bunyan.

Who do you choose? Do you turn to a builder/contractor who perhaps also designs or has an architect on staff? Or do you select an architect outright who bids out your design to a builder/general contractor or developer? Or, do you try to find the burgeoning group known as design/build, which combines these disciplines? Then, there are also the various types of builders, from the production to semicustom and custom professional.

A *builder/contractor* thinks of himself as a hands-on craftsperson who hires subcontractors to do much of the specialized work, says Allan Freedman, Management Services Division, NAHB. An *architect* thinks of himself as a builder's creative arm who takes his cues from your lifestyle and all the important design trends. An *interior designer* may be called in to oversee the entire project or just one area of the home he may specialize in such as kitchens or bathrooms. A *build/design group* offers one-stop shopping. You choose them, and they in turn hire everyone else to do the job from start to finish.

SALLY QUINN AND BEN BRADLEE (Washington, D.C.)

There are good and bad contractors, and Sally Quinn, author of *The Party,* who is married to Ben Bradlee, former executive editor of the *Washington Post,* says she's worked with both. "The last architect we used was a woman and we chose a male contractor with whom we had worked before. It was a disaster because the contractor was a male chauvinist pig. He couldn't stand working with two women and he was constantly arguing with us. It's best, we learned, to allow the architect to choose his or her own contractor."

BUILDERS

One type of builder is the *production builder* who works on a high-volume basis and is used to working quickly, which may result in less leeway for you to make choices and change designs. Higher volume also usually means lower individual costs. A semicustom builder typically works with an existing plan, but is more willing to adapt it to your needs than a production builder. The downside? Most charge more than a production builder, though less than a custom builder. A custom builder tries to work like an architect and design a home for your needs and pocketbook, often with an architect on staff or through a consultation, which usually leads to a higher pricetag, but greater flair and flexibility.

DESIGNER

Any design professional you consider should meet with you face-to-face so you can outline the scope of your project. This meeting will be a good test to see if your aspirations and tastes jibe, and if there's chemistry. You'll be working daily with this person so chemistry should not be viewed lightly. One homeowner joked that she saw her contractor more than her husband during the nine months of construction.

Getting the designer to understand what you truly want can be tricky because not all homeowners can pinpoint and verbalize their desires when they begin the process. Talk frankly with the designer about how much you're willing to spend, what design and size you envision for each room in your house, and develop a work timetable and fee schedule that are acceptable. Show pictures of favorite rooms, as well as ones you dislike.

CHRISTOPHER AND SHEILA BERNER KENNEDY (Chicago, Illinois)

Christopher Kennedy, son of Ethel and the late Robert F. Kennedy, says that when it comes to decorating, if it's not your bailiwick or you don't have time, use your mother, as he and wife Sheila have done when fixing up their suburban Chicago home. "There are a few advantages. The process is exhausting since there are so many choices. You won't make any mistakes and you won't get criticized. My mother did a great job though she tends to make the same selections for all our homes. There's a rug she likes at the Stark showroom and the same rug has turned up in my house, in my sister's home, and in my brother Bobby's house. . . ." At least her taste is consistent.

To determine if the designer understands your ideas enough to conceptualize and draft them on paper, peruse other homes he's done. Some designers specialize in certain types of designs and styles. You wouldn't want someone who designs only contemporary homes to fashion a traditional house unless you're certain he's capable of that. You might not want a kitchen specialist to build your entire home. Your local NAHB and AIA chapters will be pleased to provide you with names of talented designers.

FINDING AN ARCHITECT WHO'S BOTH DESIGNER AND TEAM MANAGER

Most often the designer of your new house or room will be an architect. Most architects graduate from a five or six year college program and sometimes attend a graduate architecture school. After graduation, most intern for three years to become eligible to take a state licensing exam. They must be licensed to sign drawings. (This is necessary when applying for building permits to verify that the plans are architect-authorized and the seal is the original belonging to that architect. This also prevents any copying of plans.) The architect must know the nuts and bolts of building such as load structures, quality of materials, stress levels of materials, and how design distributes load. Design is only a small segment required; knowledge of site planning and architectural history are also necessary.

After passing the test, the architect is positioned to design an entire project from the germ of the idea through completion. To stay on top of the latest trends and technology, architects are required to earn 36 learning units per year, some of which must be public-safety oriented to maintain membership in the American Institute of Architects. The AIA accredits each continuing education workshop or course offered to make sure it complies with the AIA's health, safety, welfare, business management, and marketing standards.

Architects are multitalented, left brain and right brain. There's an old-fashioned misconception that they only design luxury million dollar homes. Not true. Like a homemaker clipping coupons from the Sunday paper, most architects scout for ways to cut costs and create more value for their average homebuilder clients. Some may only take on projects worth X amount of dollars, but many, including those starting out, are happy to design a single room.

Most do far more. Their skills range from designing a renovation or an entire new home to choosing a site (turning a difficult lot into a successful building locale); designing the interiors; analyzing costs, energy, and maintenance efficiency; and overseeing construction or construction management.

Many give the homes additional value through their innovative designs and choices. You may say, "I really love marble floors, but they're so expensive." The architect will suggest ways to achieve the same effect and quality with a different material such as ceramic tile that's less expensive. This allows you to put extra money back into another building element. Or, you may say, "I want a big bay window." The architect may respond, "I can achieve the light you're looking for in your new family room but do it in a way that will not take up the entire wall, giving you more usable living space."

ZELMA LONG AND PHILLIP FREESE (Northern California)

Use a design team, advises Zelma Long of Simi Winery, who with her husband Phillip Freese, rebuilt a home. "Use a contractor and architect who like working together. To that team we added an interior designer, and all three met with us at the start of the project to review the redesign of the home, each providing his or her own perspective. That approach improved the original design significantly and enhanced communications as the work was being done. In terms of the interior design, Phil and I resolved that no decision would be made that was not approved by both of us and our designer. That team of three sometimes disagreed, but we found that by working through the issues we came up with design conclusions that we were all happy with. And as a result, the project was a wonderful—and sometimes humorous and frustrating—creative experience that resulted in a home that fits us and suits us."

The architect can also build in functional variances that allow the home-owner to maintain the integrity of the home's original design while altering it to his changing need. A nursery may later become a mother-in-law suite or a home office if not designed with cutesy cabinets and detailing, which would be expensive to remove later. The architect also designs with a total life-cycle cost analysis in mind, which accounts for expected future operating and maintenance costs.

JUDY AND SHELDON COHEN (Ladue, Missouri)

The Cohens slept in the basement during their extensive remodeling until it got too cold and they had to move upstairs to a tiny room the size of a closet where they slept for months on a queen-size mattress on the floor with their youngest son. "Men were in our house while we were trying to shower and get dressed in the morning. And there were so many glitches—doors the wrong height, granite in one of the bathrooms cracked after two weeks. The delays were unbelievable." They wanted a fireplace in the entertainment room that went through to the living room and the contractor said it wasn't possible. "An engineer came in after the fact and said yes, it could have been done. Lesson learned: next time we use an architect."

How do you find the right architect? Ask friends, real estate agents, and local decorating sources such as tile shops and marble suppliers where the architects shop. Scan newspaper and magazine articles for names. Call the architecture school at a nearby college or university or the local chapter of the AIA to get a list of architects in your area, though there's no rule that says you can't hire someone based in another city as long as you understand you'll have to pay airfare, lodging costs, and meals. If you drive by a house you like, knock on the door and ask the owners who designed it. They'll be flattered.

The AIA suggests interviewing at least three architects face-to-face. The organization publishes a list of 20 questions homeowners should ask themselves before beginning (see the test at the end of Chapter 1). What do you want to change in the space you have? Why do you want to build a house? Why do you want to renovate your current home?

Homeowners should pose another round of questions to the architect before making a final selection. Why do you need an architect? How and how much does an architect charge? When do you bring an architect in on a project? You want to be sure your architect can translate your pile of magazines and newspapers clippings, photographs, and articles into a three-dimensional, functional, and affordable reality.

CONSTRUCTIVE TIPS

Questions to Ask When Hiring an Architect
(Edited from Answers Provided by the AIA)

1. *How do I find an architect?* The challenge is to find one who is right for you! Look around at houses and renovation projects that you like and find out who did them. Call your local chapter of The American Institute of Architects and ask for referrals. Get recommendations from friends and colleagues who have worked with architects.

2. *What questions should I ask?* Find out how busy the firm is and make sure the architects have the time to focus on your project. Ask who will personally design your new home or renovation and make sure you meet directly with that person. Discuss how long the project will take to complete. Make sure you talk budget. Ask about the different charges the architect anticipates and discuss any budget constraints upfront.

3. *How do architects charge for their services?* That varies. Some architects charge an hourly rate, others set a fixed fee, and still others charge a percentage of construction costs. Sometimes the architect suggests a combination of the above. Whatever the method, discuss the payment plan early and make sure there's an agreement before the process begins.

4. *Should I get everything in writing?* Definitely! The American Institute of Architects has a variety of standard contract forms that are used widely throughout the industry. An easy way to obtain them is by calling the AIA at 800-365-ARCH.

CONSTRUCTIVE TIPS (continued)

5. *I'm having second thoughts; tell me again why I need an architect?* Would you go into surgery without a doctor? Would you embark on a court case without a lawyer? An architect can help you clarify and define your wants and needs. The architect is the one person who has the education and training to guide you through the entire process. Secondly, the architect sees the big picture. Whether it's a new home or a renovation, the architect can help you create your dream— and do it within your time frame and budget.

6. *But isn't it more expensive to work with an architect?* Not in the long run. A well-designed home can be built more efficiently and more economically and can add to your selling price when it's time to move.

7. *What can I count on the architect to provide?* That depends on the scope of professional services required for your project as well as what you and your architect have agreed on in advance. But services can include preliminary (schematic) design, design development, preparation of documents, and administration of the agreements between you and your builder or contractor.

8. *How do I decide between architects?* Evaluate finalists. Consider your candidates' track records in general, as well as their direct experience with projects similar to your own. Determine who can best complete the undertaking within your stated time frame and your budget. If it's feasible, visit a few homes designed by your finalists. There's nothing like looking at the actual work of a candidate to discover if you are a match. Interview two or three final candidates for the job. See if your personalities mesh, as well as your concepts of the project. Clear up any questions about the proposed schedule, the fee structure, and areas of responsibility.

CONSTRUCTIVE TIPS (continued)

9. *What are my responsibilities?* The owner should be clear on design objectives, constraints and criteria. A well-defined budget at the start is critical. The owner should also provide any legal, accounting, auditing, and insurance counseling services that are needed for the project.

10. *Any tips I can follow to ensure that this is going to be a successful relationship?* Yes—keep talking! It's vital to keep the lines of communication open during the course of the project. It's critical that you and your architect have a relationship that will withstand the inevitable bumps in the road that will occur along the way. Make it your business to be involved. Remember that it is easier to solve a small problem quickly than to have it develop into a big one.

The wish list you give your architect should not only include the total square footage of the house, but also very specific details about rooms, amenities, building materials, and even rough layouts.

He will put together a rough draft or *schematic plan* (typically on a scale where ⅛-inch equals 1 foot) of the interior, as well as how the house or addition sits on the property. He may run it by a contractor and subcontractors to get ballpark estimates of costs to use as a rough gauge. Don't panic if you don't like what you see; the drawings are just a first stab. They will be redone with your input on a larger ¼-inch scale, with greater detail that may include elevations and a materials list. At this point, you'll probably also ask others for input, which can be either helpful or more confusing.

The final drawings are called working drawings or blueprints. They are literally blue, usually drawn in ¼-inch or ½-inch to 1 foot scale, and detail the elevations, floor plans, finish schedules, wall sections, lighting plans, cabinetry, roof lines, and all necessary specifications. The builder uses the blueprints to bid out the project and guide the construction. Blueprints are also used to acquire the necessary approval and permits.

At this point, the budget may be addressed and the project rebid from the plans at hand. These bids are apt to be much more reliable and realistic than early ones. With a better handle on costs, you and your architect will then know if there's extra money for a fancier countertop or oven, or if some things need to be eliminated, such as a bar sink, walk-in closets, or marble floors and walls in the master bathroom.

Once changes are determined, pricing can be finalized and the drawings are signed and stamped complete. At this stage, you might also receive a work schedule and construction contract. If you're buying a production home, these plans will have been finished before you arrive on the scene and your builder may not allow changes.

Now it's time to bring forth the design or purchase agreement. This is a set of contract documents drafted by the AIA, that architects provide to clients. The contract directs you and the architect to answer all questions before work begins so everyone knows what to expect at the starting gate.

The architect's fees are among the contract's most important data. Fees can be derived in various ways: a percentage of the total construction cost, which typically ranges from 6 to 15 percent (the amount usually depends on the breadth and intricacy of the job); a fixed fee for a defined scope of work; or an hourly billing rate that can range from $50 to $150 or higher on East and West coasts.

Is any one route better than another? St. Louis architect Thomas Yanko with Myers & Yanko, LLC., says, "From an owner's perspective, it's probably safest if the architect charges a fixed fee because that way he can define the scope of work and how much it will cost him. If the scope of work changes, so does the fee."

Although you may be eager to figure building costs on a per-square-foot basis, most architects feel there are too many variables that factor into that formula. For instance, some architects waive their fee for the initial interview if they're later hired, while others don't charge an interview fee at all. Per-square-foot arrangements also make it hard to compare the quality that you're getting for the price (more on this subject in Part Two). The contract will also spell out the types of drawings to be provided, how many copies will be provided, and who owns the copyright to the drawings should the project be terminated.

It's now time to put your money down by providing a retainer of 10 to 25 percent of the total architect's fee. The amount of the retainer will depend on where you live (state) and the scope of the job. At this point, you and the architect face another big decision. You may ask the architect to *bid out the project* to two or three contractors. The completed blueprints will serve as a vital building map for the contractors because they are accompanied by specifications of the materials including brand names, item numbers, and prices. The architect may also decide to bid out the project to a contractor himself. There are pros and cons. While architects don't build actual structures, they know good builders and can determine who's best for each job and budget. They are also adept at establishing a construction budget.

The contractor you hire will then negotiate the best price for materials and workmanship and hire whatever labor is needed. The contractor will oversee the budget, manage the construction and work within a guaranteed maximum price, though he may charge some additional fees depending on the contract. (When you change your mind or the builder encounters unexpected obstacles, it can cost you an extra 15 to 25 percent.)

Many homeowners prefer to find their own contractors because they feel they can get a better price and find a more objective third party who will readily assess the plans and make any necessary changes without offending the architect's delicate ego.

CARL J. CIRCO (Overland Park, Kansas)

Carl J. Circo, a real estate attorney, says, "An honest and solvent contractor is worth more than anything that appears in a contract. But I'm not the best source available to check out the contractor. Word-of-mouth and an architect are better."

CHRISTOPHER AND SHEILA BERNER KENNEDY (Chicago, Illinois)

Christopher Kennedy, executive vice president for the Merchandise Mart Properties Inc. in Chicago and son of Ethel and the late Robert F. Kennedy, learned from his family's experience. "A plumber, who was a grade school friend of my father, hooked up the toilets to the hot water heater on the Fourth of July. By the end of the weekend, we had nothing but steam. So my advice is sometimes not to use a friend."

Even if you've gone the spec-house route, you still may be gaining an architect-designed house. An NAHB membership survey with more than 16,600 respondents found that 53 percent of single-family spec-house builders used the services of an architect for some or all of the project. The architect typically provided the builder with design options. According to the AIA, 57 percent of the work architects do today is new construction, 34 percent is remodeling.

STOCK PLANS

If you have a definite idea of what you want in a new home, you may be able to bypass the need for an architect and go directly to hiring a builder. Mass-produced or stock home plans from a magazine, home plan book, catalogue or website may be fairly rudimentary, but some builders have expertise in design or they have a copyrighted set of plans from homes they've already built. Chances are builders who use their own plans can give you a more definite idea of costs. Caveat: some municipalities require that an architect prepare the plans. Your local building department can cite the law.

Many of the readily available plans typically come with specs, a materials list, and blueprints. The *Southern Living Historical House Collection* showcases charming old-fashioned southern-style homes including working drawings for the foundation and floor-framing plans; dimensioned floor plans; electrical plans; typical wall section; exterior elevations of the front, rear and sides of the house; interior elevations; door and window sizes; and suggested interior and exterior finish schedules. *Southern Living's* prices, like many other companies, are $275 for one set of drawings and $375 for five sets.

Overall, the costs can be as low as $200 but mostly range from $300 to $700 for the whole packet. *Home Plan Ideas,* published by *Better Homes & Gardens,* offers fairly large two-story, three- and four-bedroom homes with one-set package prices between $350 to $590; four sets, $395 to $635; eight sets, $455 to $695; and a reproducible set from $555 to $795. There are also additional costs for identical blueprints, reverse blueprints, and mailing charges.

With any of these plans, be sure they are appropriate for your lifestyle. If you like to cook and eat informally, look for a large kitchen and breakfast area. If you work at home, be sure there's room for you to set up a home office.

Stock plans save you time and money. But choosing the right stock plan that works for your lot can be risky. The plans are not tailored for a specific site, soil type, or elevation, such as a sloping property. Most plans are designed to be modified by a builder. There are disclaimers and warnings that also require adjustments. You are warned to heed local building codes, heating and plumbing guidelines, zoning requirements, and state regulations. *Home Plan Ideas* notes that in Nevada homes must be redrawn by a Nevada-registered professional. *Southern Living* offers this disclaimer: "Square footage estimates include exterior wall thicknesses. They are approximations. Accurate construction-cost estimates should come from the blueprints."

HOUSE KITS

Little has been written about house kits or modular homes. Basically just the shell of a home, these kits include several modular blocks and steel structural components. There are blocks for modular windows, door systems, the roof, and wall systems. One company includes all doors, windows, wiring, and plumbing behind the walls along with pipes and fittings, circuit panel, electrical boxes, metal studs for interior wall partitions, foundations, steel roof rafters, and floor joists. There are custom house kits as well in various styles, sizes, and configurations. Modular houses can also be expanded or reduced in size.

Home kits were very popular around the turn of the century, and Sears, Roebuck and Co. was the best-known seller of these kits. Today they are starting to reappear. The ready-made housing units are advertised in magazines, catalogs and on the Internet. Some of the large home product supply centers and hardware chains offer them as well. The homes range from humble to high-end styles, with mostly log cabin construction, and are sometimes even designed by architects. Most are accompanied by a full set of plans which your builder can personalize.

Before you buy, add up all finishing/installation costs and be sure your bank is familiar with this type of home and the way it's processed. Modular homes must meet all building codes for the areas to where they are shipped.

If a home kit is purchased from a builder, he may expect you to hire him to put it together. You're under no obligation, especially when you don't know anything about his credibility. Have the kit builder show you other homes he's built in your area. Check out his background, his credentials, and find out who assembles and finishes your home on the site.

DAVID HOFFMAN (Northbrook, Illinois)

Although he's in the building business, David Hoffman, who works and lives in Illinois, knew to find a local general contractor when he started building a vacation house in Colorado. "Don't try to outsmart yourself; every locality has its idiosyncracies, and it's better to let someone earn his keep for doing a job right. The weather conditions—such as snow loads and moisture accumulations—are different in Colorado than Illinois. The air is much drier, and when the sun hits, the snow stays on the ground longer. A roof has to be designed properly."

Never gamble or take short-cuts with the builder you select. He will become either your new best friend or your biggest nemesis. Don't be dazzled by cheap prices. Also, be wary of contractors or designers who leave cards or flyers in your mailbox, or send you ads with special promotions saying, "We'll be in your neighborhood on Tuesday and we'd like to bid on doing some work for you." It's fine to consider them, but check them out diligently.

The best way to find a reputable builder is to pick up home guides from an area supermarket, then drive around and look at homes, says builder Charles Schagrin, a developer with a degree in architecture and an MBA, who heads a build/design group called Amherst Corp. in St. Louis. Make sure the builder designs the type of home you want. Like architects, builders too often specialize in styles and types of homes—some build for active retirees, some for baby boomers who want $500,000-plus homes, some for vacationers. Interview those who seem like good prospects, and ask for references. The same process can be used for choosing a builder for a remodeling project. Go see some of his finished projects. Jot down what you find appealing or take snapshots. Then ask questions and get references.

If you don't know a builder, call your local NAHB or NARI and ask for a list of active builders who have been around for several years. You can also get names from job site signs, local media, seminars, home shows, and magazines. And of course, friends are always great sources.

A good litmus test to determine if a builder is worthwhile is to tell him you are considering a specific building project and you haven't decided whether you should do it yourself or use a professional. Give the professional a chance to earn your respect and business by helping you gather accurate facts.

Once you find a builder who answers all your questions satisfactorily and who seems to be capable and imaginative, you should meet to see if there's chemistry. If you get along and he offers you good counsel, you then face the nitty-gritty fact-finding mission.

Check the contractor's background.   A builder's credentials can be all over the lot. A typical builder may have started out as a subcontractor earlier in his career, but some builders have degrees in architecture, engineering, law, or business. Others have no college credits on their resumes, but something perhaps more valuable—years of hands-on experience.

JULIE AND DENNIS SINGER (Palos Verdes Estates, California)

Julie and Dennis Singer, an oil broker, had a chain of mishaps when remodeling their home. The Singers say it seemed like every contractor and sub who entered their home left damage behind. "The hardwood floor refinisher ruined the freshly painted baseboard moldings. We needed the painter to repair them. The wallpaper guys killed our phone lines and shorted out several electrical outlets. We needed the electrician and the phone company man to fix the wiring. The kitchen cabinet refinishers ruined the hinges on our cabinet doors. We needed the carpenter to install new hinges. The carpet guys scratched the walls. We needed the painter— again. The air conditioner installers left big black scratches on the ceilings and walls. We needed the painter—again. Our daughter then put a washcloth down the bathtub drain. We needed the plumber to retrieve the washcloth. While trying to remove the washcloth, the plumber punctured a pipe. As a result, water came through the ceiling into the guest bedroom below. We needed the plumber—again. He cut a hole in the guest bedroom ceiling, which was the only way he could replace the punctured pipe. We then needed the drywall man to patch up the hole. The drywall guy patched the hole. It looked terrible. We needed the painter—again. Then our daughter put a washcloth down the bathtub drain—again. At that point, I considered not allowing her to take a bath again until she is married and living in her own home. It's a miracle we kept our sanity."

Weigh all the information.　There are no federal regulations governing who can be a builder. It's up to each individual state to determine if a builder needs more than a deft pair of hands. In some states, anybody can hang out a shingle. This is more common among remodeling contractors than new home builders, however. In other states, becoming a builder requires licensing, continuing education, proof of insurance, and bonding.

Neighboring states may have regulations on opposite ends of the spectrum. California has some of the oldest and most stringent laws in the country. Builders must pass an exam to get a license. Each applicant must also provide a financial statement and pay fees, and there's a penalty if a builder operates without a license. Colorado, on the other hand, has no licensing of residential contractors. Some states only require registration. In Georgia nonresident contractors must be registered and Kansas requires registration with the Department of Revenue to collect business taxes. In many states there are also local requirements—licensing for county and/or city jurisdictions.

Check licensing.　Licensing adds another level of protection to consumers because it takes into account the financial viability of the individual and firm. Licensing ensures the contractor is insured against claims of workers' compensation, property damage, and personal liability. Call to verify the contractor's insurance coverage after you get the name of the carrier and agency.

Licensed builders are also more aware of building codes, which protect health and safety, although there are seven states in the United States, including Arizona and Hawaii, that do not have building codes.

To check city and state requirements, call the city or county government office. Also, call your local home builders association to inquire about licensing requirements and other regulations in your area. There are more than 900 state and local NAHB affiliates throughout the country.

Run a complaint check. Call your local better business bureau. In 1996, the second most common inquiry was about home remodeling contractors with a total of 240,986 inquiries filed, says Holly Cherico, spokesperson for the National Council of Better Business Bureaus. People are suspicious of contractors because of the reputation of the industry, the great variance in talent, and the steep investment remodeling represents. Of the businesses that received the most complaints, general home remodeling contractors were fifth on the list with 6,829 complaints. But the good news is that those numbers represented a drop from third place the year before.

Certification. Another safeguard against trouble is certification. The NARI offers three certifications to remodelers nationwide that follow the contractor's name: Certified Remodeler (CR), Certified Remodeler Specialist (CRS) and Certified Lead Carpenter (CLC).

Receiving certification can be tougher for a contractor than rehabbing a landmark apartment building in New York City. According to *The Master Plan* magazine published by the NARI, a contractor must be currently employed and have been in the remodeling industry for at least five years. He must offer a resume of experience that is notarized and/or letters of recommendation. He must complete a one-day written exam (NARI offers study groups before the test), and must complete continuing education courses. In addition, each member of the NARI pledges to follow a code of ethics. If a tradesperson is willing to make this commitment to receive certification, it's a sign of professionalism.

Continuing education. Some states also now require builders to enroll in continuing education courses. The industry is in flux and in order to be competitive, builders need to be aware of fresh and innovative developments and learn when and how to use and install new materials and gadgets. The NAHB has an annual convention in Dallas that almost 60,000 industry personnel attend.

They come to learn about new products and building techniques through educational programs and exhibits.

In addition, there are more than 131 schools of construction around the country accredited by the American Council for Construction Education. Some schools have an NAHB Student Chapter or membership in the Associated Schools of Construction.

Bids. Regardless of credentials, consumer advocates recommend you see written bids and the work of at least three builders before you hire anyone. Compare numbers and quality. Get comfortable with prices by comparing the same items on each bid: building specs, materials, labor, and time needed to complete the work. If your state requires licensing and one of the bidders doesn't have a license, the playing field is not level. The unlicensed builder can offer a better price because he's not paying licensing fees and may not be paying for insurance.

With three bids you sometimes get involved in a money game. It may be better to find one contractor who you know does good work and then negotiate his price. Too many homeowners take the lowest bid and run. Do not hire a contractor solely based on price. You'll be sorry in the end if the quality is subpar and the work has to be redone.

DANNY MEYER (New York, New York)

Danny Meyer, co-owner of Union Square Cafe and Grammercy Tavern in New York, learned through experience. When renovating his first apartment with his wife Audrey, he paid the contractor 80 percent of the fee, but the contractor skipped town after doing only 55 percent of the work. "We found someone who had to redo a lot of his work. It was a real disaster." When they found their new apartment, they also found a wonderful contracting firm that consisted of several brothers. "Much more important than saving a bit on the price here and there is basing your decision on whether you could imagine sitting across from the person at a table for a year since that's how often you may be meeting him. Remodeling is an incredibly emotional experience and it requires an emotional connection between you." In working on his last restaurant, Meyer says he learned to negotiate a contractor upfront with both the architect and contractor and pay a fixed fee rather than a sum tied to the construction costs, because the latter always involves a conflict of interest—the work staff makes more when prices escalate. "It's the reason the city decided to make taxicab drivers charge a fixed fee for rides from JFK Airport into Manhattan rather than the varied amounts, depending on how little the riders knew about getting into the city."

If you do compare three bids, discuss them in detail to determine why there are price variations. There should be no more than a 20 percent price difference between the highest and lowest bids. If there is, either the builder is desperate or he doesn't want the job. Or, maybe he's made an error, which may seem to be in your favor, but may ultimately cause changes down the road in order to complete the work. Building does not come cheaply, nor does labor. But you want to know the specific costs and whether they're related to materials, time, labor, or all three. It's often smarter to opt for expensive labor rather than expensive materials, according to the NAHB. Many contractors split labor and materials in half. When it's not divided 50-50, find out why.

Be as thorough as possible when analyzing each bid. When you bake you follow a recipe, buy the best ingredients, and use the right equipment. The same care should be taken here. Any builder can toss out a ballpark figure based on square footage (which can be measured in various ways) and inferior materials, but there are too many variables, such as fixtures and appliances, that comprise the final figure that you can't afford to ignore. An appliance package alone can have a $5,000 to $10,000 swing. And there can be a 700 percent difference in plumbing fixtures.

References.   It's also a good idea also to check references of subcontractors. If you're hiring someone to custom craft cabinetry for a paneled library and the level of wood working expected is high quality, insist on seeing that sub's completed work before you allow him into your home. One sample tells you little. The dollar value of the project may also affect your level of expectation. If the project is a $50,000 kitchen, check out the sub's cabinetry work. If it's only a $5,000 rework of a single cabinet, it might not be necessary to inspect the work, but many homeowners will still feel more comfortable doing it.

Spell out the contract.   The national average construction cost per-square-foot of a typical two-story 2,000 square-foot home in 1996 was $63.55, according to the R.S. Means Company, Inc., a provider of construction cost information, products, and services. For a luxury home with the same dimensions, the per-square-foot costs rose to $94.10, and one St. Louis, Missouri, homeowner quoted costs per-square-foot for custom housing between $150 and $165. Of course many factors, such as architectural details, either pump up or deflate these figures.

The customer's expectation is also important, but it has to be communicated. Often, the contract is the best communicator. Other esoteric items often overlooked in a contract are starting and ending dates, additional fees, time schedules, payment schedules, and warranties. Write into the contract that you need a face-to-face meeting with the contractor each week to discuss progress—and problems. Put in an arbitration or mediation clause to resolve conflicts. If possible, include as many specs for materials, fixtures, appliances, and finishes as possible.

Don't forget to learn all facets of the fee schedule. Most builders charge 10 to 20 percent over the total figure for changes. When a builder requests large cash advances, a red flag should signal you to check if the builder has met his representations in timing and cost overruns.

Calculating and controlling the costs of a remodeling are more difficult than building because the remodeler often doesn't know what the job will entail until he opens a wall or pulls up the floor. Even a good experienced remodeling contractor won't be able to give an accurate estimate in all cases. Instead, he should say, "We won't know what's above the ceiling until we open it up." Most will recommend that you set aside some of your budget, 5 to 10 percent of the job, for the unexpected. However, major cost increases don't come from inside a wall. They usually result from additions or changes you make during the job. Many builders prefer to bill these additional costs separately from the fixed initial bill.

If there is any confusion with the contract, or you have a large, complicated job, an attorney, preferably one schooled in real estate or construction law, should review the documents before you begin. (Some homeowners prefer having an attorney review any contract, large or small.)

Pick a start date, sign the contract, hand over a deposit check—typically 5 to 15 percent for new home construction and 15 to 30 percent for an average remodeling. Usually, the smaller the job, the higher the percentage required for downpayment. After you sign the contract, you have three days in which you can legally cancel the contract. This is called the Right of Recision. Think long and hard during this period, especially if you have any reservations. Once the three days pass, the contractor will begin to apply for permits and order materials. When the materials arrive and work begins, it's harder to turn back.

WHAT'S A BUILD/DESIGN GROUP?

"A typical builder is a person you go to with a set of drawings that have been designed by an architect," says Edgar W. Ellermann, a St. Louis developer with an MBA who is also head of a St. Louis build/design group. A build/design group, on the other hand, can offer full-service one-stop shopping from finding a lot to completing the design and building the house.

The head of a build/design firm is usually a remodeler or builder/developer who provides a design service, or an architect who provides a contracting service team. These teams work like the part of the brain that transfers information back and forth between the left and right hemispheres.

A developer does everything from the ground up. He buys the land, subdivides it, puts in utilities and prepares it for construction. He then finds a client or the client finds him. "I'll bid on a set of plans, but it's a far richer solution if a client comes to me and says I want to build a house and how can this best be accomplished," says developer Schagrin. People hire build/design groups to build custom houses (and occasionally spec houses) and to renovate.

What is the difference between a developer who heads a build-design group and a builder? Typically a developer owns a piece of property and tries to match a client to the site, says Ellermann. "We agree to work together. The first professional brought in on the project is an architect, on staff or independent, who plots the design and works within the owner's price range. After meeting with the architect, it becomes a turnkey project. We take a person through the process and say here's what we have to decide and here are the people we're using—I hire the engineer, the construction manager and the crew—here's the schedule and here's what we must do to meet it." A build/design group saves you time and leg work.

Some build/design groups are headed by architects, who may not do the blueprints but are in on much of the early planning. Schagrin designs the initial floor layout. "I have taken on more of the role of the interiors person as well, although I'm not an interior designer. The nature of the houses in the last eight years has changed. Houses are larger, budgets are bigger, interest in detail is greater and opportunities are vast," he explains.

The biggest single risk of using a build/design group is that you don't have the objective third-party to act as your advocate when problems arise that you have when you hire a separate architect and builder or contractor.

THE INTERIOR DESIGNER

To understand the role of the interior designer, you have to see what drives the demand. Despite computer programs that allow consumers to view room arrangements on a screen and shop for furnishings on the Net or at a myriad of affordable design showrooms or retail stores, busy homeowners today often want a live person with design credentials to do it for them. They like the repartee and the relief they get from not having to make all decisions and do all the leg work.

ALICE AND KENNETH STARR (McLean, Virginia)

Independent counsel Kenneth Starr and his wife Alice base their renovation advice on the work they did in the early 1990s when they added a two-story addition, which included a kitchen and master bedroom, onto their 20-year-old home. They found it wise to use a decorator because a builder does not always consider how furniture will look or fit in a room. "Builders are more concerned with structure, while decorators can visualize the amount of light in a room and enhance a room with small improvements such as skylights, windows, moldings, recessed lighting and special finishes," says Alice, a marketing expert. "Unless you plan for the outcome, it may be too late to make the changes once a room is built. Our decorator helped design our new master bathroom and found a wonderful corner whirlpool bathtub. By knowing exactly where it was going to be placed, the builder extended the pipes and retrofitted the plumbing and floors for the tub. The builder also designed a long rectangular room to increase our children's bedrooms. But the decorator thought it more important to add skylights to the new addition downstairs and suggested a smaller addition to the children's rooms upstairs. She also recommended that we have recessed lighting in each room, which would not have been as easy to do if we had decided after the rooms were built to make the addition. She was right."

With bigger purses and a national penchant for building with greater detail, more people are hiring designers, who balance understanding of structural necessities with the complexity of making sure a room is built to house furniture, accessories, and people. Many building $500,000+ homes today are starting to use interior designers from start to finish. The designer becomes your insurance policy, another expert to review the layout of your home before construction. Those with ASID (American Society of Interior Designers) following their names have earned a college degree, completed an apprenticeship, and passed a design licensing exam, though many designers feel such accreditation is not worthwhile. You can feel comfortable using designers without such training, if you prefer their style, prices, and the way they work.

Designers are also used in varying degrees. Some rearrange furniture, find new furnishings, or add final touches to a room, charging only for their time. Others drive a project from beginning to end, acting like a contractor. John Robert Wiltgen in Chicago falls into that latter category. He often plans a home's spaces, works with the architect, creates a total interior and exterior design, develops working drawings that include foundation plans, electrical details, cabinet layouts, and framing layouts for the floors, walls, and roof, and even oversees the construction team, if asked.

From the start, you must clarify the designer's role. The designer must learn how your family intends to live in the house and how long you plan to stay there. He must develop a work timetable, set fees and payment schedules, and decide if the budget is reasonable for what's to be done.

The budget is based on the scope of the job and the extent of new furnishings to be purchased. Some designers charge by the hour—typically between $75 and $125—and occasionally a percentage of the products purchased on top of that. Some charge retail prices for the products, while others use a cost-plus fee or charge the wholesale price of materials plus a consulting or design fee, which ends up being close to the retail price.

All designers should give written estimates for work to be performed, products to be purchased, and any taxes and shipping charges. Most ask for a 50 percent deposit on carpet and labor costs, and 100 percent for fabric. A big advantage of using a decorator is that he will correct errors, often before the homeowner sees them. When work is done improperly or the wrong furniture is delivered, you don't have to spend hours on the phone with manufacturers or argue with professionals to resolve problems.

Contrary to popular belief, when an interior designer is used, your house may reflect your personality better than if you did the work yourself, says Marilyn Raines, ASID, owner of The Final Touch in Springfield, Missouri, and a designer for 25 years. "Using us, the client is so much more able to incorporate her things. We'll reupholster, or remat the picture, use the chair in a different room. We choose colors that can make a huge difference. It doesn't cost any more money to paint the right color than a wrong color."

A good designer also has a pipeline to some of the best or more unusual products, and to specialists such as painters, carpenters, and electricians. To find a reputable designer, call ASID, ask friends, go to local showcase houses, study model homes, and visit the interior design sections of department stores to view various designers' work.

Also be aware that many architects have become involved in designing interior rooms, doing everything from selecting molding to arranging and choosing furnishings. If you work well with an architect, you may like the continuity that this arrangement provides.

SIDESTEPPING THE EXPERTS

Are you overwhelmed by the idea of working with one or more professionals? Here is some good news. It is possible that you don't need one—if you think you can handle the details of a construction job. According to the United States Census Bureau, 78 percent of remodelings were done professionally, 18 percent were do-it-yourself projects, and 4 percent were buy-it-yourself jobs, in which homeowners bought materials, but hired others to do the work.

TREY AND ERIKA ELLIS (Los Angeles, California)

After watching a contractor take six months to remodel their California kitchen, author Trey Ellis felt he "could go it alone next time." So when he started redoing the master bathroom, he was his own contractor. He laid most of the tiles and did much of the demolition. "My wife, Erika, also an author, kept asking for a larger bathroom window while we were at it, but I said that it was too much extra trouble and expense. Besides, I felt as if I were already being a superior husband. I'd picked out a pricey, Japanese-style soaking tub/jacuzzi for her since she's addicted to taking baths. I'd thought I'd measured everything perfectly and the new tub was just going to fit into the old space. Well, when the deep, square-shaped tub arrived, I realized immediately that I had not thought at all about how I was going to actually get the monster into the room. I didn't have a choice about the window any longer. I took a sledgehammer to the existing window. The new, much bigger bathroom window, is now perhaps the best part of the bathroom." What a window of opportunity!

Many do-it-yourself projects are tackled during vacations. For a small job, that's fine. In remodeling especially, people can often do it themselves. NARI lists some jobs that are manageable if you are patient and handy, such as painting, cleaning out gutters, and even building a deck.

But beware. Avoid electrical or structural tasks. When a new roof you put on leaks or the ceiling falls in because you forgot to use the proper supports the cost of the damage far outweighs the do-it-yourself savings. At some point you have to say, "This is more than I can handle myself." If it's a large project, it doesn't make sense to learn on the job.

Being your own contractor requires more knowledge than you may think, and in some cases you could risk your life (there are safety precautions you may not be aware of without proper training) and your life savings. A common mistake is leaving out necessary portions of work in your original bid that you end up paying more for later when changes are made. And if a mistake is made by your subs, the buck stops with you. You eat the cost to correct it.

If you decide to proceed, this can become another full-time job. Before you begin, research your project to learn where to find ideas and financial worksheets. You will also need to know how to arrange construction financing, do cost analysis, complete contractor forms and subcontractor agreements, hire subs, schedule, and manage the project. One man read all the Time-Life books on home building and remodeling. Then he and his wife, both of whom are very handy, tackled their remodeling themselves. There were glitches, but the gutting of their vintage home turned out to be quite successful—at least it looks great and no one was injured.

Once research is accomplished, plan the job, purchase the right tools and learn how to use them, prepare or obtain drawings, apply for building permits, follow codes and other regulations, hire and monitor the subs (you may not be able to find the best ones), schedule workstaff, handle product delivery, arrange inspections, test soil for water content during the process, and plan for unforeseen problems. In addition, you must pay for materials, worry about insurance, and accept the fact that the work will not be warranted.

If you can handle all this—fine, though the experts say it's probably easier and cheaper in the long-run to hire a team of professionals if the job is extensive. Regardless which route you take, your level of involvement in the project is up to you.

CONSTRUCTIVE TIPS

Five Resources to Get You Started

Want to feel smart and in control? Much like doing stretching before a hard workout, here are five exercises to get you in shape and revved up for your building or remodeling project.

1. Read shelter and trade publications such as *House & Garden, Better Homes & Gardens, Metropolitan Home, Architectural Digest, Traditional Home, Remodeling Magazine* and *Home Remodeling* to get ideas.

2. Check out computer programs for budgeting, designing, and landscaping ideas.

3. Watch videos. There are a number of how-to videos you can rent, check out from the library, or borrow from a trade association, that will show you how to do-it-yourself, whether you are putting in a floor or building a treehouse. If you opt to order a house, gardening, lighting, or greenhouse kit, get one that is accompanied by a video that demonstrates installation.

4. Get professionals' numbers. There are phone books on CD-ROM that offer residential and business listings, street addresses, 800 phone numbers, and fax numbers: *The 300 Million Ultimate Phone Directory* by American Business Information ($59.99); *Powerfinder Phone Disc* by Phone Disc ($79.99); *Listings Deluxe* by Pro CD ($44.99).

5. Skittish about using a computer or don't have a CD-ROM drive? Now all you have to do is dial local information for any number in the country.

✔ CHECKLIST 1

What to Ask a Reference

Questions to ask when checking a tradesperson's references (as suggested by National Association of the Remodeling Industry, Inc.).

❑ Did the builder communicate well?

❑ Were you pleased with the quality of the work?

❑ Were you satisfied with his business practices?

❑ Did the crew show up on time? Did they clean up?

❑ Were you comfortable with the subcontractors?

❑ Was the job completed on schedule? On budget? If not, why?

❑ Did the builder fulfill his end of the contract?

❑ Did the contractor stay in touch throughout the job?

❑ Were the final details finished in a timely manner?

❑ Would you use the contractor again without hesitation?

✔ CHECKLIST 2

What to Ask the Tradesperson

In order to get to the heart of what you need to know, you have to ask the builder several probing questions (as suggested by National Association of the Remodeling Industry, Inc.).

❏ How long have you been in business?

❏ Have you ever been sued? (If he says no, you can call the Better Business Bureau to double check.) Make sure he provides warranties and insurance and check policy numbers.

❏ Who will be assigned as project supervisor for the job?

❏ What is your approach to a project of this scope?

❏ How do you operate? Do you come every day at the same time? Weekends? Nights? When do the workers arrive and leave? What about delays or changes in the schedule? Will I be contacted? By whom?

❏ Is your company a full service or specialty firm?

❏ Do you offer design services?

❏ What is the timeframe for starting?

❏ What percentage of your business is repeat or referral?

❏ How many projects like mine have you completed in the past year?

❏ Who are your suppliers?

3

Your Lot in Life

Where do you want to live? Do you like old established neighborhoods such as Ladue, Missouri, Chestnut Hill, Massachusetts, Beverly Hills, California, that teem with shade trees, sloping lawns and vintage homes with personality? Or do you prefer the sticks where you can design and construct a new home on a larger lot in the woods, which may be more affordable than an established neighborhood.

MICHAEL AND BENITA ROMANO (River Forest, Illinois)

Benita and Michael Romano turned what could have been a disaster into a bright spot. "Our house is built on a hill and we thought we'd build it up higher, but the village of River Forest made us build the house lower. The builder should have known this in advance. We were left with a 12-foot wall of mud. I terraced that mud and built an English garden. It turned out to be a godsend. It keeps our house so private. In fact, it's so beautiful people think we did it on purpose."

Where you build is as important as what you build. The mantra of anyone building or remodeling should be "Location, location, location." But the location you desire can be quite different from what your Uncle Harry might like. So take the time to carefully select the right lot in the right location.

DEBBE DUNNING (Del Mar, California)

Debbe Dunning, who plays Heidi on *Home Improvement,* recently married two-time Olympic gold-medal volleyball player Steven Timmons, who owns Red Sand Clothing Company, headquartered in Encinitas, California. The couple moved into his ramshackle bachelor pad in Del Mar just north of San Diego, according to Dunning's publicist John Zaring. Debbe completely redecorated the home's interior and then the couple tackled the exterior. The house sits on a huge hill which overlooks the ocean. They had the hill terraced and then proceeded to design and landscape it pretty much themselves.

GREEN COMMUNITIES

Does it require more green to go green? And how involved is the process? Consider this: Hardwood and ceramic floors are more expensive than synthetic versions, like processed wood or vinyl flooring, but the real McCoy gives off fewer fumes and lasts longer.

Many builders are thinking green because consumers are demanding it. But the cost to do so doesn't have to rival the national debt. Several new communities that are ecologically correct are popping up across the country. The tiny town of Stelle, Illinois, for example, maintains its own utilities that harness renewable energy, and many residents have environmentally friendly and energy-conscious passive solar homes. The town was founded 25 years ago by the nonprofit Stelle Group and is now overseen by the Stelle Community Association.

The Fellowship for Intentional Community, a nonprofit organization based in Rutledge, Missouri, publishes a quarterly magazine, *Communities,* that addresses unusual communities. Each issue is devoted to a theme such as sustainable building or ecologically correct communities that use reusable resources. The organization also publishes a directory listing more than 600 communities that have been set up for people to live and work together while pursuing a specific goal such as ecology, spirituality, or shared political beliefs. About one-third of these communities have an ecological connection. For example, Dancing Rabbit Ecovillage, also in Rutledge, provides a sustainable lifestyle of farming and manufacturing for its 12 residents; Firius in Shutesbury, Massachusetts, offers educational and work programs with a strong ecological focus to its 50 residents.

For additional information on how to be ecologically correct when building or remodeling, check out the website of the U.S. Healthy House Institute under Internet resources in the Associations list at the back of the book.

SETTING YOUR SITES

Everybody has a different dream when looking for the perfect community. And each community presents a different package.

Some builders sell the lot with a home already constructed on it. Some people buy a lot and then build on it. Some don't want to move at all. They choose to add on or remodel, making their homes grander and more comfortable, so they can stay in their school district or neighborhood.

Setting your sites is crucial. Make a list of must-haves, maybes and can-live-withouts for any potential neighborhood. "The most desirable characteristics today," says the NAHB, "are places that capitalize on pleasures of public life and are safe." Based on a 1996 NAHB survey, people are looking for jogging trails, park areas, outdoor swimming pools, playgrounds, and lakes.

To find your idyllic spot, start by reading newspaper ads in your area or an area where you think you want to live. Take a drive. Perhaps you will find yourself in the country looking at a lot you love smack in the heart of farmland in a newly developed area. Or maybe you catch a glimpse of rolling hills and a run-down house through a stand of tall pines. Your fantasy may be fixing up that house.

Daydreams are fine, but what do you really know about the area? Is it in close proximity to stores, public transportation, public parks, sidewalks, churches, and temples, or hospitals? How far is it from your place of work? A long commute can quickly grow weary. Find out the property's resale value, the status of the schools, and the crime and safety records of the area. Check the costs of utility hookups and sewer service. If you are really serious, have a survey done. Listen for the sounds of trains, planes, and traffic during the day. Go back at night. Find out who's going to collect and dispose of your garbage, do snow removal, maintain roads, and provide fire and police protection. Where will you find new friends, and will your current friends and family come to visit or is the new home too far away?

If you're really serious about a property, learn as much as you can about it and the neighborhood. Check out the neighbors by knocking on doors, visiting the area's retail shops to see if there's a healthy mix of the people you like to have close to you, attending a community meeting, and chatting with people about the pros and cons of the area to get a feel for who lives there and whether you'll fit in.

Snoop around city hall. Find out what's going on. What's the tax base? Is it an established area or one that's growing? Are there are any road changes planned such as connecting streets through the subdivision around the corner? Make sure the area isn't connected to an interstate highway ramp. You should understand exactly what you are buying and pay accordingly.

Visit the area several times, at different times of the day and during different seasons. Yes, according to some shrewd salesperson, the property may be gone in a flash if you don't put down a deposit, but it's better to be safe than sorry.

When you're looking at your possible lot in life, visualize how the home you want to build (or remodel) will look on that plot of ground. Are there trees, hills, streams, brooks? Can the house take advantage of sunshine? Building the house so windows are positioned on south-facing walls will increase the sunlight inside. Sunshine helps offset low temperatures and decrease high heating bills.

Now dig deeper. It's mandatory to consider what kind of ground you will be building on. Soil and water conditions should be examined by an engineer. "If you're building a home that is part of a subdivision, such as model 'A' on lot number 6, the builder/developer is probably constructing 50 to 100 at a time and had his engineer do the soil work already as well as the structural design of the home. All you're doing is paying for the house," says Patty Brown of the American Society of Civil Engineers (ASCE), which represents more than 120,000 civil engineers worldwide.

THE ROLE OF VARIOUS ENGINEERS

When you build a custom home or an addition, an engineer should be consulted to make sure the land will be suitable. Brown cites the example of a woman in Houston who built an unattached garage. "The city didn't approve it because she didn't have a certified professional engineer verify soil conditions."

Engineers come in a variety of flavors, depending on what needs to be done. Like architects and builders, they are registered and certified by individual states by passing an exam, which earns them a P.E. after their names. Most have either a bachelor's or master's degree. In terms of homebuilding, only certain engineers have the expertise to check the layout and composition of the land before designing a structure.

Civil Engineer

A civil engineer designs municipal utilities and roadways. He is brought in at the inception of subdivision development. Surveyors divide the property and actually formulate the platted subdivision, then the engineer plans a corresponding set of blueprints for water, sewers and storm drainage, roadways, and earth movement. The public utility companies such as gas, electric, cable, and phone add their lines after that.

Geotechnical Engineer

Once an area is developed, a geotechnical engineer will be hired to analyze the soil and make suggestions to the structural engineer on how to design the foundation. Geotechnical engineers calculate bearing capacity and/or permeability of the soil. "We study the earth movement so the underlying soil we build on is structurally suitable," Brown says.

SOIL TYPES AND FOUNDATIONS

There are no absolutes about soil types in any one area of the country. Variances in soils exist within the same area, says engineer Jeff Palmer, vice president of land development for Town & Country Homes in Westchester, Illinois. Palmer pigeonholes soil types, however, as clay, silty, sandy, organic, or rocky. "Most important, soils must be compactable and must develop some type of bearing strength."

In many parts of the country, predominantly the Gulf Coast region and parts of California, *expansive soil* conditions exist. "Expansive soil doesn't have rock close to the surface and is sensitive to shrinking when dry, and swelling when wet," says Palmer. This may cause the ground to heave and could crack a building's foundation.

Most *clay and silt soils* are highly expansive, says Palmer. Before building on certain clay soils, it's important to obtain an estimate of the depth and degree of soil dehydration. Taking this into account, a foundation depth suitable for new construction may then be calculated. Typically the house will warrant a post-tension concrete slab foundation which is comprised of steel cables that run crosswise and are tensioned and fastened permanently to each side of the foundation. As the soil expands or contracts, the slab moves as an entire unit preventing differential movement that can crack a home's foundation.

Concrete slabs are regulated by local and national building codes. Post-tension slabs have to be structurally designed by an engineer and the thickness and design determined by the square footage, number of stories in the house, and how much weight it has to support as stated in the local codes.

Sandy soils such as those found in Florida can be difficult to build on if they get too wet. On the other hand, the compaction of the sand can provide a good sturdy soil that is usually not a problem. These soils typically require a specially engineered concrete slab floor poured directly on the ground, and a foundation that includes footings underneath bearing and permanent walls. Some homebuilders in these areas want crawl spaces instead. These are typically constructed of grade beam with a perimeter foundation wall and interior pier foundation to support beams under the foundation.

Essentially, crawl space and basement-type construction are similar. A crawl space is smaller and not as susceptible to expansive soil problems because it has deep footings below any fluctuations and water content. The crawl space must be protected from ground moisture with special foundation vents, and treated wood is used to obviate termite damage and decay. Footings for the perimeter and piers of a crawl space can be used in any type of soil as long as they go down deep enough to bearing soil to provide bearing capacity for the footing.

Basements are just a deep foundation with concrete footings or concrete or block walls. Thickness of walls is dictated by the height of the basement wall and local and national building codes.

Organic soils or topsoil or areas adjacent to wetlands aren't good places on which to build foundations because that soil, comprised of decomposed organic materials, will continue to decompose and settle. The same is true of a home built on a land fill, which can shift. This situation can be rectified by removing organics and replacing the soil with an overlay of better material such as stone or clay.

Rocky soils are ideal to build foundations on because they drain well, but can create problems for landscaping. If there are huge boulders in the soil, which is sometimes the case in California, the area might have to be blasted by drilling holes in the ground, pouring in a liquid, and using dynamite as a catalyst.

TYPOGRAPHY, WATER ABSORPTION, SEEPAGE, AND DRAINAGE

In any type of building, typography, water absorption, and seepage are significant. Do you want a flat lot? If so, what about water runoff? Good surface drainage will prevent flooding and soil shifting. A home site has to be built high enough so when dirt is filled in around the house water drains away from it. You might check out the lot after a rainstorm to see if this is the case.

You must also determine if the sewers are adequate and who maintains them? Is the area in a flood plain? Your local building department or Federal Insurance Administration office can give you the facts on flooding. (You can find phone numbers in the back of this book.) It's important to also check out soil erosion, and the prevalence of landslides or earthquakes.

An underground water table too close to the surface is a problem for basements. Many homes in Florida or Arizona, for example, don't have basements for this reason and structurally don't need them. There's no problem with frost in these areas which can change the volume of the foundation, hoist it, and move the house. Also, the high ground water could cause a house with a basement to flood. But in an area like Chicago, basements are *de rigueur* because the foundation must extend four feet below the frost line.

It's not only necessary to check the water table before construction, but during building as well. It's monitored to make sure that soils are compacted within specifications. As the earth is placed, it's tested. Any soft areas are removed and replaced by hard clay or stone.

BRING IN MORE ENGINEERS

Structural Engineer

Once a geotechnical engineer determines the soil type and water absorption, the information is fed to a structural engineer who will help an architect with the blueprints. He designs trusses and the foundation and decides what size beams are needed and where bearing walls should be placed.

Architects understand some rules of thumb, but more intricate homes or creative designs need the analysis of a structural engineer. Talk to the architect and make sure you are happy with his choice of an engineer, then contact the local chapter of ASCE for verification of the engineer's background.

For a remodeling, your need for the analysis of a structural engineer depends on whether plans involve structural changes such as adding on to your home, or moving walls that will change the support system or add substantial weight. A home has critical points. If not supported properly, it will settle incorrectly and structural failure could result. Fortunately, homes are built so systematically today that structural problems rarely develop.

Electrical Engineer/Utilities

Once the blueprints are drafted, an electrical engineer designs the indoor and outdoor wiring throughout the site.

BOB AND RANDY COSTAS (St. Louis, Missouri)

"The hardest thing about building a house is mapping out the electricity," says Randy Costas, wife of sports announcer Bob Costas. "The day I had to plan the electricity, I flew in from New York. It was freezing cold and when the electrician asked me where I wanted the sockets, I was too cold to think about sockets. I should have put a switch at the top of the basement stairs to turn the lights off in the playroom. Now we have to run downstairs every time to do it. So I suggest that you do your electricity in the spring when you're not thinking about how cold you are. And do a thorough walk-through."

MICHAEL AND BENITA ROMANO (River Forest, Illinois)

The biggest mistake Benita and Michael Romano made when building their new house was not installing enough electricity. "We put up a million Christmas lights and we're always blowing a fuse. They gave us the minimum. The electrician asked, 'Is it enough?' And I said 'yes.' However, when they tell you something, perhaps triple it." Another error, says Benita, is the noise. "The new house is not made of plaster and we used PVC pipes. We should have used cast iron because we can hear every toilet flush all over the house."

Before you lay the foundation, look into access to public utilities. How do you get to them? Make sure trenches are dug to accommodate utility lines. It may be more expensive to run the lines if your house is on a hill.

If you're in a rural area, you may also need a septic system. Talk to neighbors or the health department to find out if there are rules governing septic systems and learn how far they have to be from your home or a well. Water absorption rates will affect the type of septic system you can have and where it can be placed. If you have to dig a well, you'll also need to know the specifications and costs.

ENVIRONMENTAL CONTAMINANTS

Are there environmental concerns in the area where you plan to build? An environmental engineer will verify that no contaminants exist on a site prior to acquisition. If you purchase a farm, the environmental engineer needs to analyze the barnyard area to make sure no underground diesel tanks are present. If they are, they need to be removed and the problem remediated. These engineers also check for radon (a radioactive gas) in the soil before and after you build your house. They will examine wetlands and do a species evaluation, often with the help of a biologist.

THE RESIDENTIAL BUILDING INSPECTOR/ENGINEER

If you buy an existing home to fix up, you still must go through the paces. You need to call in a licensed residential building inspector, who may also be an engineer. He can tell you if the home is a smart purchase for your prospective remodeling project. Get his comments in writing. If problems exist, try to negotiate corrections with the seller, or at least agree to split the costs. The strength of the real estate market will affect the seller's compliance.

AREA RESTRICTIONS

Whether building or remodeling, the area's restrictions such as zoning, size of lots, setbacks, variances, and any historic guidelines must also be explored. You must find out what percentage of the lot the house can occupy, also called the footprint. And the footprint must fit within the building envelope, the space left after setbacks and easements are taken into account.

Zoning

Check with city hall (the local zoning officer, commission, or planning board) or the local library to learn the area's master plan. Find out about lot sizes and whether the area is zoned residential or industrial. Will there be room left on the lot for later expansion within the setback requirements? Setbacks are the mandated distances between a building and its lot lines. Most municipalities establish their own setback requirements. What about parking? If a house already exists on the lot, check with the municipality for any known setback violations. You need a survey to calculate this.

You'll also need to know whether you can legally operate a business out of your home. Are there any federal environmental constraints? Any future plans for the area? That beautiful open field nearby may be killed by a shopping center to be constructed three weeks after you move in.

The Survey

It might behoove you to get a real staked survey rather than a spot one before you sign on the dotted line. A staked survey, where iron pipes are positioned in the ground, allows you to see the parameters of the lot with setbacks plotted. The survey also shows easements and encroachments. It should be done by a registered state land surveyor whose name you can get through your state government office. A site plan must be submitted to city hall along with building (or remodeling) plans for building permit approval. The site plan is mapped to scale to depict dimensions and angles of lot boundary lines. It also indicates dimensions of existing structures and their distance from property lines and from each other, direction of slope or drainage, elevations, easements, and sewage disposal or septic fields.

EASEMENTS AND ENCROACHMENTS

If an owner has given permission for limited use of his property to a neighbor (unrecorded) or the government (recorded), this is known as an easement. Be aware of any easements on the property you buy.

An encroachment is when adjacent property, such as bushes or a garage, extends beyond your property line into the neighbor's yard. If you build a bay window or a deck that sticks out beyond the setback, that's an encroachment. You, as the encroacher, may compensate your neighbor for the land you're using. The property survey will pinpoint any easements or encroachments.

VARIANCE

If you encroach, you might be able to get the city to grant a variance (permission to use land that encroaches on a neighbor's property because it may not conform to an area's setback restrictions) but the process is mired in red tape. If a variance is not granted, then you will have to tear down that bay window or deck. If you buy a house that has existing encroachments that you haven't checked out, you, not the former owner, are accountable. One man bought a home with a deck attached on the back that was built by the previous owner. The house was adjacent to an empty buildable lot that was owned by the neighbors on the other side of the property. When the neighbors decided to sell the lot, a survey was done. The homeowner learned that the deck encroached on the empty lot by several feet. The city told him he would have to tear it down.

Before buying any lot or existing home to remodel, it might be judicious to talk to a neighborhood trustee to determine whether there are any violations or pending lawsuits involving the previous owner. You can also get this information through the municipality's records. And again, it would be wise to have a real staked survey done.

Covenants/Trust Indentures

Covenants are rules governing the type of house that can be built and the way in which you can use the land. These are mandated by the neighborhood association, developers, or local governments to maintain a certain look in the community or to protect your property. Perhaps you cannot have a fence or trampoline in your yard. Or you may be required to build a fence around a swimming pool.

Building Codes

If you are moving a wall, it must be done according to code to ensure the structure will still be stable. This code is for your safety. Codes also regulate the style of house you can build, and prohibit any type of structural changes without a building permit.

MARY ANNE ROTHBERG ROWEN AND ANDY ROWEN
(New York City/Upstate New York)

Mary Anne Rothberg Rowen and her husband Andy, an attorney, had just built a home in upstate New York that was a successful experience. They assumed then that remodeling three rooms of their historic New York City cooperative would be easier, less costly and less time-consuming. Wrong! It took almost as long to remodel the three rooms, and on a per-square-foot basis was more expensive. "It's easier to start with something new rather than trying to make something old look new again and living in a mess. Stripping and finding pieces that match with what you have whether trim, tiles, fittings, or flooring is difficult," says Mary Anne. "We were constrained by covenants in the landmark building. We could not change anything on the exterior such as the windows. If we needed to install through-the-wall air conditioning, it had to be done according to the building's master plan. We could not move a bathroom and put it over a public space because of potential leaks. And we could not just stick a dryer or stove hood vent anyplace, but had to go through the Landmarks Commission to get permission."

HISTORIC PROPERTY

If you drool over a home in a historic district that you want to remodel, stop before you start. Owners of single-family residences that are landmarks, that sit in landmark districts, or are built in planned communities, first need to make their homes compatible with the guidelines of their communities. To learn these rules, contact your local planning commission or historic association.

Some ordinances dictate what building materials or colors can be used, as well as the height of the buildings and what structural changes can be made to existing homes. Be sure you obtain a copy of your community's regulations before you plan and build. Some homeowners have been forced to remove additions or parts of their homes that did not comply with regulations.

It's also important to check into federal regulations. *Standards for Rehabilitation and Guidelines for Rehabilitating Historical Buildings* are issued by the Secretary of the Interior, United States Department of the Interior, which governs what you can and cannot do. There are ten standards that cover everything from building exteriors and interiors to the site and district/neighborhood.

Contrary to what you'd expect, an addition to a historic building has to be distinguishable from the historic structure. Most homeowners unwittingly try to make the addition match, but this is considered falsifying the historic character, explains Esley Hamilton, St. Louis County Department of Parks & Recreation, Historic Preservation. The implication is that the remodeler is making the original structure look larger than it was during its period of significance.

Some local municipalities are more relaxed about these mandates. If you're lucky, preservation restrictions may be limited to only the exterior.

One boon for homeowners is that those who own historic houses can receive a property tax assessment freeze for 12 years when they rehabilitate their homes, including the exteriors, as long as they follow the guidelines. Call your local or state historic preservation agency for a copy, the National Trust for Historic Preservation, or the Secretary of the Interior for a copy of these guidelines.

CHECK THE TRUST DEED

One final check, which is usually a contingency in any real estate contract, is to investigate the trust deed on your property to ensure the title is clear. A title insurance company will run a complete title search to uncover any liens or lawsuits on the land. This eliminates the possibility of a bizarre inheritance where one sibling gets the house that another sells without ownership. Title insurance covers easements, encroachments, and other restrictions, but will not pay to remedy zoning or subdivision violations.

INTERSTATE LAND SALES ACT

Subdivisions of 100 lots or more on undeveloped land which is sold across state lines falls under a public disclosure law requiring the seller to provide the buyer with a property report on the land offered prior to the purchase, says John Kuzava, examiner with the RESPA/ILA division of the Office of Consumer and Regulatory Affairs, U.S. Department of Housing and Urban Affairs.

WEDDING YOUR HOUSE TO ITS ENVIRONMENT

Okay, you've checked soil types and water tables, municipal regulations, and public access sources until you're blue in the face. And you've established that the physical site is buildable. Now what?

It's time to indulge a bit of fantasy. Sit back and picture the house you want to build and decide how you might want to position it on the lot. Some people center a building, some turn it sideways, but what's now important is to leave room for your house to grow with your family.

Think about where to put the kitchen, what views you want to have from the family room, and the best and safest location for a pool. If you put in a pond or greenhouse, what type of backyard spaces will be left? Where will the driveway go and how will it lead to the garage? Do you want sun in the morning or evening—and in which rooms? Do you want maximum privacy when you're outside barbecuing or sunbathing? Spend time walking around your property at different times of the day, and if possible, in different seasons to make these decisions.

A lot is the landscape of your dreams where what you construct on that land turns into a home. Like Dorothy said in *The Wizard of Oz,* "There's no place like home." But don't start clicking your heels together just yet. Once you've done your homework and have an idea of what your project will look like, where it will be located, and what it will cost, it's time to figure out how you're going to foot the bill and still sleep at night. No matter what your dream, you don't want to overextend yourself in the here and now.

CONSTRUCTIVE TIPS

Country Mouse versus City Mouse Syndrome

You hear about a great city condo or townhouse, close to shops, restaurants, and main thoroughfares, and your heart begins to palpitate like a just-caught fish on a line. The thought, however, of moving to the suburbs with lots of greenery and few neighbors sends your spirits plummeting and your nerves a twittering. You're definitely an urban folk. But how do you really know whether you're a country mouse or city mouse? Sometimes, you don't, until you're in one environment or the other. The following test may help you sort it out. True or false:

1. You prefer to walk or use public transportation rather than drive.

2. The idea of having two or more cars gives you hives.

CONSTRUCTIVE TIPS (continued)

3. You love having restaurants, bookstores, dry cleaners, a drugstore, and a grocery store within walking distance.

4. You don't mind crowds and, in fact, get nervous when you are alone on the street.

5. You enjoy community living and are happiest when you get to know your neighbors well, though you don't mind being among strangers at times.

6. You're content to exercise on a treadmill or stationary bicycle in your home or at a health club. You don't need a park or country trails for jogging.

7. You enjoy being on the cutting edge of trends, whether it's hair styles or hardware.

8. You want to be near restaurants, shops, and movie theaters that stay open late so you will always have something to do at night.

9. You love to cook, especially with exotic and ethnic ingredients, and you enjoy shopping at specialty markets where they know what arrugula and cilantro are.

10. Your idea of a wonderful Sunday is to head out for a caffe latte while reading the paper, then tour the latest museum exhibition, watch a foreign flick with subtitles, view a parade, or go to brunch at a soul food restaurant.

Answers: If you said "True" to most of the above statements, you're definitely a city mouse. If you want to move to the country, try it out on a temporary basis (rent a place) before you move permanently.

PART TWO

Moving Forward One Square Foot at a Time

4

What Do You Mean "Price Per Square Foot"?

You like to save a buck. You haggle over prices at car dealerships, appliance stores, antique shops. You know what you can and cannot afford. Somewhere in the back of your mind you've unconsciously budgeted a figure for these items. So why be a wimp when it comes to budgeting for your new home or remodeling? Whether a clothing allowance, grocery allotment, or entertainment quota, budgets provide some stability and control over how we spend our hard-earned cash.

Some panic at the thought of budgeting, however. They're skittish about the math and accounting involved. But today computer programs have helped simplify the process of drafting a budget by eliminating trial and error, serendipity, and unreliable formulas. Programs like Planix 3D Deluxe Home Designer by Autodesk, 3D Home Architect from Broderbund, or Dream Home Designer by Alpha offer budgeting features as well as help with design and materials. All are in the price range of $45 to $60-plus.

Some still prefer to calculate a budget longhand with pen and paper. And that's fine, too. Whatever works and keeps you on the financial straight and narrow.

JUDY AND SHELDON COHEN (Ladue, Missouri)

Judy Cohen and her husband Sheldon Cohen, a dentist, did a remodeling that cost three times what they spent for their home. "We added a pool, entertainment room, a new kitchen, a master suite, and updated bathrooms." They figured it was worth the price because they planned to live in the house at least another eight to ten years. "It wasn't worth the aggravation," says Judy in retrospect. "Our kitchen went smoothly, although the family was cooking French toast and pizza on the barbecue pit all summer. But the upstairs reconfiguration and first floor entertainment room, which was supposed to take six months, has taken more than a miserable year of construction."

How do you size up a budget? Many homeowners about to remodel, add on, or build a home begin by thinking about the price per square foot. Often developers and builders quote prices that way. This approach sounds appealing, but it's a bit too pedestrian. This measure can also fool you. It may be a starting point for new construction, but other factors should be taken into account. And it's a less accurate measure for remodeling.

On a per-square-foot basis, it costs much more to remodel than to build for several reasons. Remodeling is more labor intensive and involves more time. Workers must deal with existing structures and unknown conditions. And the job site is much more complicated because furniture has to be moved, rooms kept clean, and resident's schedules considered.

Per-square-foot cost is an empirical formula that can have many compositions, similar to different cookie batters. This measure falls short of accurately conveying the quality of materials or level of craftsmanship a homeowner will get for a certain price. These must be fleshed out in greater detail with brand names, descriptions, and measurements.

LESLIE SCALLET AND MAURY LIEBERMAN (Washington, D.C.)

Go with the best labor not the best price, which is a lesson learned by Leslie Scallet and her husband Maury Lieberman when they redid the master bathroom in their Washington, D.C. townhouse. They hired a small unknown contractor to do the work and soon after completion water started dripping through the ceiling. The contractor came back to fix the problem, but a few days later water came cascading through the ceiling into the living room. "The pipes weren't hooked up correctly," says Leslie, an attorney. The couple admit their mistakes. "We didn't check the contractor's qualifications, we didn't write some important elements into the contract like a starting and finishing date, and we didn't go see samples of his work." They brought in someone else to fix the problem.

Furthermore, per-square-foot pricing depends on costs of materials and labor, which can differ drastically in various parts of the country, in urban versus suburban areas, and even between different craftspeople in the same area. One Midwestern painter was known to quote different fees for different clients, depending on how much he thought they could pay. In New York City and other urban areas where the cost of living is much higher, many contractors build additional costs into their higher prices to pay for the parking tickets they anticipate receiving when they're forced to double park their trucks in front of a client's apartment building on a crowded Manhattan street, or to cover the losses due to urban theft.

There is a better way to calculate the cost of your project that won't be like playing a slot machine, where you keep trying until you score or run out of money. Simply choose a final figure you can live with. It's a more comfortable way of arriving at a price. The figure should be based on your finances and the resale value of the house. If you are building, you should come up with the final price for your new home, which includes the cost of the lot, based on your finances and the neighborhood.

Once you have a ballpark figure in mind, start to develop a detailed wish list of the furniture and appliances that will go in each room to get an idea of how large the room will need to be. Before you ask your architect or contractor if the project is feasible, you should visit some building showrooms on your own to get an idea of what is available and how much things cost.

Like anything else you do, the more leg work you've done up front, the faster the job will go. That's why it's smart to compile a list of appliances, equipment, materials, fixtures, and furniture you like. Go to more showrooms and compare selections and prices. Try to find a wholesaler willing to sell to your professionals, if not to you directly. Doing so before a project gets off the ground may seem like a lot of work, but the more information you provide to your work crew, the more likely it is that they can submit a bid that won't elicit gasps of surprise or send you into cardiac arrest.

Here's a hypothetical example. You've got a 16-by-20-foot kitchen that you want to redo. You hate your old kitchen and want a totally new work/eating space. You plan to gut the room back to the studs, move the plumbing around to better take advantage of a new bay window, and change some framing and firring so the new walls are plumb and true. Then you will add new recessed lights, a new hardwood floor, new hardwood stained cabinets with nice pulls, ambient and task lighting with a hanging fixture over your new breakfast area, and built-in bookshelves for all your cookbooks and food and wine magazines. Because you like to cook and your family likes to gather in the room, you have in mind some restaurant-grade equipment—stainless steel appliances and marble countertops—a few handpainted tiles on the backsplashes to add personality, and some fancier crown and baseboard moldings. It's beginning to sound pretty spiffy and worthy of one of the glossy home-shelter magazines, isn't it?

In addition to hiring an architect and contractor, you'll also need a cabinet-maker or millworker for the woodwork and built-ins, a painter, a plumber, and an electrician to hook up electrics and install new wiring for the enhanced lighting. Your architect breaks the news to you gently—the room could run $100,000 or more depending on your location. You swoon. You may not be able to spend that much, or you may not want to because you know your $500,000 house would never sell for more than $600,000 in your neighborhood.

Who needs such a nice kitchen anyway? you rationalize. You then bake some brownies for the work crew and ask them to redesign the space for half the price—which may also cost you an additional fee. You want to find out what you could end up with for about $50,000?

To minimize the headache of a new project and stretch your budget, replace the old linoleum floor with inexpensive vinyl or wood rather than ceramic or slate. Replace dingy cabinets with less expensive cabinets that have fewer details and use ¾-inch high-pressured laminate instead of ⅝-inch real wood for the shelves. Solid-surface countertops can be used instead of stone. Buy equipment that's readily available in appliance stores instead of commercial-grade items. And a chandelier or hanging lamp will add a gleam to your kitchen without the cost of recessed lighting. You will probably also have to keep the plumbing and electrical work intact. And forget about moving walls.

If you calculate the cost on a per-square-foot basis, the higher-priced version is more than $300, compared to $150 for the more affordable solution. So you see the dichotomy that can exist. In either case, by adding up the materials and labor, you better understand all that's going into your project.

When it comes to building a new house, the price-per-square-foot can be easier to determine because starting from scratch doesn't present as many unknowns. Once again, the per-square-foot price is only a starting point.

The questions your architect or builder should ask you are how large you want your house to be and how much you want to spend. The latter question may be much easier to answer than the former. If you have no total size in mind, start by making up a list of rooms and their measurements. If you still have no clue, measure your existing rooms and decide whether they need to be larger, smaller or the same size. Then throw in some hallways and bathrooms. Most architects and builders don't include basements, garages, or attics in the total square footage number—those are extras you get gratis, unless you live in the city where they're sometimes included at an extra cost. It's important to define exactly what you want.

Add up the measurements and you're closer to having a total square foot figure. But remember to think for the long term. Have vision. If you're building a one-story house, it might prove economical to add a second floor now—even if you don't finish the space right away—because it will be cheaper than adding it later. Similarly, even if you don't want a finished basement, it's smart to have the space excavated when the foundation is being dug rather than after the house is built. And you may also want to rough in the basement plumbing because it's very expensive to add later.

Of course, you want to keep furnishings in mind. The more space you add the more furniture you need to purchase. And heating and cooling all your fabulous new spaces are other costs to consider.

DEAN AND JANICE LEVY (New York, New York)

Dean Levy learned that quality has many different definitions. When they remodeled their New York City cooperative apartment, the Levy's expectations of quality were not the same as the contractor's. Levy, one of the owners of the family antiques business, Bernard and S. Dean Levy, kept trying to explain what the couple expected. But the painter never understood and just thought the couple was difficult to work with. When the painter finally finished, the results were less than satisfactory. "We probably should have fired him long before, and I would advise others to do so before it's too late," Dean Levy says.

In addition to the size of the rooms, you also need to define the quality of materials and equipment, which greatly affect the price. Since quality is a bit subjective, this can be very difficult to verbalize. That is why per-square-foot cost is not a good measure for new homes. Many builders and developers in the Chicago area quote new houses at an average price of $165 per square foot, but each builder's formula includes materials that vary in quality. Some offer laminate countertops but not Corian or granite, vinyl or carpeted floors rather than oak strip, a bit of marble tile in the master bathroom instead of all marble, and bi-fold closet doors instead of solid-core or raised panel ones.

Often it's critical to see samples or get written descriptions to fully understand the differences in quality and price. For example, there will be a significant difference in price between a simple ceiling-mounted fixture versus recessed low-voltage halogen lighting on a sophisticated dimming system, or between ¾-inch plastic laminate open bookshelves with ½-inch thick fronts and 1½-inch-thick shelves with the same size fronts that have an exotic wood veneer and concealed lighting to illuminate rare books.

As the prices of these elements are added to the mix, your costs will escalate, raising the price per square foot. Another reason the per-square-foot cost is inaccurate is that not all rooms are created equal—or constructed for the same price. Your kitchen and master bathroom are likely to be built at a much higher per-square-foot price than your basement or child's bedroom. More tradespeople are involved in the work and more equipment, appliances, and detailing go into finishing them. Also, when you're remodeling, don't forget to factor into the budget the cost increase when your homeowners insurance policy is adjusted to reflect the added value of the addition.

As you begin to understand how the final pricetag evolves, you'll realize that there also needs to be some give and take—sacrificing some amenities in one area to afford those in another. This is what design professionals call prioritizing. If you insist on a wide 54-inch stairway with wrought-iron railing that has brass fittings, you may have to construct the treads in oak or maple rather than marble or limestone so you don't exceed your budget. You also may have to do without a separate formal dining room, a built-in vacuum cleaning system, a second bar sink in the pantry, glass-fronted cabinets in your kitchen, and the French doors between your den and patio.

DAVID HOFFMAN (Northbrook, Illinois)

David Hoffman, president of Red Seal Development Corporation in Northbrook, Illinois, said the single biggest reason for delays in new construction is the customers' inability to make their selections—or changing their minds after selections are made. "As professional builders, we could build in half the time . . . if the customer made selections upfront. While it seems easy to do so, the truth of the matter is that when a customer is presented with three marble floors, three colors for granite countertops, or three shades of wood stain for kitchen cabinets, they think they know what they want but keep changing their minds. While it might seem prudent for them to make selections way ahead of time, they won't. Who does their tax return by December 31, for example?"

Don't despair though, you're not starting from ground zero every time you add or remove something. Instead, view this task as a sort of juggling act. Some experienced homeowners like to get out a big sheet of paper and make a list of must-haves, maybes, and can-do-withouts. Review your list and move items from one column to another. You'll find you won't be willing to budge on some items, while others you'll eagerly give up for the right savings. Eventually, the juggling will give you enough of your wants while keeping you within your budget.

SALLY QUINN AND BEN BRADLEE (Washington, D.C.)

Sally Quinn and her husband Ben Bradlee bring different strengths to a homebuilding or remodeling project. "I have a way of seeing a room and imagining it becoming a fabulous place. Ben gets more excited and involved after the architect does the drawing. Once the drawing is complete, we both work together."

CONSTRUCTIVE TIPS

**Decision-Making Style:
Are Men from Mars and Women from Venus?**

He wants an elaborate home theater and you want a European-style kitchen. You fight, you bicker, you sleep in separate rooms because you're so angry. Building or remodeling is a highly-charged emotional time. Power comes into play. Who will get his/her way? St. Louis psychotherapist and marriage and family counselor Michaeleen Cradock has detailed the five individual personalities that emerge when couples make decisions.

1. *The authoritarian.* This person takes over with posturing like, "I'm right and this is the way it will be and there's no discussing it."

2. *The shrinking violet.* This person won't make any decisions and says, "It doesn't make any difference to me." The underlying message however, is, "when you make the wrong decision, I'll be pissed."

CONSTRUCTIVE TIPS (continued)

3. *The bulldozer.* Sort of like taking down a hill, this person keeps pushing the dirt around. Typically, one person wants the power and control. He wants a deck, and she says "no." He keeps pushing, and she finally relents. "Once she says okay, heck, it's not so much fun," says Cradock. "They're not fighting anymore." The decision process represents a power game and with power lost, they both lose interest.

4. *The pouter.* This person acts like a martyr to punish the other person after losing the power in the relationship. When this happens, the other person doesn't really enjoy the outcome of the decision.

5. *The compromiser.* This is the best way to make decisions because each person gets something they want. "If you want the living room chocolate brown, I'll go along with it even though I don't really care for brown. Then, when it comes to the shower upstairs, you let me get the double shower head I really want. Each person prioritizes their wants and lets the other person know.

The first four personality types can learn from the fifth that prioritizing your wants, communicating, and compromising allow both people to benefit and feel satisfied with the decision.

5

Prioritizing Your Room Investments

A house is a place to live in and enjoy, and its value and appreciation are not meant to be checked daily in the same way you would check the value of your stocks and bonds. But given the high costs of remodeling or building today, it would be imprudent to tackle any project without evaluating the potential investment based on a number of factors.

First, consider the most important projects on your wish list. The rooms and amenities that you are really going to use, and will help improve your life emotionally, functionally, and aesthetically should get top priority. If you've always wanted a walk-in closet the size of a room, go ahead and convert that fourth bedroom, even though your real estate agent and best friend say it makes no sense from a resale point-of-view. But change it in such a way that it can be converted back to a fourth bedroom if the need arises. The operative words are "flexibility" and "resale."

Second, decide how long you may stay in your home. Certain big-ticket remodelings make more sense if you can spread the cost out over a longer period. Many architects say it's foolish to totally redo a kitchen or bathroom if you're not going to stay in the house at least five years. The exception is if you make the changes neutral enough that the next buyer will likely find them appealing—like painting the rooms beige instead of red or blue.

Third, it's important not to overimprove the house and price it out of the real estate market. Because you will not likely stay in your house forever or pass it down to the next generation, too many improvements will be a waste of money that you won't be able to recover in resale.

How do you know what a prospective homebuyer will really want? You don't. But you can get a handle on the most popular home furnishings trends—which change very slowly—by reading home-shelter magazines and newspapers, visiting showhouses, scanning the Internet, and perusing the vignettes and models in department and home specialty stores. Designers are also constantly taking the pulse of homeowners and offering new ideas.

One sure-fire way to understand what people want by reading *Remodeling* magazine's annual "Cost vs. Value Report," which analyzes the 12 most popular remodeling projects each year. The magazine provides the average number of projects, the cost of each job, its resale value, the cost recouped in terms of percent returned on investment, and the specific costs and values in each region of the country. To order copies of this report contact *Remodeling* Reprints, One Thomas Circle, N.W., Suite 600, Washington, D.C. 20005.

According to the last survey done in 1997, the greatest dollar return on investment was from a minor kitchen remodeling—one where existing cabinets were refinished, a new energy-efficient wall oven and cooktop were installed, new laminate countertops were laid, a mid-priced sink and faucet were added, a new wall covering was hung, resilient flooring was put down, and the room was repainted.

Nationally, the job averaged $8,395 and 102 percent of that cost was recouped. In different markets those numbers varied. In Ridgewood, New Jersey, the cost was closer to $10,000 but 183 percent of that cost was returned. In West Palm Beach, Florida, the cost was closer to $7,500 and the amount recouped was down to 87 percent.

SHERRI AND BEN MILLER (St. Louis, Missouri)

When Sherri and Ben Miller remodeled his parents' home in suburban St. Louis for the younger Millers' empty-nester years, they cleverly added a second showerhead over a bench in the large master bathroom shower for washing feet after swimming and for shaving.

Other remodeling changes that proved to be wise investments include adding a bathroom, doing a major kitchen remodeling, adding a master bedroom over a crawl space, putting on a two-story addition with a first-floor family room and second-floor bedroom, adding a bedroom in the attic, adding a family room, remodeling a bathroom, adding a deck, replacing siding, adding a home office, and replacing windows—which cost the least nationally at around $6,000, but also brought the lowest return at 68 percent.

Though basements have become popular remodeling projects, *Remodeling* magazine does not include them in its survey because basements do not have a broad appeal across the country. They are much more popular in the Northeast and Midwest than the South and West, particularly in homes worth $150,000 and more. For the last decade, the percent of new single-family houses in the Midwest with a partial or full basement has ranged from a low of 73 percent to a high of 83 percent, with the variation due to relocation of homeowners from areas where basements are not popular. In contrast, during the same decade, only between 14 and 20 percent of houses in the South were built with basements. The NAHB attributes the variation to climate, topography, water tables, and different life-styles. Homeowners in the Northeast and Midwest are less able to enjoy their yards year round and much more dependent on the interiors of their homes for recreation.

Even projects that don't appeal to you can offer a bonus—they often help to sell a house faster than one without the improvement. A basement can differenti-ate one house from another, particularly if it offers such sought-after features as extra storage, a home office, exercise space, or a teen's haven from adults. (See more on basements in Chapter 11.)

LESLIE RICHMOND SIMMONS (Milton, Massachusetts)

In redoing her family's main residence in Milton, Massachusetts, and her vacation home on Martha's Vineyard, Leslie Richmond Simmons has found she's been able to cut expenses by going to close-out sales and buying at large discount home sup-ply centers. "You can find great faucets and wallpapers for much less, particularly if you keep most choices to white and simple designs." She also found that it is sometimes better to buy new than refinish. She resurfaced an old tub, but it never looked right. "I could have bought a new one for $250 and been much happier," she says.

HOW TO PERK UP YOUR HOME FOR LESS THAN $250

There are many effective changes you can make to your house to perk it up. Many—like the 25 suggested below—cost less than $250. These ideas were offered by designers, architects, and homeowners throughout the country.

1. Put up new decorative tiles along a backsplash in the kitchen or along the main wall of a bathroom.
2. Buy inexpensive posters or even postcards from favorite destinations, then put them in quality frames, and hang them in a novel arrangement such as a grid.
3. Change the color of the accessories in a bathroom with new towels, toothbrush holder, soap dish, cups, cabinet knobs, shower curtain, and mat. Or add one great colorful vase to a kitchen table.
4. Add new throw pillows to make a room look brighter, softer, or more dramatic.
5. Clean up your cluttered rooms by getting out a garbage bag and throwing away everything you don't use or no longer like.
6. Add crown or baseboard molding.
7. Cut patterns from leftover wallpaper rolls, glue them to your walls, chests, desks, chairs, or other furniture.
8. Take dishes or teacups and use them to create a mosaic on a wall. If you don't own enough dishes or cups to do this, attend a flea market or estate sale where your costs will be minimal.
9. Arrange fresh flowers throughout the house on a regular basis. You can buy them at a flower market to save money.
10. Group your collections in one room rather than dispersing them so they become a focal point.
11. Hang an old family quilt or other large textile on a wall as the focal point of a room.
12. Poise a set of stainless steel address numbers by your front door or buy a new mailbox.
13. Install a new laminate countertop in a spiffy color or pattern.
14. Change one light fixture or shade, change the color of the bulb for another twist.
15. Add some nostalgia with a martini cart, shaker, and old cocktail glasses.

16. Paint is the least expensive and most dramatic way to change a room. Paint the ceiling a color that contrasts with the walls; paint an entry door a new bold hue; paint the window and door frames contrasting colors; paint the floor in a splatter or checkerboard design.
17. Place a folding canvas screen in an important area of a room and use it as a revolving bulletin board or picture gallery.
18. Put a new large plant in a wicker basket or ceramic pot.
19. Rearrange artwork to alter the look of your room.
20. Recycle leftover fabric into a table runner, placemats, or napkins.
21. Rubber stamp a border pattern near the ceiling or baseboard molding using stamps readily available in art and gift shops.
22. Wash old kitchen cabinets with a watered down acrylic paint using a sponge to add an aged look.
23. Drape remnant fabric over a pretty decorative rod. You can find the fabric at a second-hand shop or large fabric store; many hardware and home furnishings centers carry the rods.
24. Organize your closets with shelves and drawers that you can install yourself or have a closet company do it. At the same time throw out clothing you haven't worn in the last five years.
25. Remove some of the books from a bookshelf and organize your collectibles in an artful display. They needn't be expensive—even snow globes look great when massed together.

CONSTRUCTIVE TIPS

Overimprovements

Unless you plan to stay in your house forever—and few of us will—it's smart to not overimprove it. But what improvements won't return your investment during resale? The following are overimprovements to avoid, many compiled by Chicago real estate agent Jennifer Ames. Caveat: In some higher-priced markets, these won't be considered overimprovements.

1. Carpeting every room wall-to-wall, especially when covering beautiful hardwood or ceramic floors.

2. More than two of the same appliance in the kitchen—more than two dishwashers, wall ovens, refrigerators, or freezers.

3. Mirrored surfaces, except those on the back of closet doors, over a fireplace, or over a dresser in a bedroom or bathroom. Also other heavy glitz, including too much marble and granite.

4. More than 25 percent of your house surfaced in marble or granite, including floors, countertops, walls, bathtubs, and showers—they make the place look like a mini-Versailles.

5. Gold-plated faucets.

6. So much recessed lighting that you feel you're being interrogated.

7. Elaborate window treatments in every room, including having draperies and blinds on the same window. Have you got something to hide?

CONSTRUCTIVE TIPS (continued)

8. A master bathroom that mimics a bathroom at a Ritz-Carlton or Four Seasons with a phone, TV, two vanities, toilet and bidet compartments, a shower and tub, heated towel rack, and marble everywhere.

9. So much dark wood paneling that others think you deforested Yosemite.

10. Expensive built-ins and cabinetry, or wallpapers and faux paint treatments, which rarely work for the next buyer who will discount their value when making a bid (and make you incredibly hurt and angry).

✔ CHECKLIST

Wish List to Use When Prioritizing

❏ Living room, fireplace, bookshelves, china cabinets

❏ Dining room, fireplace, china cabinets

❏ Kitchen, cabinets above and below countertops, island with extra sink or cooktop, range, sink, microwave, refrigerator, warming drawer, pizza oven, pastry center

❏ Breakfast room or area, fireplace, bookshelves

❏ Laundry room, storage, sink

❏ Family room, fireplace, bookshelves, built-in surround sound speakers, bar

❏ Den, fireplace, bookshelves, music center

❏ Home office, bookshelves, built-in desk, computer station

❏ Master bedroom with *X* closets, fireplace, bookshelves, desk

❏ Master sitting room, fireplace, bookshelves, desk

❏ Master bathroom with closet or medicine cabinet, vanities, shower and tub, toilet, dressing area

❏ Bedroom 2 with closets

❏ Bedroom 3 with closets

❏ Bedroom 4 with closets

❏ Bedroom 5 with closets

❏ Bathroom 2 with closet or medicine cabinet, additional entrances (shared with another bedroom), tub and/or shower, toilet

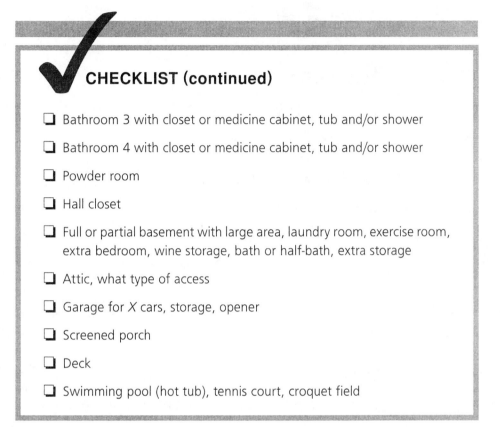

CHECKLIST (continued)

❏ Bathroom 3 with closet or medicine cabinet, tub and/or shower

❏ Bathroom 4 with closet or medicine cabinet, tub and/or shower

❏ Powder room

❏ Hall closet

❏ Full or partial basement with large area, laundry room, exercise room, extra bedroom, wine storage, bath or half-bath, extra storage

❏ Attic, what type of access

❏ Garage for *X* cars, storage, opener

❏ Screened porch

❏ Deck

❏ Swimming pool (hot tub), tennis court, croquet field

6

Tackling the Nitty-Gritty Details of Your Budget and Timetable

Your family goes to the grocery store hungry. The first mistake! You have a detailed budget, but your children or spouse pile groceries in the cart when your back is turned—sugar-coated cereal, sparkling bottled waters, and a big tub of ice cream. You're also a bit hungry and can't resist buying some of the new cookies you spied on television. Before you know it, you've spent much more money and time than you had allotted for your weekly trip to the grocery store.

COLLETTE DOWLING (suburban New York)

Collette Dowling, author of *Cinderella Complex* (Simon & Schuster) and *Maxing Out: Why Women Sabotage Their Financial Security* (Little, Brown), let her renovation get out of hand because she mistakenly thought that money would keep flowing in. "Let's go for it," she told her contractor. Unfortunately, there wasn't enough money, especially after she split from her partner and bought out his share of their 1775 colonial, saddling herself with enormous expense. She thought it would be better if she didn't take on too much change at once. "I thought I needed the comfort of staying in the house to maintain my equilibrium," she writes in *Maxing Out.* But she couldn't afford her tax bill. "Learn to stick to a budget and be sure your contractor gives you a definite price so you have a limit." Dowling has also found that many women experience power by decorating excessively and have bought into the romance myth that a house will make them happy, and life perfect. "I felt like my father handing out payroll money when I had a work crew; it was an empowering feeling."

HOW TO BUDGET AND WHAT TO SPEND
FOR BUILDING OR REMODELING

Remodeling and building a house are not dissimilar in terms of budgeting. You plan to keep the costs of redoing your bedroom to $750–$1,000 for a new bedspread, sheets, blankets and pillows; $1,500 for the paint job; $2,000 for new blinds and curtains; $2,000 for new wall-to-wall carpeting; and $1,000 for two new bamboo night stands. But after seeing your best friend's new master suite, you know you wouldn't be happy unless you could trade in your brass headboard for a more up-to-date iron one and replace your overhead crystal light fixture with soft, romantic illumination from wall sconces.

If your project is large or if you're building, multiply that one room's expenses by the number of rooms in an entire house, and your overloaded post-holiday credit card bills will pale in comparison.

Before you even come up with a dollar amount for remodeling or building, base your allotment on two factors: what you can realistically afford and what the neighborhood will tolerate.

The old rule of thumb used to be spend 2½ times your annual gross income on a home, but the newer more lenient rule is to spend 3 or even 3½ times your income. Mortgage lenders are allowing higher debt-to-income ratios especially for those borrowers with large downpayments, higher incomes, and clean credit bureau reports, because they think these homeowners can handle more debt.

Other guidelines also come into play. Mortgage lenders used to hold home-owners' borrowing for housing—the principal, property taxes, and insurance—to 36 percent of their gross monthly income and to 36 percent of their gross monthly income for their housing plus fixed monthly debts such as car loans or leases, student loans, and outstanding credit card balances. Those numbers may seem a bit low, but they took into account that people also needed money for daily purchases such as grocery shopping, eating, working out, hopping into a cab, parking their car in a garage, and taking a vacation.

But as mortgage money became more plentiful and the thinking about how much money was safe to loan loosened, lenders began allowing that 28 percent to rise to 33 percent and the 36 percent to 38 percent. Borrowers with six-figure incomes can take these ratios even as high as 44 percent.

Whether homeowners take advantage of the larger funds often depends on their mindsets. Some willingly forgo filet mignon for macaroni and cheese nightly in order to live in the castle of their dreams because they know their incomes are rising, while others know that due to their positions or ages their incomes are no longer climbing and may even be dropping dangerously. Some owners are also willing to live a bit more on the edge than other more conservative folk.

Part of the decision should also hinge on how much savings you have squirreled away. If you take a conventional loan—less than $227,150 in 1998—rather than a jumbo, you must have at least two months of your housing expenses in the bank, not including the downpayment and closing costs. If your loan is more than $227,150, the savings requirement rises to four months of housing funds, and if the mortgage goes higher than $500,000, you need to have 20 percent of your gross annual income in a savings account. The downpayment you must save is the biggest hurdle for many, even though the required amount has dropped to 3 to 5 percent over the last decade from the 20 percent once required.

Also, if comparable houses in your area sell for $400,000 with appreciation occurring at 4 percent a year—like in Chicago—and you've valued your house at $350,000, you shouldn't spend more than 5 percent of that total value on remodeling projects if you believe you'll live there for the next 10 years. If you can truly afford to spend more and don't mind risking losing some of your savings should the real estate markets turn down when it's time to sell, go ahead, but be forewarned.

Once you have used these formulas to arrive at a dollar figure, draw up a budget. Your PC can simplify the process and enable you to be miles ahead of the game. Budgeting software programs are crammed with features and data you can display in the blink of an eye and access with only the push of a button. However, it's still up to you to know what components that new home or remodeling budget should contain.

How long and detailed the budget is depends on the scope of the project. If you're remodeling a kitchen, picture the kitchen of your dreams and make a list of everything that will go into it. Some items may already exist in your current kitchen and won't need to be replaced (unless you want to) and other items will need to be purchased new. Figure 6.1 lists elements to help determine kitchen remodeling costs.

FIGURE 6.1 **Kitchen Remodeling Elements**

1. Cabinets: total number, how many above countertops, how many below, any with glass fronts

2. Countertops: total number, how long, what surface, what type of edging

3. Appliances
   - Refrigerator/freezer (side-by-side, top or bottom freezer)
   - Refrigerator drawers or compartments
   - Microwave
   - Wall oven(s)
   - Warming drawer
   - Cooktop or range
   - Sink
   - Second, smaller sink
   - Faucet(s), hot water tap
   - Dishwasher, possibly second dishwasher
   - Trash compactor
   - Wine cooler, cabinet or refrigerator

4. Flooring

5. Lighting: undercabinet, cans, pendants, cables

6. Knobs for doors

7. Pulls for cabinets

8. Specialized insets for cabinets such as spice and tray racks, baking gear, lazy susan, doors that pull out and twist to reveal shelves for large items like a blender or bread maker

9. Bookshelves

10. Painter's fees

11. Electrician's fees

12. Plumber's fees

13. Architect's design fee

14. Contractor's fee

CONSTRUCTION BUDGET

If you're building a house, the construction budget will be much more involved, more exact, and more costly. Figures 6.2 and 6.3 are examples of the detail that should go into the budget and the costs of building a 3,255-square-foot, two-story house in St. Louis and Chicago. The St. Louis figures were provided by architect/developer Chuck Schagrin, and the Chicago numbers by Roger Mande-kick of Concord Homes, a semicustom builder.

Whether you remodel or build, you should decide before you start what areas of the budget you can cut back, because it's almost a guarantee that extra costs will surface. For example, when a column could not be removed from a kitchen during remodeling, the contractor and homeowner quickly decided the area would make an ideal spot for a bar sink and liquor cabinet, even though the homeowner's family and friends rarely drink. "There was little else we could do with the space," she says. The new sink and labor added several hundred dollars to the expenses, hardly pocket change.

Even when painting a room, the painter may give you a bid based on "ideal" conditions, then charge you additional fees for time and materials needed during situations. When the painter removes the wallpaper and discovers large gaps and cracked plaster, he will need to do more plastering, which will cost you more money. Are you prepared to pay an *extra* $750? Or, if you change the nature of the work—choosing to use a glossy enamel rather than a more expensive glaze, will you receive the credit you anticipate?

Many architects and contractors suggest setting aside at least 5 to 15 percent of the total cost of the project for "miscellaneous fees," which can cover a host of contingencies from "oops, we have a problem" to "we may as well add these additional items" to the simple change orders that occur for better materials.

The earlier you can make changes the better because it will lower labor costs and material costs, and decrease delays in the project. It's important to put all changes in writing. Also ask your contractor for cut-off dates after which time making changes is impossible. And find out if he is going to charge a fee simply for making a change. Some do. Rick Bechtel, vice president of Chase Manhattan Mortgage Corporation in Chicago, says he always assumes costs will run 10 percent higher, so he bases his loan approvals on that fact. "We never assume people will be able to find those extra funds. They may have borrowed some from Mom and Dad, but Mom and Dad may be trading up their house so their children shouldn't count on them," he says.

FIGURE 6.2 Preliminary Construction Budget (St. Louis)

1. Fees, Insurance
   Builders Risk Insurance. . . . . $ 1,000
   Permit . . . . $ 2,000
   Sewer connection . . . . $ 1,040
   Total . . . . $ 4,040

2. Engineering and Surveying
   Site plan, house stakeout. . . . . $ 650
   Soil report . . . . $ 200
   House plans. . . . . $ 6,000
   Total . . . . $ 6,850

3. Utilities, Sanitation
   Temporary utilities . . . . $ 1,000
   Portable toilet . . . . $ 525
   Trash disposal . . . . $ 1,000
   Total . . . . $ 2,525

4. Excavation, Foundation
   Backfill, rough grade . . . . $ 4,000
   Footing and foundation $16,000
   Waterproofing. . . . . $ 2,500
   Perimeter drain . . . . $ 900
   Drive and culvert . . . . $ 2,000
   Fine grade. . . . . $ 1,000
   Total $26,400

5. Frame, Exterior Trim
   Frame lumber $21,240
   Exterior trim and deck . . . . $ 7,400
   Trusses . . . . $ 7,000
   Beams and posts (steel) . . . . $ 1,000
   Frame and trim labor $35,000
   Vinyl siding . . . . $ 7,000
   Total $78,640

FIGURE **6.2** **Preliminary Construction Budget (St. Louis) (Continued)**

6. Mechanical

Plumbing	$ 9,000
Plumbing fixtures (allowance)	$ 8,000
HVAC	$12,000
Electric	$ 9,200
Electric fixtures (allowance)	$ 3,500
Fireplace (zero clearance)	$ 1,500
Total	**$43,200**

7. Roofing, Gutter

Roof	$ 4,200
Gutter	$ 1,500
Total	**$ 5,700**

8. Flatwork, Masonry

Basement, garage, flatwork	$ 6,000
Driveway, porches, walks, flatwork	$ 5,000
Brick veneer (front)	$ 7,760
Total	**$18,760**

9. Insulation, Drywall, Paint

Insulation	$ 3,000
Drywall	$12,000
Paint (allowance)	$10,000
Total	**$25,000**

10. Doors, Trim, Windows

Entry door	$ 1,100
Windows, patio doors	$ 9,000
Interior trim material (Doors, base, casings)	$ 7,000
Hardware (allowance)	$ 2,500
Garage doors	$ 1,700
Total	**$21,300**

11. Cabinets, Tops, Mirrors

Cabinets, laminate tops, (cultured marble bathtops allowance)	$10,000
Mirrors/shower doors (allowance)	$ 1,500
Total	**$11,500**

FIGURE 6.2 **Preliminary Construction Budget (St. Louis) (Continued)**

12. Appliances, Floors, Ceramic Tile

Appliances.	$ 3,000
Carpet.	$ 4,000
Hardwood/vinyl.	$ 4,000
Ceramic tile baths (2½ bathrooms with 4-by-4-inch tile).	$ 4,000
Total	**$ 15,000**

13. Miscellaneous

Labor/cleanup	$ 4,000
Final clean	$ 1,000
Landscaping, tie wall	$ 5,000
Seed	$ 1,000
Mailbox.	$ 75
Total	**$ 11,075**

TOTAL HARD COSTS.	$269,990
Contingency	$ 3,000
Profit and overhead (15 percent)	$ 40,500
TOTAL	**$313,490**
Cost per square foot, excluding lot.	$96.31

DEVELOPING A TIMETABLE

Remodeling and building are never slap-dash events and generally take anywhere from a few months to more than a year. But getting through the project becomes much easier if you and your work crew develop a realistic timetable based on prior experiences, which almost always include some unexpected disappointments along the way. Someone may get sick, materials may not arrive on time and products may come in wrong or be damaged.

FIGURE **6.3**   Preliminary Construction Budget (Chicago)

1. Fees, Insurance
Builders Risk Insurance	$ 600
Permit	$ 2,500
Use tax	$ 3,200
Well	$ 9,500
Septic	$ 3,500
Total	**$19,300**

2. Engineering and Surveying
Structural	$ 850
Site plan	$ 350
House stake	$ 125
Improvement survey	$ 125
Grading certification	$ 100
Soil report	$ 400
Footing inspection	$ 55
Steel inspection	$ 55
Drain inspection	$ 55
H_2O proof inspection	$ 55
House plans	$ 3,500
Total	**$ 5,670**

3. Utilities, Sanitation
Power usage	$ 150
Propane tank and fill	$ 1,000
Snow removal	$ 500
Portable toilet	$ 510
Trash disposal	$ 550
Total	**$ 2,710**

FIGURE **6.3** **Preliminary Construction Budget (Chicago) (Continued)**

4. Excavation, Foundation

Excavation	$ 1,150
Backfill	$ 450
Rough grade	$ 300
Fine grade	$ 300
Drive and culvert	$ 2,000
Foundation	$10,750
Deck and porch caissons	$ 525
Waterproofing	$ 265
Perimeter drain	$ 900
Total	**$16,640**

5. Frame, Exterior Trim

Frame lumber	$21,240
Exterior trim and deck	$ 7,400
Trusses	$ 6,870
Beams and posts	$ 750
Frame and trim labor	$15,000
Stairs	$ 250
Total	**$51,510**

6. Mechanical

Plumbing	$ 8,500
Heating (w/AC)	$ 6,800
Electric	$ 5,120
Light fixtures	$ 1,800
Fireplace	$ 1,150
Total	**$23,370**

7. Roofing, Gutter

Roofing	$13,250
Gutter	$ 850
Total	**$14,100**

FIGURE **6.3** Preliminary Construction Budget (Chicago) (Continued)

8. Flatwork, Masonry

Interior flatwork	$ 3,280
Exterior flatwork	$ 2,400
Precast concrete products	$ 0
Stonework	$ 7,760
Total	**$13,440**

9. Insulation, Drywall, Paint

Insulation	$ 2,600
Drywall	$ 8,030
Paint	$ 6,080
Total	**$16,710**

10. Doors, Trim, Windows

Entry door	$ 900
Windows, patio doors	$ 9,090
Interior trim labor	$ 2,656
Interior trim material	$ 3,855
Hardware	$ 815
Garage doors	$ 1,330
Total	**$18,646**

11. Cabinets, Tops, Mirrors

Cabinets	$ 7,285
Cabinet installation	$ 535
Countertops and installation	$ 1,715
Mirrors, shower doors	$ 850
Total	**$10,385**

12. Appliances, Floor Coverings

Appliances	$ 2,350
Carpet	$ 3,970
Vinyl, hardwood, tile	$ 4,390
Total	**$10,710**

FIGURE 6.3 **Preliminary Construction Budget (Chicago)**

13. Miscellaneous

Equipment rental	$ 350
Cleaning	$ 815
Landscaping, tie wall	$ 1,600
Mailbox	$ 75
Total	**$ 2,840**

TOTAL HARD COSTS	$206,031
Lot cost	$ 50,000
Warranty claims	$ 1,545
Contingency	$ 3,090
Profit and overhead	$ 46,000
TOTAL	**$306,666**

Cost per square foot, excluding lot	$94.21

ED AND NANCY GREENBERG (Freyburg, Maine)

Hone your communication skills, say Nancy and Ed Greenberg, who learned how to do so while remodeling their home and inn on multiple occasions. "Being able to convey what you want to those involved is vital—to carpenters, electricians, plumbers, everybody. Even a terrible drawing is sometimes worth a thousand words. We were very fortunate in this regard because we worked very closely with the carpenter/contractor, and we seemed to understand each other. We spent many hours discussing and looking at the rooms that would be renovated so we could come up with the ideas and plans we wanted completed. We were here every day, so if there was a question, we could provide an answer," says Nancy.

A key to maintaining your sanity with a smile on your face is to keep communicating with your work crew on a daily or weekly basis and/or have someone—such as your architect—assigned to oversee the project. If a snafu occurs—you're called out of town and don't want work to progress while you're gone for fear that something will go wrong; someone you've hired has a problem; a crisis on another job develops; rains are so torrential that workers can't dig the foundation; or the European faucets you ordered get stuck in customs at Kennedy International Airport in New York—alter the timetable right away.

Some homeowners also like to offer a financial incentive if the project is finished ahead of schedule. An appropriate amount is typically $1,000 to $2,000 for a $50,000 project, and so on. But St. Louis builder Chuck Schagrin says that rarely happens. More likely it is the client who delays completion. "A client will say, 'Oh, I'll go choose my cabinets next week,' but then he delays it for whatever reason and the timetable gets pushed back . . . and back."

There are also those who prefer negative reinforcement. They impose a penalty if the job is way overdue—perhaps a month. Not all builders/contractors will agree to such a penalty. Schragin, for one, says the difficulty is that it's hard to pinpoint who's at fault in most problems. If you feel strongly about an incentive or penalty, certainly bring it up with your contractor before you sign a contract and work gets underway. Figures 6.4 and 6.5 are examples of building and remodeling timetables.

SALLY QUINN AND BEN BRADLEE (Washington, D.C.)

Sally Quinn, author of *The Party,* and her husband Ben Bradlee, former executive editor of the *Washington Post,* love to fix up houses and entertain in them. Quinn contends that "too many people use remodeling to repair their marriage, analogous to the way couples have a child to hold their marriage together." She advises against this.

FIGURE 6.4   **Rough Timetable for Building a 3,255-Square-Foot Home**

This is a realistic but somewhat rough plan for building the 3,255-square-foot house discussed earlier.

- Talking—several meetings to discuss the scope of the project, including a possible budget
- Walking the lot or choosing the lot
- Writing and agreeing to the contract, including a time frame (1 to 2 weeks)
- Design stage (30 to 60 days for schematics and 30 days for design development)
- Another discussion about the budget
- Final design or construction documents (30 to 60 days)
- Final budget (2 to 3 weeks for all work to be bid)
- Securing a building permit (2 to 3 weeks)
- Getting approval for plans from your community and any associations (2 to 3 weeks and can be done in conjunction with building permit)
- Ordering materials
- Clearing the site and preparing it (2 to 3 weeks)
- Inspection (ongoing)
- Excavating and pouring the footings and foundation (1 to 2 weeks)
- Framing the house (3 to 4 weeks)
- First floor deck put on, second floor deck added (part of framing)
- Roofing—trusses and sheathing, papering and shingles (1 week)
- Plumbing work, rough-in (2 to 3 weeks)
- Pouring slab (1 or 2 days)
- Additional plumbing work
- Rough-in mechanical systems (2 to 3 weeks, same time as plumbing)
- Electrical work (2 to 3 weeks, same as plumbing and mechanical)
- Inspections
- Insulation (1 week)
- Drywalling (2 to 3 weeks)
- Interior trim, floors and cabinetry (4 weeks)

FIGURE 6.4 **Rough Timetable for Building a 3,255-Square-Foot Home (Continued)**

- Paint and stain (2 weeks)
- Finish work, including light fixtures, countertops, appliances (2 weeks)
- Cleaning of construction site (1 week, but ongoing)
- Punch list (1 week to establish, 1 day to go over)
- Final inspections (1 day)
- Moving in (about six months to one year after starting)
- Check-in thirty days after the move
- Check-in eleven months after the move

FIGURE 6.5 **Rough Timetable for Remodeling a Master Bathroom**

This is a realistic schedule for remodeling a master bathroom. Some of the steps are the same as in building, but the timetable is much shorter.

- Talking—several meetings to discuss scope of project and possible budget
- Looking at existing house
- Preliminary design stage (2 weeks)
- Design development (2 weeks)
- Working drawing design final (2 weeks)
- Looking at equipment and appliances to use (several outings)
- Bid pricing (1 week)
- Permit (2 to 3 weeks)
- Ordering equipment, wallpaper, lights, flooring (1 to 2 weeks if in stock)
- Packing up furnishings, etc.
- Gutting the room (1 week)
- Plumbing rough-in (2 days)
- Electrical (2 days)
- Mechanical systems (2 days)
- Insulation (less than a day if it exists)
- Plastering (I week)
- Laying the floor (1 week)
- Installing equipment, cabinetry (1 week)
- Painting (3 days)
- Installing lights, mirrors, details (same week as above)
- Punchlist (1 day to develop and 3 days to complete)
- Painting (3 days)
- Moving back in (three to four months from start to finish)

CONSTRUCTIVE TIPS

Budget Busters (Honey, I shrunk the budget!)

Talk about grounds for major warfare. One person saying, "Oh, it's just a minor thing to change all the door hinges to solid brass," can lead to huge expense when you consider how many doors you have in your house. If you sit down and look for alternatives, you will be amazed at how much money you can save, says Roger Mandekick, executive vice president of sales and marketing for Concord Homes in Palatine, Illinois. "Don't go for different unless you're sure your different choice is worth it and will look okay in the future. Stick to standard finishes and door styles. Be humble and it will get you a long way." The following are some areas where you can lower your budget:

1. *Driveway.* Your wife has to have a paved driveway, usually bricks or cobblestones, that could cost more than a new sports car—$25,000 to $30,000. She tells you the Greens have one and it's gorgeous. Forget it, you say. There are alternatives, thank goodness. For less than $10,000 you can have an asphalt driveway with concrete sides, and then paint or score the concrete to look like bricks.

2. *Roof.* Your husband has read that slate roofs are the absolute best and last a lifetime, but you find out it will cost $35,000 to $45,000. Alternative: Use architectural-grade asphalt shingles with a neo-slate design that give you a similar look and are architecturally pleasing. Even more pleasing is the cost: about $8,000.

3. *Roof pitch.* You've seen a beautiful Tudor home down the street with a high-roof pitch that may be 12' × 12' instead of the more standard 8' × 12' or 6' × 12'. You love the look, but the higher roof pitch can cost one-third more than a standard pitch due to labor and material costs. An 8' × 12' will not look that different and will save you money that can be better spent elsewhere.

CONSTRUCTIVE TIPS (continued)

4. *Fixtures.* You just have to have European fixtures after you saw them in a showcase home on a house tour, except they can cost between $12,000 and $15,000. But wait. There are lower-priced copies of these fixtures, and the cost difference can be compared to buying a moderately-priced dress that copies a Vera Wang design instead of the real thing. The look is similar, but the price is thousands less. If you go up five grades from commercial/builder's grade, you can get the same European look for only $4,000.

5. *Countertops.* You've always wanted granite, but you never knew the price. Granite, you discover, is prohibitive at a cost of $14,000. Instead you can choose one of the copies in laminate, one of the solid surfaces, or Corian knock-offs such as Swanstone that mimics granite or marble. The knock-off solid surface may be only $5,000 or $6,000, saving you more than half. This is more money for new his-and-her golf clubs or a much needed vacation.

CHAPTER 7

Down to the Wire

Signing the Contract and Checking Warranties

Even among the country's fraternity of custom homebuilders, the irrepressible Lieberman brothers of St. Louis had style, numerous clients, and top-notch reputations. They sailed upstream most of their working lives. But who knew they were peddling dreams to homebuyers who would never see those dreams realized.

The brothers operated in the spirit of outlaws. They began to overspend and illegally dipped into the millions of dollars they collected from homebuyers' down payments, using the money to pay off their debts while never building their clients' homes. The brothers were caught and federally indicted, but fled the country. One landed in jail; the other committed suicide in Chile. Homebuyers, banks, contractors, architects, and decorators in several states were left holding the bag—empty.

Given the somewhat shaky condition of the construction and remodeling industry—where anything can easily go awry—you need protection. A written contract offers a smidgen of security, but should be carefully crafted by an attorney.

For many, contract-signing time is nervewracking. Why do this to yourselves? There are ways to avoid stress at contract time. One is by doing copious research to assure yourself that the architect, contractor, or builder is reputable and credit worthy. Another safeguard is to draft a contract as airtight as possible and have it reviewed by a real estate or construction attorney. If you don't know an attorney who specializes in these areas, check the Yellow Pages, which lists attorneys by specialty or call your local bar association or the American Bar Association in Chicago.

Before you even contact an attorney, however, rely on your gut feeling to determine whether you need professional intervention. The moment you decide to build or remodel, envision the worst case scenario, says real estate attorney Richard Nikchevich of the Chicago law firm of Barack Ferrazzano Kirschbaum Perlman & Nagelberg. "Say to yourself, 'Well, there's a one in one million chance something will happen' or 'It's a big risk and I need to figure out my comfort zone.'" If you're not equipped to do this, seek help, he adds.

IS A CONTRACT NECESSARY FOR A SMALL JOB?

It's important to know that you may not need a contract for something as simple and clearcut as a $3,000 paint job, although some painters and homeowners prefer one. In many cases, the painter slips you a piece of paper with his fees and seals the deal with a handshake. Of course, risk here is reduced if you've checked the painter's reputation as well as his work. Make sure you understand what you're getting.

A simple handwritten contract should spell out exactly what type of paint he'll use (including brand names), what type of preparation work he'll provide—plastering and patching, for example, how many coats of paint he'll apply (at least two), what type of cleanup he offers, his typical work hours, a final sum, and who will be responsible for any problems that may arise. If you're really savvy, you'll also add in how long the job will take, how long he'll be held accountable for the work, and how any disagreements will be resolved.

But you also should allow for contingencies, especially if you're refurbishing. The walls may need extra plaster, sanding or special paint, and cracks may need to be sealed—all of which can ratchet up the cost.

And be forewarned, small construction projects often produce the worst dilemmas later for a lawyer. Many construction projects seem so routine or too small to justify the time and expense of legal assistance. But, when work goes awry, even these tiny projects can have horrendous consequences, and you may have wished you had spent some money on a consultation.

WHEN A CONTRACT IS A MUST

If you proceed with a contract, know that all construction contracts are not the same. Some cover only a specific type of home or job—a production or tract house, semicustom house, spec house, custom-built house, or a remodeling project.

Some construction contracts end up being more twisted than a soft pretzel. "A contract for new construction is the most complicated document in the home-buying process," says attorney Nikchevich. "Basically it's two transactions in one. You're buying a piece of real estate and negotiating for construction of something that isn't built yet."

An attorney's fee for reviewing a contract may seem high, but it's only a small fraction of what he would charge to assist you after a project has gone sour. Such legal scrutiny is labor intensive. A real estate lawyer typically spends twice as much time with a new construction contract as he would with a contract for the sale of an existing home. He must apprise you of the risks, and then work with the builder to add in extra protections such as how to settle possible disputes, how often you need to make payments and when you can withhold fees, how to handle delays, insurance, bonding, building codes, and warranties (some builders must give any warranties other than what the manufacturer offers for appliances or equipment).

To understand how the various construction contracts really work, you may also want to study standard contracts published by the American Institute of Architects.

PRODUCTION HOME CONTRACTS

Production builders provide the bread-and-butter business of the home-building industry. They work on volume and turn out houses fairly quickly, in a matter of several months. If you choose this route, your hands are pretty much tied in terms of making contractual alterations. These homes are virtually mass-produced for speed. Glitz and glamour aren't a production builder's main focus. He sells very nice homes, but as a package.

The contract reflects this. Usually you start with a builder's document, cast as a purchase and sales agreement. This form has a probuilder slant because, as a rule, the builder owns the lot and the house until closing when the home is complete and ownership is transferred in exchange for a nice big check. Because new construction is a litigious field, builders and their attorneys want to protect themselves from such liabilities as late construction, product imperfections, and home-buyers who will not complete the closing transaction by withholding payment.

What changes to the contract will a production builder allow before you enter into an agreement? You need to understand what you're really buying and determine whether it's right for you and your family because most builders will only make minor design changes—if any. Sometimes the builder's ability to make changes depends on the types of warranties he offers. Warranties are legally binding written guarantees. There are full warranties, limited liability general warranties, and highly limited warranties. Some builders will try to give a limited warranty covering only typical construction problems like nail popping.

Others push liability off to a third party warranty company. Your sole recourse is then against that firm. Also, if the builder uses a third party firm, that firm has its own contract form and the builder may not have flexibility to change it. If the builder uses a builder-only warranty, he will have more room for negotiation with you.

The most flexible part of negotiating with a production builder is the punch list, which details items that are incomplete, don't meet specifications, or need to be corrected, adds Nikchevich. A key sticking point is whether the homebuyer will hold back funds at the closing until the punch list is satisfied. NARI suggests you check the following areas before creating the punch list: gas and water are hooked up; all HVAC systems are operational; appliances work; doors, windows, and skylights function; screens and storm windows are in place; cabinets and drawers align and open easily; tile, grout, countertops and flooring are even, without scratches, and have matching seams; walls are painted and free of nail holes; molding is in place; ceilings are plumb to walls and without cracks; built-ins are firmly affixed to walls; and all spaces are broom clean.

You may want to have money in escrow to provide a level of assurance that the builder will come back after the closing to fix whatever is unacceptable. Most production builders don't allow this, however.

Welcome to the real world of production homes. Now is when it is crucial for a client to check out the builder. Talk to someone in the same subdivision and ask how the process went. The risk of being duped is heightened when dealing with mom and pop contractors who don't have the name recognition of the major homebuilders or the deep pockets to wait out construction delays, problems with materials, or uncooperative weather.

One production home job in a Midwest suburb blew up in homebuyers' faces because they didn't dig deep enough into the builder's background. Several homebuyers put their life savings into these tract homes. When the work was done, buyers found hairline cracks in the foundations, sinking yards, leaking basements, and drainage and electrical problems, according to the *Post-Dispatch* newspaper. They stormed city hall. The builder was called before the Planning and Zoning Commission and admitted to financial difficulties. He said that the ground on which he built the homes had trash pits underneath. He had been misled by the seller of the property and the soils engineer. The commission denied issuing the builder permits for further development until he corrected his mistakes.

SEMIPRODUCTION HOME CONTRACTS

A semiproduction builder, sometimes referred to as a semicustom home builder, also constructs tract homes but allows a little more leeway in the contract for negotiation and custom requests, which can sometimes cause production delays or hold up a closing.

Most semiproduction builders use their own contract forms. Some builders require big down payments or earnest money—usually 10 percent of the purchase price—at contract signing.

Generally, after the home is built, most of the bigger well-known builders will offer at least a one-year warranty covering all problems with construction or materials. Like an extended warranty on your car, a third party warranty company insures the structural integrity of many homes from year two through the tenth year. It is spelled out in the contract that when a buyer accepts this warranty, he waives any right that may be granted by law to make any claims against others.

Another leg of the typical contract includes provisions for change orders. When there are 20,000 different components going into a typical house, some people can't visualize what the finished house will look like. Many companies try to comply with changes, but only up to a certain point. "We charge only for what is changed not for making the change, such as a light fixture in the kitchen. If it's not ordered and not in place, we can switch it. The customer is charged if it's more expensive. If it's past a certain point in the homebuilding process, such as custom cabinets that have been made and are on the truck ready to be installed or if it's something already installed and you want us to rip it out, this requires additional labor. We have a late charge order fee of $200 for each modification," says Bob Meier, general counsel of Taylor-Morley, Inc. in St. Louis. But each builder has his own policies and fees.

There's also a clause that lets a buyer off the hook at any time before closing if there is a disagreement between the purchaser and seller as to the quality, nature, and character of the work in the sales contract, says Meier. "The builder will return all deposits or down payments to the buyer and cancel the agreement. The same is true if the builder hits rock while digging the foundation. This is an extra cost passed on to the buyer. He has 10 days to get out of the contract, if he doesn't want to pay. All money is returned," adds Meier.

If there is not a legitimate reason for backing out of the contract, the builder will retain the earnest money, put the house back on the market, and work out damages. In some cases, the builder may refuse to cancel the closing.

One buyer, who was moving to St. Louis to take a new job, built a $650,000 semiproduction home. The contract was completed and the man decided at the last minute not to take the St. Louis job. He asked to be let out of the contract. The builder told the client he would have to take the house and either sell it or have his company sell it. The buyer and builder closed on the house and the buyer turned around and sold it for $40,000 more than he had paid.

While your home is being built, your complaints can pile up like a chain reaction car accident on a slick road. Holding back final payment at the closing offers you some form of assurance that the job will be finished correctly. Most production and semiproduction builders who assume all the financing until closing won't allow this, however, once a home is substantially complete—that is, after the municipality takes down the approved sign and the structure passes inspection.

"We cannot allow a buyer to escrow certain funds. We say, 'Look, it says in the contract that we'll paint the outside of the house, lay sod, pour the driveway, fix broken systems, and repair construction defects because of the warranty, but the home is still habitable. The only time we'll deviate from this is if the lender requires us to set up an escrow specifically for unfinished items of a substantial nature such as a certain floor covering or kitchen cabinets. We ask that the money be released automatically upon installation and not at the discretion of the buyer," says Meier.

Misunderstandings between builder and client are a major headache. Some believe in binding arbitration, but Taylor-Morley does not. "We are not going to let a third party tell us what is or isn't right. We try to satisfy the customer. If we haven't and we can't, our philosophy is to let the court decide," Meier says.

THE SPEC HOME AGREEMENT

Not all roads lead to production and semiproduction homes. If you are interested in a spec home—a single home nearly or totally complete that is put on the market by a builder—the legal transaction is less convoluted. You are dealing with fewer construction items because the house is closer to being in move-in condition. But there may still be some construction issues that must be addressed—the builder might have to finish putting in sinks or commodes—and it's important to check the warranties.

THE CUSTOM HOME CONTRACT

If you want more control over the finished product, custom building is the best option, though be aware that it's also the most costly. The degree of difficulty of negotiating a true custom home contract is determined by who owns the lot.

If the builder owns, you buy the lot and the contract becomes a bifurcated transaction, which means it starts as a land contract and changes into a regular construction contract. In some cases, the builder will retain title to the lot, build the house to your specs, and then transfer the property at the closing. In either case, you make regular progress payments along the way.

You can keep better control over your money with some guidance because progress payments can be as difficult to monitor as your personal debt. "If you own the lot, you're paying the builder as a general contractor through these payments. You need to know the money is going to pay the contractor's subs and suppliers. Otherwise there's a risk of lien waivers," warns attorney Nikchevich.

Make sure your contractor isn't drawing funds in advance of completion. It's hard for most of us to judge construction progress. It might be a good idea to have an architect on board because he can not only design the house, but inspect the work in progress as well. Write into the contract that the architect is your representative who will oversee the project. The architect will charge for this service, but it's worth it to have him make sure the contractor is doing the work properly and not get ahead of himself in the payment schedule.

If you're looking to build a custom house on a lot you own, first find the contractor and architect, and then establish your own construction contract and financing.

If you seek a construction loan, the lender will insist on a chaperon—a title or disbursing company. A loan escrow will be set up and draws will not be dispersed until inspections are made. The lien waivers come from the subs and others who get paid. This is a form of security for you, but mostly for the lender.

JACKIE PRESTON (Miami, Florida)

Writer Jackie Preston had to put a new roof on her home after a corner blew off during hurricane Andrew in 1992. "Water went under the roof and began to destroy every ceiling in my house. I wanted the repair done quickly before too much more damage was done. The new roof cost $6,000. When the roofer was done, I asked if it had been inspected. He said that the state had allowed contractors to do their own inspections and that my roof had passed. I believed him. Then five years later when I went to sell the house, the inspector told me the roof didn't pass code. He asked where the certificate of inspection was and I told him what the roofer had said. He laughed and told me that the roofer had gone out of business and left town. I had no recourse. Lesson learned, don't believe what a tradesperson tells you. Check everything. I should have checked with the state to confirm his inspection story."

TYPES OF INSURANCE FOR BUILDING OR REMODELING

A contractor carries public liability insurance to protect him and his business from third party claims such as property damage or bodily injury—should an injury occur at the job site due to the contractor's negligence. Find out if you can have an endorsement placed on the contractor's policy whereby you are named as an additionally insured party, if this liability is not already part of your homeowner's policy. There are always exclusions and limitations in any insurance contract. Check with your insurance agent and lawyer to determine which liability coverage is right for you.

DON AND DEMETRIA CHESTNUTT (Winnetka, California)

Don Chestnutt, an executive with Warner Bros., and his wife Demetria, had to make some remodeling decisions after the 1994 California earthquake. Their condo, one of 73 units in a townhome development built in the '70s, shook like hell. The quake cracked tiles in the kitchen and damaged walls throughout the house. All residents of this development were required to fix the damage and, at the same time, bring the building up to '90s code. The condo association took out a 30-year SBA loan, and each family was assessed about $17,000. One year later, a common decision by the association was made to hire a contractor to do minimal repairs. Fortunately, the Chestnutts' homeowners insurance covered temporary housing expenses so they could move out of their home while work was completed. Residents were told repairs would take four weeks; they took four months. But a bigger surprise was the poor quality of the work. The contractor took all common walls down and attempted to put them back in livable shape. Says Don, "They were going to repair only part of one wall which left an edge. We had to hire someone else to do the replacement dry wall, reprime, resand, and repaint. We had to pay for all painting, wallpapering, floor redos, and new carpeting."

Worker's compensation is also the contractor's responsibility. It covers all his subs in case of injury or death during the building of your home. Ask to see the worker's compensation certificates for all subs. If you hire the subs yourself, make sure they are covered and have it written into the contract. Be sure to get policy numbers for your records.

DON AND DEMETRIA CHESTNUTT (Winnetka, California)

Don and Demetria Chestnutt say, "Don't ever let contractors know you have insurance, because the estimates will jump. They charged us almost $7,000 just to paint the house which is less than 1,900 square feet. Our insurance, minus the deduction, paid for most and even covered half of our assessment, but California insurance laws have changed. We have to carry a separate policy now. The deductible is so high that our house would have to fall to the ground and burn before it would pay for us to put in a claim."

A contractor/builder also carries builder's risk insurance. It covers the structure from the time the foundation is poured until the home is complete and turned over to you. Find out what's covered and get a copy of this policy. If your builder includes you on his policy, this may negate the need for you to obtain separate liability insurance. You will have to purchase your own risk coverage if you own the lot and are paying for the construction. For your protection, the policy should cover the builder and his subs.

Title insurance is another protection that comes in two forms: owner's and lender's coverage. Owner's insurance covers deeds; wills; trusts with improper and incorrect names; outstanding mortgages, judgments and tax liens; easements; and incorrect notary acknowledgments. For example, if you buy a home and it comes out later that the seller's brother is the real owner, your owner's title insurance will protect you from loss by paying the full purchase price. "Usually this insurance is issued in the amount of the real estate purchase. This ensures that the title is as stated and protects you against a faulty title search. It contains an inflation rider that increases the level of coverage as the value of the property escalates," says Gary Garrity, Vice President of Public Affairs for American Land Title Association, a national trade association of some 90 large and small title insurers.

DON AND DEMETRIA CHESTNUTT (Winnetka, California)

Demetria Chestnutt says she became obsessed with the remodeling of her condo after earthquake damage. The condominium's contractor came in, tore down everything, and left it half finished. When the contractors pulled out the walls, they literally destroyed the closet doors and closet framing in the back bedrooms. They said they'd fix it. "I wanted to put mirrored sliding doors in their place and handed them the bill. They said we were trying to rip them off. I had a 20 minute screaming match with the contractor. I told him he had 24 hours to get the hell out of my house and that I'd bill him for the damages later. We brought in another contractor to correct the shoddy work and to convert our loft into another bedroom. If I could do it differently, I'd take two months off of work and monitor progress every step of the way."

Obviously, you don't need owner's title insurance for a small job where the payment flow is more ad hoc. The cost of the title company escrow might be the same as the cost of the job.

If the dollars are big enough, though, these bells and whistles might be warranted. It will also depend on what part of the country you're in, the type of job, and the custom of the builder.

The seller of the property may also provide owner's title insurance for you. In some cases, the builder may even decide to offer this as part of the closing costs built into the purchase price of the residence. But in most cases, you will need to purchase your own insurance. The insurance will cover the house as long as you or your heirs own the property.

Garrity says that the number of people buying their own title insurance is on the rise because buyers are becoming more savvy. "The buyer has become the ordering influence of title insurance rather than a broker or lender ordering it for them."

At the time of closing, lender's title insurance is issued. In most states you foot the bill. This protects the lender against any title claims or legal fees should there be a claim on the title. If the lender loses the legal battle and the property, this insurance covers the amount of the mortgage. Coverage decreases as the loan is paid down.

Sometimes you can lump the lender's and owner's title insurance together on the same search to reduce cost. Ask a local title insurer for the local rate card. Rates do vary.

Mortgage insurance is required if you borrow more than 80 percent of your home's purchase price. (See Chapter 10 on loans and mortgages.) There are alternatives to this insurance such as a piggyback mortgage, where the mortgage banker or broker allows you to mortgage less than 80 percent and then borrow an additional 10 percent from him as a second mortgage at a higher interest rate.

In case of a disability or untimely death, you can carry term personal mortgage life insurance, which lasts for a certain time period. This would pay off your home without leaving your heirs or estate responsible. As you pay off the principal on your home, the value and premium of this insurance decrease proportionately.

Homeowners insurance kicks in at the closing. Your lender will require proof of this insurance to protect your home against fire, theft, and damage. A special or deluxe form of homeowners insurance will cover earthquakes, floods, and tornados. If you live in a flood plain or on a fault line, your lender will most likely mandate that you purchase separate flood or earthquake insurance. These special policies or riders can be expensive, so plan ahead when you buy property or build a new home.

WARRANTY PROTECTION

Warranties are the forms manufacturers or contractors use to guarantee workmanship before and after a house is built or remodeled; they also help you sleep better at night because warranties can cover construction defects. However, exactly what they cover, and for how long should be stipulated in the contract that a lawyer has carefully reviewed in advance.

Confusion often arises because all the warranties for the work, materials, building components (such as a roof or windows), and all the appliances and equipment typically differ in length. Floorboards might be covered for 30 days; a roof for 15 years. Some warranties also cover installation while others do not.

In addition, there are all sorts of nitty-gritty questions regarding warranty coverage. If a warranted window is installed improperly, is the manufacturer liable? If no, who is? A reputable builder should correct such a defect, but the warranty should clearly state so. It's smart to compile all your warranties in a file including the name of each person or manufacturer responsible, the address of the party who honors each warranty, and the outside date of coverage.

Many builders back their own warranties on workmanship and materials, typically for one year. Others offer warranties backed by an insurance company.

Typically, a builder will make two service calls during your first year of ownership to repair nonemergency problems covered by the warranty.

It's important to understand that like doctors and lawyers, architects can give no warranties because they can never guarantee an outcome. They can, however, be held to a reasonable standard, which means they must exercise care and skill. Otherwise, they could be held liable. They do, however, carry errors and omissions coverage in case they err. Contractors, on the other hand, can warrant that the materials and equipment they provide reflect a good quality, that their work is free from defects, and that it conforms to the contract document's requirements. Their warranty excludes damage or defects caused by abuse, improper operation, or normal wear and tear.

The toughest part is usually deciding who's responsible for a problem. For example, peeling paint may be the result of too much heat or moisture in the house, improper preparation, or inferior paint. Usually, though, the problem will be easy for a professional, objective, third-party painter to diagnose.

BONDING

Bonding is a financial transaction—rather than an insurance policy—that has three parts: the surety or insurance company, the principal or the person being bonded (usually the contractor), and the performance, which is a guarantee that work will be done in a timely fashion and in accordance with the specifications of the bid.

Find out who is giving the bond and include its terms in the contract. Also find out if the bond names you as an additional insured, and determine what kinds of protections you will receive. A bond may protect you against poor work that doesn't comply with building codes, but it may not protect you if the contractor doesn't finish the job.

A bond doesn't mean the contractor is bonding your job per se. Ask about this. Some contractors will bond a job, and then bill the cost into the job. If the contractor files for bankruptcy, goes insolvent, or takes all the money and doesn't pay his subs, it can be horrific.

In this case, a surety company bond obtained by you might offer some recourse. It will step in to find another contractor to complete the job, or in rare cases, pay you damages up to a maximum called the penal amount of the bond. As a rule, these bonds are the preserve of commercial, public works, and government projects because the cost can be staggering.

The price you pay is determined by the size of the project and the credit worthiness of the contractor. A good rate is $10 per $1,000 of the building cost. But if the contractor has impaired credit, or is a mom or pop operation without much access to capital, you'll pay a higher rate because there's a higher degree of risk to the bonding company.

REMODELING CONTRACT

A remodeling contract is one part of a whole, but requires certain provisions to safeguard your current home and property. It's important to establish the kinds of insurance you and your contractor have as well as any warranties and bonding.

When you hire a babysitter for the first time, you tick off the rules of the house. The same is true here. Include some threshold items in the contract about clean up and protection of your household goods.

You may not want to add all these points into the contract, but you should nicely tell your contractor what you do and don't expect before he starts—not to block any driveways, not to use your home phone (especially if you work from home), and not to trek dirt through your finished rooms. Also, don't forget to tell him to secure the construction area for safety so it is off limits to children and pets. Mention which bathrooms he may or may not use, what areas of the house he should stay out of (including your refrigerator), whether it's okay for him to smoke in your home or to help himself to a soda or coffee, and also if you want him to have a set of house keys or your alarm code while he's working on the premises. Always keep him informed of when you'll be home, at the office, or out of town (post the phone numbers), and let him know the hours your municipality or building will allow him to work.

In any remodeling, as with a new home building, sort out your objectives. Develop a comfort level. Check out the remodeling contractor thoroughly. Talk to other clients to find out if he's honest and competent, inspect samples of completed jobs, verify insurance and bonding.

And be aware of red flags. If a job costs $3,000 and the remodeler wants to be paid in full up front so he can buy $1,000 worth of materials, make sure you can trust him to come back with the materials. Use the same protections that are available in any construction contract.

ARCHITECTURAL CONTRACT

The American Institute of Architects has standard construction contracts used by architects, custom builders, and developers who head build/design groups. They are architect-owner documents and are very specific, containing all or some of the following provisions (some may be part of the owner-contractor agreement): the blueprints, specifications, color selections, lighting schedule, site drawing, warranties, soil report, financing information, prices including allowances, contingencies relating to price or materials, inspection schedules, cleanup provisions, settlement and possession information, insurance, and alternative dispute resolution.

These documents are written to protect the professional, so you want to have your lawyer review them and make the same changes that you would in any construction document.

Rarely do you have a contract that will give you 100 percent of all the legal points you want. "As a result, I tell my clients that they must feel comfortable with whom they've chosen to do the work. But if everything goes to pot, make the contract as good a document as possible," says Nikchevich.

Be sure that any professional you hire has sufficient insurance coverage. Again, an architect should have professional liability insurance; a contractor should have a payment and performance bond.

Also document progress and conversations along the way. Should a problem occur, careful records of talks (you might want to tape record conversations) and photographs can easily settle any heated he said-she said arguments. Homeowner Sandra Thomas, who built a house in Chicago with her husband Robert, kept a spiral notebook, which she dubbed her "house book." She made notes of all meetings, including dates, and wrote down every vital piece of information discussed such as model numbers for pieces of equipment ordered. "Doing so reduced the 'I said, you said,'" she found.

In the end, even a well-drafted contract may not keep you out of arbitration or court. But as with life's other unknowns, it's better to be safe than sorry.

You might also impose penalties for construction delays. However, most contractors will not allow them. If they do, have a lawyer write into the contract, "If the house or room addition is not built by X date, liquidated damages will be built in. The amount will vary depending on the size of the job." For example, you might say the builder pays $50 a day for each day of delay after X date. The price of the job then gets reduced by the liquidation amount.

CONSTRUCTIVE TIPS

Finding an Ace Real Estate Attorney

How do you ferret out an ace real estate attorney? Beside asking friends and colleagues for recommendations and checking with your state or national bar association, you need to ask potential hirees the following questions suggested by real estate attorneys Steve J. Holler of the law firm of Hopkins & Sutter and Carl J. Circo of Stinson, Mag & Fizzell.

- How long have you been in practice?
- What type of real estate work do you specialize in?
- Do you charge for an initial consultation? How much do you charge per hour?
- Is there a maximum limit to your charges?
- Do you charge for telephone time as well as in-person conference time?
- Will you be working on my contract/closing or will one of your partners or associates do the work?
- Are you familiar and comfortable using standard industry forms such as AIA's or do you prefer to draft your own? (Certain situations will call for different forms.)
- Are you familiar with this builder, developer, or architect?
- Have you worked in the municipality in which the remodeling or building is taking place?
- Will you do a project for a flat fee rather than an hourly rate?

✔ CHECKLIST 1

General Construction Contract

As a rule, experts say a generic rock solid construction contract designed to protect you should include the following:

❏ The contractor's full name, address, phone number, and professional license number (if required in your state). Be aware, however, that many contractors do business under more than one name and through more than one legal vehicle, Circo says.

❏ Descriptions of all work to be done, spelling out in detail all materials (size, color, style, brand, number), and upgrades.

❏ Agreed upon starting and completion dates.

❏ A statement allowing you to visit the site at designated times. Most production and semiproduction builders don't want you hanging around except at preordained times. However, if building a custom home, it's important to stay on top of what's being done on a regular basis.

❏ Breakdown of the total costs of labor and materials.

❏ Agreed upon payment schedule, if you're paying the builder during construction. Keep the downpayment on a new home as small as possible, but if the builder is financing construction, he may insist on a larger one. The downpayment on a remodeling is usually one-third. Schedule additional payments after completion of each phase. Normally construction draws are paid monthly.

❏ A release-of-lien clause to ensure the contractor pays the subs.

❏ Building codes, permit restrictions, and fees necessary to complete the work. A permit requires that you have someone review specs for work and inspect the job at completion, giving you some level of comfort.

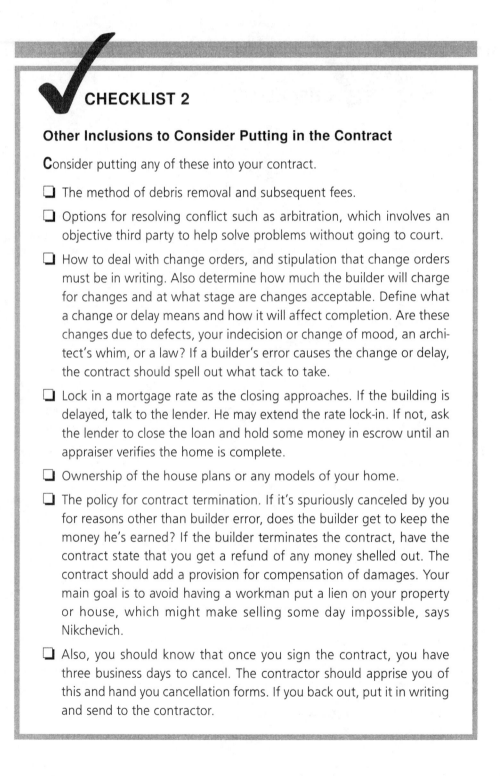

CHECKLIST 2

Other Inclusions to Consider Putting in the Contract

Consider putting any of these into your contract.

❑ The method of debris removal and subsequent fees.

❑ Options for resolving conflict such as arbitration, which involves an objective third party to help solve problems without going to court.

❑ How to deal with change orders, and stipulation that change orders must be in writing. Also determine how much the builder will charge for changes and at what stage are changes acceptable. Define what a change or delay means and how it will affect completion. Are these changes due to defects, your indecision or change of mood, an architect's whim, or a law? If a builder's error causes the change or delay, the contract should spell out what tack to take.

❑ Lock in a mortgage rate as the closing approaches. If the building is delayed, talk to the lender. He may extend the rate lock-in. If not, ask the lender to close the loan and hold some money in escrow until an appraiser verifies the home is complete.

❑ Ownership of the house plans or any models of your home.

❑ The policy for contract termination. If it's spuriously canceled by you for reasons other than builder error, does the builder get to keep the money he's earned? If the builder terminates the contract, have the contract state that you get a refund of any money shelled out. The contract should add a provision for compensation of damages. Your main goal is to avoid having a workman put a lien on your property or house, which might make selling some day impossible, says Nikchevich.

❑ Also, you should know that once you sign the contract, you have three business days to cancel. The contractor should apprise you of this and hand you cancellation forms. If you back out, put it in writing and send to the contractor.

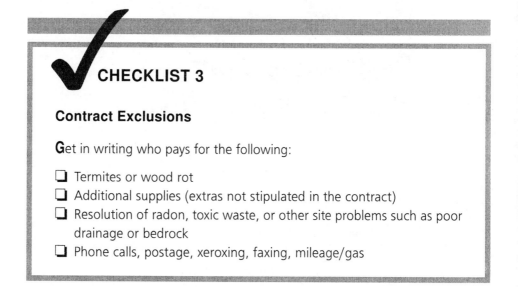

CHECKLIST 3

Contract Exclusions

Get in writing who pays for the following:

❏ Termites or wood rot
❏ Additional supplies (extras not stipulated in the contract)
❏ Resolution of radon, toxic waste, or other site problems such as poor drainage or bedrock
❏ Phone calls, postage, xeroxing, faxing, mileage/gas

CHAPTER 8

Reading the Signs and Granting the Nod

There's a definite moment of excitement when your architect or builder calls to say he has a preliminary set of plans for you to view. It's best to know how to read a blueprint so you can understand and critique what you're about to be shown. But you may have never been exposed to a building facade on paper, elevations, or lighting and electrical plans, all of which are vital elements for you to peruse before you okay the drawings.

Here's a crash course. *Floor plans* are usually drawn to the scale of ⅛-inch, ¼-inch, or ½-inch to one foot, depending on the stage of the project. Rooms are typically abbreviated such as *lv* for living room, *dn* for dining room, and *kt* for kitchen. Various symbols are used as well for the lights, outlets, water heaters, furnaces, and walls. Figure 8.1 lists most of the important symbols that you should recognize on a plan, and Figure 8.2 includes a sample blueprint for you to examine.

There's also an art and science to learning to read the other types of plans, including *facade and elevation drawings, electrical and lighting plans.*

Stock blueprints. You may feel comfortable and be quite successfully working with stock plans that you order from a magazine or catalog. They can definitely save you money and time, especially if you like the completed designs. You may then adapt them to the site, your needs, and the community and neighborhood rules. But again, it helps to know what you're looking at.

FIGURE 8.1 **Blueprint Symbols**

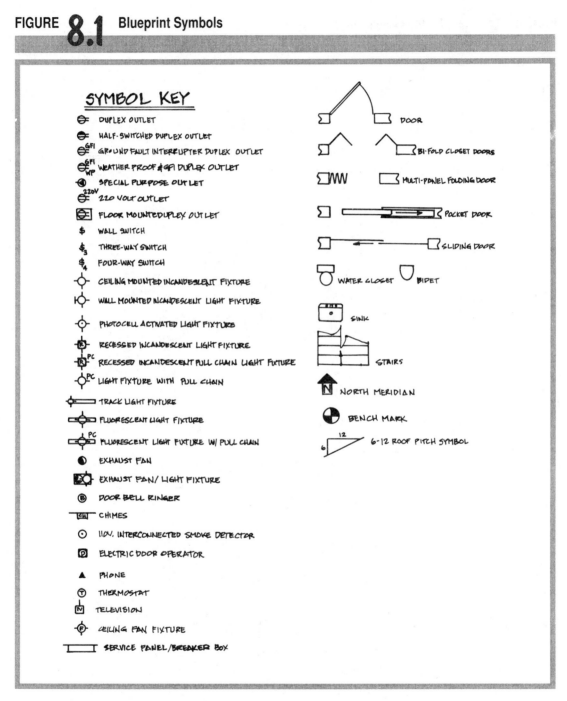

Source: Red Seal Development Corp., illustration by Brian Connor

FIGURE 8.2 Sample Blueprint

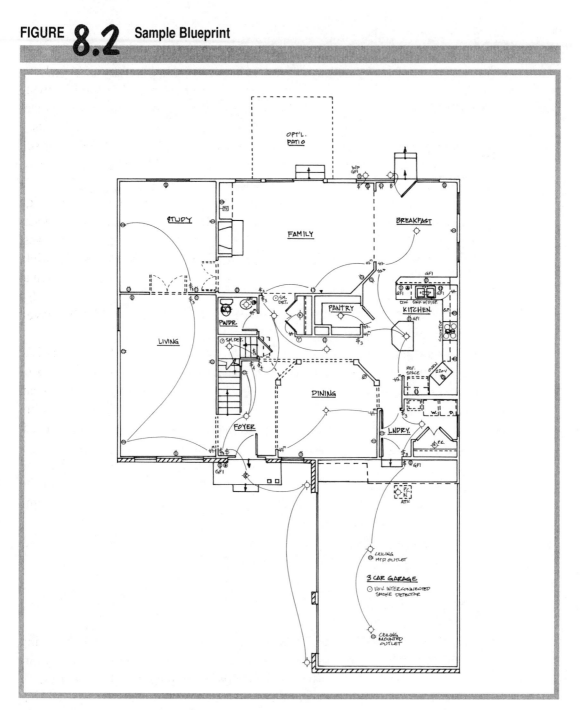

Source: Red Seal Development Corp., illustration by Brian Connor

House Beautiful editor-in-chief Louis O. Gropp built from stock plans years ago. He took a solar plan that New York architect Al DeVido developed for a plans company and adapted it to meet his needs for a vacation house in Long Island, New York. Would he do it again? Yes, says Gropp. "Although knowing and working with Al was helpful in building our house from plans, there are other advantages: the huge variety to choose from, a way to get an estimate on costs, a faster timetable," he says. A downside, he adds, is that most services that sell plans do not carry cutting-edge designs or designs with the uniqueness of a custom home.

One of the caveats of using stock plans is that you must be sure your design can be adapted to local building codes, your community's ordinances, and setback requirements. Some communities such as Clayton, Missouri, 12 miles west of downtown St. Louis—developed about 100 years ago—require all-brick, stone, or stucco facades. The city is considering allowing frame homes, which at one time were permitted, but today are not on the approved list. The city is also fairly strict about the exterior design. Some plans have not been approved because they were not compatible with existing homes in the neighborhood.

In addition, find out your community's regulations regarding permissible work hours during the week and on weekends. If you live in a condo complex or apartment building, there may also be strict rules regarding work hours. Rules can vary greatly, and you don't want to incur the wrath of your neighbors. In certain cities, homeowners also need to take into account equipment that can be used. One older apartment building in Chicago does not permit jackhammers.

After you have a plan in hand, you may be able to have your architect and designer provide a computer-generated three-dimensional image of what the home will look like when it is finished. You may even be able to "walk through" the virtual home design.

Before long, you'll be reading blueprint symbols like a pro. However, it's still easy to make mistakes along the way.

AVOIDING BIG MISTAKES

This could be your worst nightmare: You okay the plans and building begins, but soon you find huge mistakes and items missing. If you protect yourself with knowledge, however, you can survive building with few worries. To begin with, before you okay any blueprints, be sure they are sufficiently documented, which means that your architect has added all measurements and specified all products and materials.

EILEEN AND JEFF GUTMANN (Bethesda, Maryland)

In redoing a hall bathroom/powder room, Eileen and Jeff Gutmann found that there's no substitute for hands-on inspection. "Someone has to check everything, including the serial numbers of any fixtures, etc., when they arrive. We found that they often didn't match and we were sent the wrong ones," Eileen says.

Detail, detail, detail is the crux of a good set of plans. "Don't allow anything to be left to the imagination," says Chicago architect Allan J. Grant. "I try to provide elevations of every view of a room or house, including walls in every room—even demolition drawings. You want to see where the toilet paper holder goes, how high the tiles run. It's not just good for the owner but for the architect in the design process and all the tradespeople on the job. Some owners may not care about the specific location for recessed lighting or the cabinet fronts and configurations. They have to help decide whether they want to be involved or not and stick with that decision."

One homeowner did not pay careful attention to the placement of an electric wall oven. She discovered only after it was installed that it was so close to the corner of a wall that its door could not be opened when an adjacent cabinet's door was used.

ED AND NANCY GREENBERG (Freyburg, Maine)

Ed and Nancy Greenberg thought they had carefully planned their remodeling, including which pieces of furniture would go in each of the four guest bedrooms they were renovating and furnishing for their Admiral Peary Inn. "We created one room from attic space at the top of the house, dubbed the North Pole. The only access was a pull-down staircase. We had to devise another way into the room. Our carpenter came up with a cute right-angled staircase. What a genius, we thought. As the room neared completion and the railing for the stairs was about to be built, some bright-minded individual thought it would be easier to move the king-sized bed, huge pine dresser, two chairs, and two bedside bureaus into the room before the railing went up. Once it did, however, we discovered that we won't be able to get any furniture out if we want to redecorate, short of tearing down the railing. Oh, well," sighs Nancy. "I guess that's our 'Oops we goofed episode.'"

BRING IN A THIRD PARTY EXPERT

If you don't feel you are able to determine whether the plans are sufficiently detailed, you can avoid a costly and irrevocable surprise by simply asking for assistance. Sometimes, it's wise to bring in a third-party architect or contractor to offer an assessment. This isn't the time to play shrinking violet. It's not on the same level as refusing to ask for directions when you're lost. We're talking big bucks. It's easier, smarter, and cheaper to make changes early on—and on paper—than later during the building process. If you don't like what you see, say so and have the plans redesigned and redrawn.

LESLIE FALK OSTERWEIL (Tampa, Florida)

Leslie, who built a house in Tampa with her husband, John, was told by a friend that only one of them needed to be the boss. "As soon as you decide who that will be let the contractor know so that he will know whom to answer to. It's annoying for the contractor to make changes for one spouse, then later that day have the other come in and totally change things."

Changing your mind may cost you, though, if your professional charges by the hour. He may also not agree to redo the drawings three or four times without additional compensation. "There's a point at which additional money is justified for revision work, though at what point is hard to say. So much depends on the relationship and the scope of work," Grant says.

LESLIE FALK OSTERWEIL (Tampa, Florida)

A funny thing occurred to Leslie during the building of her home. She was clearly the boss on the project, however, after about six months of construction, their contractor asked if Leslie was still married because he never saw her husband. "I reassured him there was just a division of responsibilities." She would bring her husband by after the workstaff left to show him the progress. "I was totally responsible for actually building the house, staying within our budget, and moving."

How do you avoid so many redos? Ask your architect or designer for as much help as possible, particularly if you have little ability to visualize what the finished product will look like. Grant tries to help his clients understand how their design on paper will look as a three-dimensional house by taking them to see actual houses, showing them pictures, drawing a three-dimensional sketch, or sometimes making a small-scale model from cardboard with a few details of doors and windows. Be sure you ask in advance how much a scale model will cost, and if you can keep it in the end. Computer programs can also help you "see" a three-dimensional object.

During this time you should also ask your architect or builder if he is willing to take you to other houses or to make a rough model at no additional charge. Many will charge you an hourly rate for additional time and $500 to $2,000 for the model, depending on the detailing.

CONSTRUCTIVE TIPS

What-Ifs

Before you sign on the dotted line, you're likely to have some second thoughts. You forgot to do this; you should have done that. Here is a list of the most common what-ifs that architects have heard—often too many times. Ask yourself whether any apply to your project. Better to make changes now than later.

- What if I move this wall over five feet and remove the beam?
- What if we eliminate all the soffits in the kitchen?
- What if we change the countertops to granite instead of laminate?
- What if we add a few recessed cans?
- What if we add a second vanity and a whirlpool tub instead of a regular tub in the master bathroom?
- What if we sand and stain all the hardwood floors instead of just those in the living room, dining room, and hallway?
- What if we add a sound system throughout the house?
- What if we finish the basement completely instead of partially?
- What if we finish the basement partially rather than leaving it unfinished?
- What if we add another 500 square feet to the plan for a fourth bedroom and third full bathroom?

9

Bidding Out the Project and Calculating the Costs

When it comes time to bid out the project, it can sometimes feel like the sky is falling once you add up all the real costs. Figuring out how much your job will cost can be tricky and time consuming. Typically, each trade contractor, supplier, and design professional involved in your project prepares a materials list, which is known officially as a takeoff. This list cites the materials needed and their costs. Then the labor costs are added and the total is presented in a bid, which is a formal written proposal. Bids are typically valid for 30 days, but can sometimes go as long as 60 days or more, especially if the bids are high and the owner needs time to reassess the scope of the project and his individual choices.

When you—or your architect or builder—add up all your bids, the figure should total the cost of your house or remodeling project. There are two major exceptions, however, that can affect the bottom line. "The three most expensive words in the English language when it comes to remodeling and building are 'as long as,'" says Chicago architect Allan J. Grant. "Owners often say, 'As long as we're doing this, we might as well do that,'" he explains. Also, some work costs cannot be calculated due to unknown conditions discussed previously such as hitting rock during the excavation of a foundation. Most of these "surprises" occur after demolition, and the added costs are usually based on time and materials, which can be estimated but not precisely determined in advance.

Most architects and builders advise you to get three bids for each type of work involved. If you act as your own general contractor, you will need to get three bids from every tradesperson involved. Or, you might get three bids from each general contractor or builder you consider hiring.

Getting bids from contractors whose work is fairly similar in price and quality will make comparison easier. Of course, you will only want bids from contractors who are experienced in the type of project you're planning such as a two-story addition with a family room on the lower level and a master suite above. Don't reveal your budget because you don't want it to influence the contractor's estimate. Also, if your insurance will be paying for a home repair, don't let the tradesperson know in advance of submitting his bid. You can always reveal your hand later and say, "Gee, we hoped to spend only $25,000 on the kitchen, not $40,000."

The bids should be submitted in writing with specific measurements, brand names, and detailed work steps, from preparation through completion. A painting estimate should include how any existing wallpaper will be removed, how walls will be patched, whether any skim coating will be done (to cover the plaster), what kind of paint will be used, and what brands will be selected. You don't want to be going through this so quickly again, so it's important to know you're getting quality work and materials.

BREAKING DOWN THE BID ITEM BY ITEM

Each bid should be broken down by components—called a line-item breakdown in addition to the lump sum or total number. You don't just want the bid to quote $50,000 to furnish and install a kitchen, because you can't distinguish the individual costs of the carpentry, HVAC systems, appliances, painting, and floors.

EILEEN AND JEFF GUTMANN (Bethesda, Maryland)

After several remodeling projects, Eileen and Jeff Gutmann know not to accept a bid solely based on a low price. "We did so in building a studio addition, only to discover that we had exposed wiring which had to be fixed, and which could have—and should have—burned the entire house down," says Eileen. "We also cut corners on quality when we redid our kitchen and as a result can't put appliances on the counter because the floor was raised too high and the appliances don't fit underneath the wall cabinets."

Typically, bids will come in at different amounts and often for more than you budgeted. You must then face the tough decision of which bid to choose. The danger of going with the lowest bid is that you could get inferior workmanship, which may end up costing you more to redo or repair. You may also get lucky and receive a low bid from a great workman who's just starting out or one who is eager to snare the work. Then again, sometimes a workman may bid low deliberately to get a job, then gradually raise the costs once work is underway.

Generally, Chicago architect Gregory Maire disregards the low bid. "I've found that it usually means the contractor hasn't understood the scope of the project and what's needed. The results will usually reflect shoddy work or the contractor will come back later and say he doesn't have enough money to finish the job properly."

On the other hand, the danger of choosing the highest bid—beside paying too much—is that you won't necessarily get the best work. It may be safer to choose the middle bid, but sometimes that is not always the case. To make the best choice, be sure you're really comparing apples to apples. That's why it's important to view each contractor's workmanship. Preferably, you should see examples that are at least six months old so you can look for any imperfections and observe how the work has held up or. Ceramic floors may look great right after they're finished, but they can crack before long if the underlayment wasn't done properly.

After you've seen examples, sit down with the contractors you like and discuss what goes into their prices. Ask each contractor if he has any suggestions for trimming costs that still seem too high. A good architect or general contractor will know how to juggle costs without compromising quality. "We always ask," says St. Louis architect Thomas Yanko, "'How can we get this down without changing the quality too substantially?' They might suggest going with a steel rather than cast-iron tub."

MIKE AND ILENE GOLDSTEIN (St. Louis County, Missouri)

St. Louis tax attorney Mike Goldstein and his wife Ilene, a teacher, came to remodel their kitchen serendipitously. During tax season a few years ago, Ilene said to Mike one evening, "You've been coming home late every night to a plate of food that's sitting in Saran Wrap ready to be microwaved. Wouldn't you like to taste this food when it's fresh? Maybe a warming drawer would do the trick." A couple days later Ilene met with a kitchen designer to decide where to put a warming drawer. Says Mike, "The next thing I know Ilene rolls out a set of kitchen remodeling plans that show walls coming down, skylights to go in the ceiling, and new large windows.

But I didn't see any place for a warming drawer. Ilene proceeded to prepare the budget for the new kitchen and itemized the list to show me. I perused it and noticed that the designer suggested very expensive cabinets. She said less expensive wouldn't last as long. Ilene had chosen Corian countertops. They would look better and wouldn't stain or scratch. She had chosen a Subzero refrigerator which cost more than my first car with a set of tires. I went through the list and finally I said, 'That's it. I'm cutting the last item.' What do you think it was? The warming drawer. You know what? I'm back to the microwave, but I'm eating my dinner in a lovely kitchen."

If the prices are still too high and you're not comfortable going with the lowest bid, go back to your original wish list and prioritize again. One owner knew she could live without granite countertops, but couldn't make do without a restaurant range. Her husband knew he could do without a bar sink but not without German hinges on the cabinet doors. Don't worry about what the tradesperson thinks.

There are also two alternatives to traditional bids that may help you avoid higher costs.

One is a negotiated contract in which costs at each stage are estimated verbally and revised as work progresses providing fewer surprises once the work actually gets underway. The other bidding alternative would be to get two "guesstimates" from the contractor each for a slightly different work plan. "If the owner wants a new kitchen that's next to a family room, the possibly more expensive option could be extending the boundaries of the existing structure, while the less expensive one might be renovating the existing space and taking over a bit of the adjoining family room," says Chicago architect H. Gary Frank.

ALICE AND KENNETH STARR (McLean, Virginia)

In renovating their home, Alice and Kenneth Starr, learned the importance of choosing the highest quality appliances. "Don't save a few dollars by getting standard equipment that the builder recommends. Get quality appliances that will last much longer and look more attractive. We did not put in the highest quality sink, garbage disposal, or dryer and wish that we had. We used ready-made cabinets, however, which look custom," says Alice. She also chose a high-quality vinyl tile floor that looks like wood . . . which they have been very happy with.

CONSTRUCTIVE TIPS

Comparing Quality

You think Granny Smiths are great apples; your husband only likes Fujis. You're content with a sparkling wine like Domaine Chandon from California, while your spouse thinks Moet & Chandon, a real champagne from France, is as good as it gets. Quality is in the eye—or the palette—of the beholder. When it comes to building materials, finishes, and products, there can be drastic differences. How do you differentiate? You can read guidebooks like *Consumers Report,* but you also must look, touch, and compare. Time and research make the greatest difference in understanding why a BMW offers a smoother ride than a pick-up truck. And you must learn to differentiate factors when comparing bids so you can make intelligent choices. Here are five examples of high quality features to look for (as suggested by Chicago designer Leslie Stern):

1. A good interior paint treatment should consist of priming and two finished coats. Quality paint should be easy to apply; show minimal roller spatter or brush marks; hide imperfections on the underlying surface; and be pleasant smelling during application. The paint job should exhibit excellent washability.

2. Three types of lighting should be used in each room: task, accent, and general. Using more than one source of light makes a room more interesting so you should consider using incandescent, halogen, fluorescent, or neon lights. To make your choice, first determine what you want the mood of the room to be. In a bathroom, you may want recessed cans for general lighting; task lighting next to wet areas such as the sink, tub, and shower; and accent lighting such as neon behind a cove or glass block wall. In a living room, you can use cans, track lights, or a chandelier for general lighting, and a can or wall sconce for task lighting over a focal point such as a fireplace, wall unit, or piano. The accent lighting can be MR 16 halogens in a crystal etagere or bookcase.

CONSTRUCTIVE TIPS (continued)

3. A great range has numerous design features. A dual-fuel range is equipped with electric convection ovens or radiant cooking and baking, plus gas cooktop burners. They come in smaller sizes such as 30 and 36 inches that are easier to work into a design than a 60-inch range. They have electronic key pads with operational graphics that don't wear off, and underglass touch controls. They come with either six burners with a grill or griddle, or four burners with both a grill and griddle. The sealed gastop burners are easier to clean, and provide a wide range of BTUs, from 400 for simmering to more than 16,000 for high heat cooking. There are different size burners for use with different-sized pans. The hot surface indicator light (electric) stays on even after the element has been turned off. A single piece cast iron grate spans two burners to allow easier movement of heavier pots and pans. These ranges also have a powerful, retractable down draft.

4. A top-quality refrigerator will have numerous desirable features. The fresh food and freezer sections should have separate controls that allow each compartment to maintain the proper temperature. An automatic door hold will keep the door motionless at a 90 degree angle to make it easier to remove food. An adjustable bin, glass shelf storage, and fully extended bins will provide easier access. Vegetable, fruit, dairy, and sealed snack storage areas should have individual humidity controls. An icemaker should shut off automatically when the ice bin is full. Custom panels and handles provide an attractive facade. Shelves that slide back and forth will make it easy to store tall containers. Freezer utility baskets can store bulk items. Rollers on the refrigerator base will make installation and maintenance easier. Movable door bins can hold gallon-size items with ease.

5. The new commercial dishwashers are quiet, can accommodate oversized plates, and are energy-efficient.

✔ CHECKLIST

Other Issues to Get in Writing

However you proceed, these are some other matters you may want to discuss and get in writing:

❏ How the unknowns will be covered. As previously stated, some contractors and architects charge according to time and materials, but this can be risky because those charges may become too open-ended. Other contractors and architects want owners to set aside a contingency sum—between 2 and 10 percent of the total cost—for unforeseen expenses such as extra plastering. The percentage amount should depend on the breadth of the project. Still others like to bring in a third-party contractor to offer an alternative price or suggestion when surprise conditions arise. Work these possibilities out ahead of time.

❏ How substitutions will be handled. Materials or equipment may need to be changed if they're not available once the project gets started. You should put in writing that you'll get materials or equipment of "equal or greater value," and you, the homeowner, should decide if the substitution is equivalent.

❏ How change orders will be priced. You need to find out what the fees for additional labor are if there are administrative charges, and the cut-off is for making changes.

❏ Payment schedules. Some contractors expect a certain amount or percentage upfront before work begins, then additional payments weekly or monthly depending on the length of the work, with the final payment upon completion. Sometimes your construction loan will determine how payments are handled. If you can, withhold about 10 percent of the total cost until the contractor or builder has satisfied everything on your punch list.

✔ **CHECKLIST (continued)**

❏ How postconstruction problems will be handled. Will they come back and correct the problem gratis if it's not your fault? Who decides who's responsible? These questions should be discussed in advance.

❏ Besides money, don't forget to consider the chemistry between you and the work crew. It can greatly influence how pleasant or unpleasant the project becomes. Ask each contractor the following questions to assess your compatibility:

    ❏ What time do you plan to start and finish work each day? (This may be dictated by local mandates. Some communities only allow workers on a job between certain hours. If they want to start very early or finish late in the evening this may annoy you and your neighbors and cause friction over time.)

    ❏ Tell me about your clean-up practices? Do you bring your own industrial vacuum cleaners, brooms, dust pans, and garbage bags?

    ❏ Do you carry a cellular phone or do you expect to use our house phone?

    ❏ Will you mind using the basement bathroom for changing clothes? Or, if you bring a portable toilet, where will it be placed?

    ❏ Will you be leaving food in our refrigerator or freezer?

Don't discount your gut instincts. If you think they are just giving you some good lines or telling you what you want to hear, they well may be. In most remodelings and certainly in all building projects, you'll be working with your crew for weeks, if not more. You need to get along with them, even if you don't become bosom buddies.

10

Understanding the Mortgage Game

Interesting side effects of the home building and remodeling industry's escalating muscle have surfaced everywhere. Signs for architects and general contractors, roofers and remodelers, painters, and tuckpointers, dot highways and stick out on lawns in new and established areas. Phones ring off the hook at dinner time with general contractors, roofers, basement waterproofers, and finance companies pushing their products and services. Mailboxes are stuffed with direct mailers. Ads on radio and TV proliferate. Headlines buzz with such news as: "Low Interest Rates Light Up Home Sales" (*USA Today,* January 20, 1998) or "The Rage to Refinance" (*Business Week,* December 1, 1997).

If you choose to jump on the building or remodeling bandwagon, why not? You've stashed away some savings for this purpose, and real estate is showing spiffy returns and steady growth—compelling reasons to invest in bricks and mortar. Of course, the catalysts behind this lively real estate market can be traced to four sources: Wall Street, the new capital gains tax, the boffo stock market earlier in the decade, and plunging Treasury bond rates—the benchmark for many mortgages and the reason for low interest rates. Because rates are at their lowest in years, lenders are competing for your dollars. What better time than now to secure a good loan or mortgage?

First, consider how much cash you can or should put down. A bigger down payment might seem attractive, but could cost you down the line. Calculate whether it's wiser to make a smaller down payment and reserve most of your savings. Too much cash down might minimize a crucial tax write-off. Home interest is the last bastion for a good tax deduction available to everybody. Typically, people put down 20 percent, the minimum required to avoid mortgage insurance—but many can now put down as little as 3 to 5 percent.

A piggyback mortgage—which more lenders are offering and borrowers are taking—allows you to circumvent mortgage insurance. It consists of two mortgages. The first mortgage is 80 percent sold off to mortgage investors, and the second mortgage is 10 percent retained by the lender. The ratio used to be 75/15. The borrower may have slightly lower monthly payments with this arrangement, depending on the rate of the second mortgage. But more importantly, you receive tax deductions from two loans. If you were to get one large loan that carried mortgage insurance, the insurance is not deductible. To calculate what's best for you, confer with your tax attorney, accountant, or lender.

After you decided on a down payment amount, next itemize and add up your monthly debts—car loan, credit cards, other loans—and divide this amount by your monthly pretax income. If the total exceeds 20 percent, you're probably aiming too high. As a rule, experts have cautioned that the total value of your mortgage should not exceed 2½ times your gross income, although recently this figure has been stretched for those in higher income brackets. (See Chapter 6.)

Then nail down how much you can realistically afford for a monthly mortgage payment. When calculating this, be sure to include all the trimmings: mortgage loan amount, interest rate, number of years financed, mortgage insurance premium, property taxes, homeowners/hazard insurance, and flood insurance (if required).

Some homebuyers put monies for taxes, insurance, and so forth in an escrow account to pay these bills once a year rather than adding these costs to their monthly payments. The lender you choose will make these payments out of your escrow account for you. If you receive a large chunk of money once a year such as a bonus check or a generous cash gift from a relative, escrow is a good option.

When creating your budget, don't forget to include the costs to furnish and decorate your new home. Trash pickup, landscaping, and lawn care are also costs to consider. Don't shoot yourself in the foot and budget so tight that you overlook emergencies such as an illness or a major home repair. You might add an extra 15 percent to your monthly total for incidentals. (For a budget, again see Chapter 6.)

Okay, now you know what you want and can afford, and you're ready to be tossed into the money marketplace to ferret out a lender. Got about a month? The sales pitches from lenders can be persuasive and mind-numbing with deals of minimal fees and no points. Mortgage providers can afford to be magnanimous because their costs to originate loans have shrunk with computerized underwriting systems and the swelling of the secondary market for secured mortgages making loans more competitive. In addition, the two mortgage mainstays, fixed and adjustable rates are now available in various incarnations.

In this vigorous game of mortgage and loan hopscotch, you must be attuned to the market or you could get burned. "There can be some nightmares out there," warns Kerry Rudin, a loan officer for Mortgage Resources, Inc., in St. Louis. He cites the case of a national mortgage company that charged customers an enormous prepayment penalty if they refinanced or paid off their loans. These borrowers neglected to ask about contingency charges and found themselves in financial quicksand.

Comparison shop. To get your bearings, find out interest rates and different deals in your area. Start with your own bank's loan rate as a reference point. Look in the daily newspapers. Flip on your computer. On the World Wide Web, you can scan listings of the best offerings and get quotes from banks in all major cities. Get referrals. The best leads can come from friends. If you don't get answers from these sources, talk to your accountant, lawyer, banker, or even real estate agent or developer.

Make a few calls to lending institutions. Say: "I have plans to build." While the lender lists your options, ask yourself, "What will I get with each, and what will I be charged for it?" The lowest rate doesn't always mean the cheapest. The tricky part is knowing when a loan is too expensive. There are some subtle clues such as prepayment penalties or points. Points are based on the level of capitalization of a loan, are equal to 1 percent of the total amount borrowed, and compensate the lender if he offers an interest rate lower than the market is demanding.

You should visit more than one bank or broker—or have them visit you— and play one off against the other to find the best deal. The corner commercial bank is only one option. These banks tend to offer more short-term loans, and fewer permanent mortgages.

SOURCES OF BUILDING MONEY

- Mortgage brokers, much like insurance brokers, are really a matchmaking service, pairing lender and borrower. They peruse options for you. With their access to banks across the country, they shop around to get you the best deal, says Rudin. "We get quotes daily on rates from many banks. We are paid by whoever who ends up servicing the loan. If we can save somebody a half point or $100 in interest a month, what do they care if that bank is in downtown St. Louis or Chicago." The servicing of broker-orig-inated loans is sold frequently, however, which may create headaches for you during the transition.

Red Flag: Brokers are minimally regulated and may be interested in steering you to the lender who pays them the most money, even if it is not the best rate for you. They also tend to have the most junk fees associated with their loans, because they receive no residual income from servicing the loans, says Rick Bechtel of Chase Manhattan Mortgage in Chicago. With junk fees there's no actual expense incurred by the lender. Such fees are underwriting, documentation preparation, or loan processing fees.

- Savings and loans are traditional mortgage lenders. They collect payments, are able to sell mortgages to other investors, and receive a fee for their services.
- Mortgage bankers (mortgage companies) specialize in making mortgage loans and sell them to a network of investors. They usually retain the servicing and perform the underwriting and closing functions in-house.
- Credit unions—available through your employer or other organizations—sometimes offer the best low rates for the first year of an adjustable rate mortgage (ARM). The amount you can borrow is usually fixed or limited. Only members of the credit union's affinity group can obtain loans from this source, however.
- Secondary markets, where lenders sell their conforming mortgages to other institutions and government credit agencies such as the Federal National Mortgage Association (Fannie Mae), Government National Mortgage Association (Ginnie Mae), and Federal Home Loan Mortgage Corporation (Freddie Mac), help maintain a cash flow in the mortgage marketplace. Conforming loans must meet certain standards and the borrower must be qualified before they can be sold on the secondary market. All permanent cookie cutter loans are eventually sold this way. This transfer of the loan to another party doesn't cost or affect the consumer. These secondary agencies do not service loans. They pay mortgage servicers, usually banks or mortgage companies, to perform the servicing function. Secondary markets also purchase mortgages insured by the Federal Housing Administration (FHA) and Department of Veterans Affairs (VA).

SHORT-TERM LOT AND CONSTRUCTION LOANS

It's time to muddle through the loan labyrinth. If you're building a home from the ground up, there are three loans that are regular fixtures in most lender's and mortgage provider's arsenals. Two are short-term loans—usually secured from a commercial bank—one for land acquisition and development, and one for construction. Then there's the permanent home mortgage.

If buying a spec home, the builder may have developed the land and constructed a new home on it already, or he may own the lot and allow you to choose the model or custom home you want to build. In either case, the builder has probably secured the lot and construction financing to be able to clear the land and build. All you must do is get a letter of preapproval from your lender to let the builder know that you have permanent financing lined up. This may cost you as much as $350 in processesing fees.

If you own a lot and want to construct a custom home, it's usually your responsibility to secure the financing for all phases. Some builders may be willing to provide their own financing for the lot and construction. In these cases, the builder then sells the finished house and land to you in one transaction. But it may be tough to find a builder large enough to carry such a loan. More often than not, finding the funding is your job.

Unless you have the cash to plunk down for the lot, you'll need to secure a lot loan. According to Mary Ellen Raymond, retail operations officer for First National Bank (St. Louis), typically the terms are more restrictive in a platted subdivision because that subdivision has been improved and costs more than a large piece of raw land. "We'll usually give a 75 percent loan with 25 percent down in a subdivision. If it's 25 acres in the woods, it's customary for us to offer a 65 percent loan to value." She adds that if you plan to build on the land within the next year, the bank might amortize—liquidate a debt by installment payments—depending on the cost of the lot. "If it's a $10,000 lot, it will be a shorter term loan than a $40,000 one. We may suggest an adjustable rate—one that fluctuates," says Raymond.

As a rule, a lot loan has a higher interest rate than a permanent loan and there may be a one point charge. There are also some added fees such as a land title policy and closing costs. Depending on where the lot is located, it may require an appraisal if the bank can't come up with a reasonable estimate of value. A survey is not needed until the construction phase, unless you plan to siphon acres off a large parcel.

You can also get a signature or personal loan for land acquisition from your commercial bank. This loan would be based on your assets held in that bank which would serve as collateral.

For a construction loan, most commercial banks will typically finance up to 80 percent of the value or the cost—whichever is less. At the time a construction loan is issued, an appraisal is done based on your proposed plans and specs. The lender looks at the plans and the lot and estimates what their value will be.

Construction loans are typically set up on a dispersing or draw basis. Construction loan payments are usually negligible at first. The borrower pays monthly interest on what has been dispersed. A dispersing department from one of the title companies or a dispersing company handles the draws. When you want to make a draw—say $20,000 to cover work, materials, labor, and so forth—the title company or dispersing service may make inspections to see that work is going on and ensure that the percentage of work performed is equal to the amount of money requested. Or, the title company will have the architect prepare a certificate of partial completion stating that the draw request is justified.

The title or disbursing company will also take care of all lien waivers—the legal right of someone to take and hold or sell your property to satisfy a debt—to make sure none have been filed. These companies ensure that when the job is finished the contractor can't come back and say you paid him but not the subs, or you didn't reimburse him for materials.

Some lenders will bypass the lot loan and simply issue a construction loan which allows the first installment to cover the property cost. If there's a balance on the lot, you pay that off with the first disbursement. There may also be additional expenses for excavation. As the project develops, there will be more expenditures for the foundation, roof, walls, trim, and more. Interest will increase as funds are dispersed. Typically interest floats at 1 percent over prime plus one point. The title company fee may be ¼, ⅜, ½, or one point.

If you want a construction loan, but still own your old house, you won't qualify for a loan because your debt ratio is too high. If you're a strong bank customer with considerable assets and good credit, however, you might be a candidate for a short-term bank loan, based on your portfolio with the bank.

PERMANENT FINANCING

After the builder is finished, you must find permanent financing for the house. This is the big league for most consumers.

Some commercial banks suggest that you obtain permanent financing first, then backtrack to get the construction loan and consolidate the two with one set of closing costs. At the closing, a conversion date is set as to when the loan converts from a construction to a permanent loan. Whatever interest rate you have agreed to locks in at that point. The land is collateral for the construction loan, and the land plus finished house are collateral for the mortgage.

Closing costs involve appraisal and attorney fees, credit report cost, origination fee to the lender, and points. The majority of mortgage loans today have zero points because interest rates are so low. Points are paid primarily to buy a lower interest rate.

Other costs include real estate sales commission, survey cost, title insurance, assumption fees, assessments (charges for county or city improvements), inspection fees, recording charges, termite inspection fee, and a tax on the deed and mortgage loan assessed upon the sale of the house or the acquisition of a new mortgage. Each state law determines whether you or the seller pays this tax.

When a construction loan is converted into a permanent mortgage, a final inspection is conducted by the appraiser who gave the original value judgement at the construction loan phase. He can compare the original plans and specs to the final result. This ensures a thorough inspection.

The permanent loan conversion also requires you to update your information such as a credit report. If a survey was done at the beginning of the project, it will be redone after the house is completed to make sure items like driveways and decks are within building lines and up to code.

VARIETY IS THE SPICE OF PERMANENT LOANS

In life, the lowest is rarely the best—unless you're playing golf. The opposite is true, however, when discussing interest rates for home loans. Because current rates are so reasonable, mortgage offerings have emerged in a variety of sizes and shapes.

There are basically two forms of loans—fixed rate mortgage (FRM) and adjustable rate mortgage (ARM)—which account for about 99 percent of all permanent home mortgages. There are six types of FRMs and several ARMs.

An FRM is predictable. What you see is what you get. Because payment amounts remain constant over the life of the loan, FRMs are most suitable for homeowners who will be in their homes for several years. There are 10-, 15-, 20-, 25- and 30-year fixed rates and FRMs with balloons up to 10 years. An FRM with a balloon offers a permanent rate for X number of years, and then is refinanced at a fixed or variable rate. Make sure there is no prepayment penalty in case you elect to pay bigger chunks of the loan as time passes to reduce the amount of the balloon loan.

Buy-downs are 30-year fixed mortgages where you pay less initially. For example, if you have an 8 percent fixed rate mortgage, you would pay only 6 percent for the first year, 7 percent the second year, and 8 percent every year thereafter. You aren't getting a discount, you are making up the difference with points or a slightly higher fixed rate. The lower initial rate makes it easier for more people to qualify for the loan, and the points you pay are tax deductible.

A buy-down, where you pay less in the beginning and then a higher interest rate, is not a graduated payment and does not show negative amortization. That occurs when borrowers have the option of making a fixed payment and then deferring additional amounts based on rate fluctuations. But when rates rise, the additional interest is added to the loan principal, so you may wind up paying more than your original loan amount.

Graduated payments are loans that increase each year because a percentage of the interest payment is postponed up front. This escalates up to a certain point. It is ideal for the homeowner who expects his income to rise in big increments. This loan typically has shorter mortgage terms. The downside is that it can also lead to negative amortization where your payments become insufficient to pay off all the interest on the loan for the first few years. Again, the unpaid interest added to the original loan amount could total more than the house is worth. Before you consider this type of loan, calculate what the highest payment will be. This payment could cause a problem if you want to sell the house and have the new buyer assume your loan.

ARMs can be as unpredictable as the weather because they fluctuate throughout the life of the loan based on current interest rates that are tied to Treasury bonds or other sources. The most popular ARMs are between one and seven years, which means they start out at rates lower than a fixed rate and adjust after an agreed upon time period based on your qualifications and needs. They can adjust every six months, once a year, or more years between adjustments. The longer period you can lock in before an adjustment occurs, the more protection you have against future rate increases. Good ARMs have a payment cap—not an interest cap—or an upward or downward ceiling.

Initially, interest rates are lower for an ARM than an FRM. Usually an ARM starts out at 1 percent lower than the current market index and margin—the percentage above the indexed interest rate. This means less income is needed up front, making it easier to qualify for a loan, so you can borrow more money, and buy a more expensive home.

ARMs are best for those who figure they won't be living in their homes more than ten years. If you're working for a large company and you know you'll be transferred after two years, why pay for a 30-year loan when you can save on interest with an ARM that's amortized over 30 years?

But first a warning. When ARMs become adjustable, they can jump dramatically, particularly if interest rates skyrocket your ARM can have a negative amortization. If interest rates stay low, an ARM can offer positive amortization. Another downside is that the borrower's interest rate varies over the life of the loan making it hard to plan your finances.

To trim the amount of your loan, some lenders offer biweekly loans. These loans can quickly build up equity. You might pay slightly higher interest for these loans because they're more expensive to service. There may also be a prepayment penalty if too much of the loan is paid off before a specified term. Some pundits consider this type of loan just a marketing ploy. Its payment amounts are really the same as making one extra payment a year on a regular loan. But with a regular loan, you're not obligated to make that extra payment. If you did make one extra yearly payment, however, your 30-year loan would be paid off in only 18 years.

According to *The Wall Street Journal,* it's even popular right now for some borrowers—who are in higher income brackets, can afford sizable monthly payments, and are earning a good return on their principal in securities—to take out interest-only 10-year loans amortized over 30 years. Before the ten years are up, they refinance, rolling over the debt into another interest-only mortgage, then repeating the process to maintain a fairly constant debt level, thus receiving a large tax deduction each year.

Some owners refinance their loans to shave interest. This means a borrower pays off the original mortgage with a new one at a lower interest rate. New loans do incur closing costs, so if you refinance, make sure interest rates have dropped enough to make it worthwhile. Find out if there's a prepayment penalty. Even an interest rate drop of less than two points might warrant a change, but you must consider how many years the new loan will be, the amount you need to refinance, the effect this will have on your tax situation, and how much longer you'll be in your home, say experts. And some homeowners may not realize that you don't even have to refinance with the same lender. Shop around for the best deal.

A convertible or renegotiable loan is another way to change your original loan agreement—maybe from an ARM to an FRM—and you can lock in an interest rate at a future date. There may be a charge for this, however.

Some owners use a reverse mortgage to borrow funds. This is mostly a tool for retirees who own their own homes free and clear and want monthly loans from a lender to perhaps downsize to a new smaller home without making monthly payments. They can borrow against the equity in their home, and only one payment is made—with interest—when the home is sold. The loan value is based on the value of the home.

For those who don't have much money for a down payment—and don't qualify for a conventional loan—there are Federal Housing Administration (FHA) loans. FHA is under the aegis of the Department of Housing and Urban Development (HUD) and is really an insurer not a lender, which guarantees repayment of a loan should you default. This guarantee is at a cost to the borrower called mortgage insurance.

FHA loans are more liberal on underwriting and allow the consumer to borrow more. A down payment for an FHA loan can be as low as 3 percent. Also, the homeowner can also borrow the closing costs. FHA mortgages may be over 15, 20, 25 or 30 years as an FRM or ARM. The FHA (and Department of Veterans Affairs, which also administers nonconventional loans) sets the guidelines for ARMs that are the same for all lenders. Percentages for margins and caps are predetermined as well as what the loan is tied to. FHA loan amounts are limited by geographic area.

A downside to these loans is that there's often a longer processesing time than a conventional loan and such loans may have higher discount points and fees.

The VA, like the FHA, also guarantees loans but only to qualified veterans and spouses who don't have enough money for a down payment. The VA pays off a loan if the veteran defaults. These mortgages come in 15-, 20-, 25-, and 30-year terms in various loan plans. The borrower usually pays a fee up front or closing costs to the lender. The benefits are a lower down payment than a commercial loan (often none at all), no prepayment penalties, and it's fully assumable and nonescalating.

Before you sign for any permanent loan, make sure your loan program won't be eliminated. Also have your lender give you the total Annual Percentage Rate (APR). This is the entire annual cost of credit over the life of the permanent loan including interest, service charges, points, loan fees, and mortgage insurance plus other charges, and therefore is higher than the base interest rate.

THE PROCESS TO SECURE A PERMANENT LOAN

Once you've chosen the type of loan you want and face-off with a lender to sign for your mortgage, don't be caught off guard or empty-handed. The lender will bombard you with questions: Who do you work for? How much money do you make? What are your debts and assets? How much do you owe—monthly payments now on current debts? What are your credit card account numbers and addresses, bank account numbers and addresses? How much money do you have to use for a down payment and where does it comes from? The government insists on knowing where the down payment money comes from to make sure it isn't laundered money.

All this information is put on an application which is usually accompanied by your tax returns from the last two years, bank statements from the last three months, and a month's worth of pay stubs. If you are self-employed or own your own company, the lender may ask for a company's tax returns from the last two years plus a year-to-date profit and loss statement. A credit report and an appraisal of the new home are also ordered. If you've had a credit problem, be prepared to explain. Behind the scenes, the lender verifies information. Once the package is complete, an underwriter either approves or rejects it. It takes from three to four weeks to close on a conventional loan and longer for an FHA loan.

MONEY FOR REMODELING

Remodeling is for those who want to breathe new life into their current home. Most homeowners today want more space, comfort, and flexible living quarters, but this can be pricey. So you're ready to begin but need to find the funding, a procedure that is different from securing funds to build a new home.

The most common loan associated with remodeling is a second-mortgage or home equity loan. This allows you to borrow a total of 80 percent of your home's market value minus your mortgage amount. To get an accurate fair market value appraisal on your home for a home equity loan, call a real estate agent and get a comparative market analysis to other homes in your neighborhood.

Home equity loans generally have lower interest rates than other types of credit. In addition, interest payments on home equity loans are tax deductible.

What if you don't have enough equity in your home to make improvements? Fannie Mae's Home-Style Second-Mortgage loan may solve the problem and is more generous than a home equity loan. It enables you to borrow as much as 90 percent of the expected value of your home after the work has been done, minus

Issues to Address with a Lender

- What are the guidelines for getting a loan?
- What do I need to bring along with me when I apply?
- If I don't qualify for a conventional loan because all my money is tied up elsewhere and I don't have any for a down payment, what are my options?
- What are the various types of loans?
- Is this the best the lending institution can do for me?
- Can you explain all about the nuances so I know what to expect?
- Please give me a handle on closing costs, what they include and how much they will total. Tell me about any other fees.
- Do I need mortgage insurance?
- How long will it take to approve my loan?

the mortgage. But you'll pay for what you get. Rates are above average because they are secured by home improvements that haven't been made yet. Closing costs may be higher too.

FHA loans for renovations may be another option available through certain banks and other lending institutions. However, FHA must preapprove the contractor. If a contractor tells you he's FHA approved, check it out instead of just relying on his word.

If you want to remodel and the cost exceeds the equity in your home but you know the house will be worth a lot more when it's remodeled, a commercial bank might issue something similar to a construction loan.

The plans and specs are given to an appraiser to figure what the house will be worth when the project is complete. This requires money to be dispersed through a title company or dispersing service to control the construction and insure the money drawn is being used for improvements and not a trip to Mexico. At the end of the construction, the homeowner flips the remainder of the loan over into the permanent loan and refinances it to bring the weighted average down. (This is an average of the total of up and down moves in interest rate for the previous years.)

If you are undertaking a small remodeling project, such as putting on a deck, the bank might offer a home improvement loan similar to an installment loan. The terms must be commensurate with what you intend to do.

With careful financial planning of your building or remodeling and good preparation in advance of breaking ground, everyone can come out ahead. Bargains for getting money require that you talk to loan officers to find the options you want. You have the advantage of dealing from a position of strength.

CONSTRUCTIVE TIPS

Budget Builders

There are ways to make your cash work better for you in the money game of homebuilding and remodeling.

- Opt for a 15-year fixed-rate mortgage rather than a 25- to 30-year loan. The monthly payments with low interest rates won't be that much more on a 15-year loan, you'll ultimately pay less interest, and you'll pay off your home sooner.
- Prepay some of the principal on your loan each month in addition to your regular mortgage payment. This reduces your interest and builds up your equity faster. Make sure there isn't a prepayment penalty though. And don't ever pay anyone a fee to set up a biweekly mortgage payment. You can achieve the same outcome yourself for free. The loan servicer should be happy to help.
- Be disciplined in your spending. Assume you'll live in the house five to seven years, which is the average. Make decisions on that basis and don't overspend. The money you will have saved by not overdoing it, invest. If you end up living in your home longer than seven years, you'll now have saved enough to do what you wanted to do in the first place.
- Consider a piggyback mortgage that allows you to borrow more and take more of a deduction. A second mortgage also allows a deduction.
- Put as little down as possible on anything you buy for your home. If someone wants 50 percent, talk them down to 10 percent max. If something doesn't work out, a smaller deposit means less money lost.

CHAPTER 11

Extra Rooms with Additional Potential

Once considered nothing more than useless boxes, garages, laundry/mud rooms, and basements are gaining new lives. And although attics have always come in a variety of shapes they too got no respect—until now.

With a little planning and ingenuity these utilitarian rooms have never been so appealing—and in such demand—even though they continue to reflect a split personality. They are among the most pragmatic rooms and can be transformed into attractive new spaces by using a clever architect or remodeling contractor, and adapting some surefire strategies that suit your taste.

THE GARAGE: MORE THAN A LODGING FOR CARS

An attached garage is *de rigueur* in new homes today and high on the list of a homebuilder's wants, according to the National Association of Home Builders. A 2-, 2½-, 3-, or 4-car garage can add great value to a home. Any bigger size than these may add panache and convenience, but little worth. (See Figure 11.1.)

There are always those who feel bigger is better, however. One owner built a 10-car garage to house his antique car collection. Another couple, who built a four-car garage, now say they wish they had included space for six vehicles, to include their son's car and their new Harley Davidson motorcycle.

FIGURE 11.1 Characteristics of New Single Family Homes: By Region

	NORTHEAST					MIDWEST				
	1977	**1982**	**1987**	**1992**	**1996**	**1977**	**1982**	**1987**	**1992**	**1996**
Total Completed (in 000s)	87	193	196	114	108	140	170	201	218	245
Central A.C. installed	17	27	48	52	64	44	43	67	77	83
2½ Baths or more	29	28	46	55	64	22	22	40	49	50
4 Bedrooms or more	26	21	25	32	34	20	17	25	28	27
1 Fireplace or more	51	40	53	52	60	54	42	59	60	60
Full or partial basement	78	74	76	85	85	83	73	77	82	76
Slab	14	17	17	11	11	6	13	13	8	12
No garage or carport	23	33	21	23	17	19	23	10	9	9
Garage: 2 cars or more	44	39	49	57	63	69	54	80	85	85
Exterior wall material: brick	9	7	5	5	5	15	11	14	13	12
Exterior wall material: wood	45	52	47	38	25	56	67	54	35	22
1 Story	37	35	25	20	19	52	51	46	46	46
2 Stories or more	52	56	70	76	79	27	35	42	45	48
1,200 sq. ft. or less	27	28	10	12	7	25	35	16	11	11
2,400 sq. ft. or more	12	19	22	31	37	11	16	23	27	27

	SOUTH					WEST				
	1977	**1982**	**1987**	**1992**	**1996**	**1977**	**1982**	**1987**	**1992**	**1996**
Total Completed (in 000s)	408	505	467	400	507	183	253	259	232	269
Central A.C. installed	80	85	92	97	98	36	53	55	54	54
2½ Baths or more	10	21	34	42	44	25	22	37	50	50
4 Bedrooms or more	19	17	20	27	30	30	19	25	30	36
1 Fireplace or more	60	59	63	65	63	74	57	72	70	65
Full or partial basement	20	14	20	19	17	32	21	16	23	21
Slab	56	63	63	55	62	49	55	63	52	54
No garage or carport	27	32	29	22	19	6	13	4	4	4
Garage: 2 cars or more	47	45	52	64	71	78	65	86	91	91
Exterior wall material: brick	61	51	34	39	38	7	10	2	4	3
Exterior wall material: wood	23	34	35	25	15	43	49	40	43	36
1 Story	77	70	59	58	56	64	60	52	48	52
2 Stories or more	18	27	39	40	42	25	31	43	47	45
1,200 sq. ft. or less	16	23	15	10	8	18	24	14	8	8
2,400 sq. ft. or more	14	14	21	30	31	14	15	18	28	26

Source: Bureau of the Census. Compiled by Economics Department, NAHB.
Note: With the exception of Total Completed, numbers are percentages.

JON AND HILDE PENHALLURICK (Placitas, New Mexico)

Health care administrator Jon Penhallurick and his wife Hilde, a CPA, don't have children and they didn't want the upkeep of a huge home. However, they built in an area where the covenants require the homes to be a minimum of 2,200 square feet. They only wanted 1,800 square feet of living space. So what did they do? "We finished our garage like the rest of the house," says Jon. "It has electricity, cable, and phone hookups, skylights, plumbing roughed in, and is heated and cooled. We told our builder if anyone questions whether our home is big enough, just say, 'I can't help it if these people like to park in their family room.' "

Whatever size garage you build, it can be positioned either in the front, side or back of the home, and can be attached or detached. "It really depends on how the builder is trying to orient the subdivision, the setback requirements, neighborhood covenants, and zoning laws," says St. Louis architect Thomas Yanko of Myers & Yanko. "If it's an area of upscale homes, generally garages are built on the side or back so people aren't driving through a subdivision of $750,000 homes and looking at several garage doors." But it costs extra to place a garage in back, and requires more land and driveway space.

Some home designs warrant a detached garage. An attached garage on a Victorian-style home might look peculiar because the original Victorian homes were never built with garages.

Garages are usually constructed out of the same materials as the home. The base is a concrete slab or foundation poured on grade, walls consist of 2-by-4-inch or 2-by-6-inch wood studs, roof framing, wall and roof sheathing, roof underlayer and covering, front and side elevations, a separation wall between garage and existent home, overhead doors, electric work for inside and outside lighting, unfinished dry wall, or unfinished studs. Yanko estimates the cost can range from $25 to $50 a square foot, but a garage's design and amenities can easily raise the roof on this figure.

If the allotted space is long and narrow, some owners build garages in tandem so one car is parked behind the other. Many owners opt to have their garages heated with separate electric units. Gas heat is not recommended around cars because it's flammable. And don't forget to consider an electric garage door opener, which will make life easier and safer, especially late at night. If your garage stands at the front of the house, also consider an interesting paneled door, or one in a spiffy color. And attractive plantings can dress it up because it's one of the first things everyone will see.

There are those who make their garages even more grandiose. One homeowner, a car enthusiast, put a full-fledged car wash in his 12-car garage. Another homeowner, whose wife kept chipping the corners of the garage doors when she pulled out backwards, had a turntable installed in the floor on her side of the garage. At the push of a button, her car rotated forward so she could pull out easily.

More typically, garages are smaller, less adorned, and less organized. They tend to become a catch-all area for old sports paraphernalia, hardware and gardening supplies, lawn equipment, paints, worn mattresses, and furniture waiting to be picked up by the Salvation Army. With so much junk in them, sometimes the cars are left out in the cold.

What a waste. The potential for storing not just cars but any items you don't want inside your home can be limitless, if you organize your garage. Decide what you need: a workshop, gardener's headquarters, sports-equipment storage area, kids' toy zone, hobby center. Some companies make specialty racks, baskets and holders for soccer balls, skis, golf bags and other sports equipment, toys, spreaders, brooms, snow shovels, and lawn mowers. Most of these can be found at hardware or home center stores.

You can also have a contractor design and install built-ins but the cost, of course, will be greater. Homeowners who live in areas not suitable for basements, such as California and Florida, are often quite willing to ante up the $3,000 to $5,000 for the right accoutrements: a work bench and cabinets, storage space for bulky items such as large cans of paint or sealants, a tool organizer, shelving to hold smaller items such as car care products, gardening tools and plant foods, and recycling bins.

This is only half the story of the versatility of a garage, however. Today's garage can also become tomorrow's new room. A single-car garage is the shell for a perfect den or small family room, bedroom, or extra bath. A two-car garage can become a single-car garage and an extra room.

Your remodeler or architect must follow building codes and have permits to make the transformation, which can be relatively fast and easy. You don't have to install a foundation, walls, or roof—they're already in place. If you knock out the adjoining wall between the garage and the house—to increase the space or your kitchen, for example—you'll need an architect or engineer to scrutinize and design the structural remodeling.

To complete the metamorphosis, frame the walls with new doors and windows, and have an electrician and plumber bring the room up to building codes. Heating and insulation must then be added, interior walls finished with drywall, and subfloors installed under an overlay of permanent flooring such as tile, carpeting, or hardwood. Next put in fixtures and interior doors, and accessorize.

Does remodeling a garage into a new room add value to your home? It depends on how well the job is done and what is lost in the process. The conversion can increase the liveability and value of your home, if you've expanded the kitchen or added another bathroom, as long as a new garage is built to replace the former one.

ATTICS: ROOMS AT THE TOP

Attics are the wallflowers of most people's homes. In older homes, the little space under the roof, filled with the family luggage, old paperbacks, and vintage clothing, is often forgotten or discounted.

BOB AND RANDY COSTAS (St. Louis, Missouri)

Randy Costas and her husband Bob say one thing they would have done differently when they built their home is to have made their faux third floor a real attic. Says Randy, "I'd love to be able to convert it into a computer room and utilize natural light." Another thing Randy would have done differently, "I would have made the laundry room three times bigger. It could never be big enough."

Usable attics are like the dinosaurs of homebuilding. They are becoming extinct in new homes because of the technology of roof construction, which consists of wood trusses—a web of 2-by-4-foot lumber—says Yanko. This type of roof cannot be altered to have attic space because it would alter the structural stability. If you want an attic, you have to construct a different type of roof, intentionally adding an attic, Yanko says.

If you opt to have one, it must be insulated and vented. There are several kinds of insulation, but the preferred type is fiberglass. There are various types of vents as well, including soffit, gable end, ridge, roof, turbines, and power. Somewhere between 10 to 15 percent of a building's total heat loss is through the ceiling into the attic. There are four considerations when installing insulation: (1) framing must allow space for insulation; (2) you must allow room for ventilation above, and for the full thickness of the insulation which is applied over exterior wall top plates; (3) the insulated ceiling needs an air/vapor barrier under the insulation, which must be sealed airtight, and (4) proper cross ventilation is required to remove moisture and reduce summer heat buildup.

Attic space, too, can be recast into a new room, but it must be done to code. The cost is in the $30 to $45 per square foot range. Putting in a bathroom will add $5,000 to $15,000, assuming the plumbing can be extended from below.

If the attic isn't high enough for you to stand in, the roof will have to be raised to a height of at least 7' above the attic floor, according to code. But this is very expensive to do, especially on an older home. It would be cheaper to add a room to a lower floor, unless there is no space left to do so.

In order to do work in the attic area, joist sizes, span and spacing must be checked by an architect and/or engineer to make sure they are adequate to support the typical loads of a finished, occupied living space. Then, subflooring must go in. Changes to the roof are made next, adding dormers and walls to increase the space. You may also need to install new doorways. The area must be insulated and dry walled, finished flooring put down (tile, hardwood, carpeting), perhaps a bathroom added, and space partitioned off for a closet, Yanko says.

Don't forget to install adequate heating and electrical systems. The heating and electrical systems in the main house can be extended to the attic or to a garage for that matter. If not sufficient, a new zoned system can be installed. The final touches involve adding fixtures, doors, hardware, decorations and voilà, you have a quirky living space with various nooks and crannies.

As for attic access, most have a pull down stairway, but some older and larger homes have a back staircase that extends to the attic. Before you add or finish an attic, though, be sure someone wants to venture up to the third floor to live because they may often be alone. Of course, your teenager may want it that way.

LAUNDRY AND MUD ROOMS

Laundry rooms and mud rooms in new homes today have earned their own space. They've grown in size as well as status. They now typically range from 12' × 12' to 12' × 14'.

Of primary importance is the location of these rooms. The location gives the perception that working in these rooms is an amenity rather than a chore. Washers and dryers in the basement are outdated. Some put the laundry room upstairs near the bedrooms in a two-story house and place the mud room downstairs off the kitchen or near the back door. But most owners opt to have the laundry room as close to the kitchen as possible for convenience, usually adjacent to—or combined with—a mud room. (Others, however, find that doing laundry in the kitchen creates ongoing clutter and noise.)

Equally important is the look of these rooms. Their presentation has improved. They can be bright and cheery, with a window, a closet, a countertop for folding clothes and even a sink. In many cases, owners don't even see their washer and dryer because they are concealed behind louvered doors.

Having the mud room and laundry room in close proximity—or even combined—on the first floor encourages practical use of these rooms. The mud room, typically an anteroom between the garage and the house, can have a coat closet or nice rack, a window to the outside, and a bench for sitting down to take off muddy shoes or wet boots. A built-in heater or radiator will not only warm the room but is a perfect spot to hang items if you don't want to use the dryer. If you do, however, laundry machines are close by as well.

First-floor laundry and/or mud rooms have also become distinctive places from which you can keep your family organized, says Dean Bordeaux of New-Space, a closet and space organization company in St. Louis. He tells about one client with ten children. As a holiday present for his wife, the client remodeled the laundry room, which was the nerve center of the house. His wife was constantly in the kitchen packing lunches and preparing meals or in the laundry room throwing in loads of clothing. They invested $5,000 to make the room as functional as possible despite the tiny space—8½' × 11'. The designers had to work around a laundry room with three doors and a huge difficult pattern.

Bordeaux and his crew streamlined and optimized efficiency and improved overall appearance. They crafted a multitier hanging coat rack area and a large, deep countertop on which to fold, sort, and distribute laundry to family members. The counter doubles as a workspace for other chores such as wrapping Christmas presents. Underneath the counter is room for bulk storage, which the family tagged their "Sam's cabinet," because they buy everything in bulk at Sam's Warehouse.

"Because the kitchen didn't have much space to store heavy appliances like a stationary mixer, we had to integrate this into the cabinetry," says Bordeaux. Cabinets and countertops were practical laminate and melamine laminate materials in bright white to keep the space light and open. The cabinets installed over the washer and dryer have integrated spaces for extra hangers. Fold out accordion-type drying racks allow wet items to be draped, and a 12″ rod was added for hanging permanent press garments that are whisked straight from the dryer to hangers to avoid wrinkles.

Some shallow cabinets were built for canned goods. A hot-iron caddie was constructed to hold the iron so it would not be left out and a slot was carved in a tall deep cabinet into which an ironing board without legs is folded. The board pulls out and can be rotated up for use. Slots lined with felt for protection were also provided for cookie sheets, placemats, linens, and table leaves. Another tall cabinet holds vacuuming equipment with baskets for the attachments.

Another idea that Bordeaux has used in a laundry room is to include a counter space with room for a chair underneath that can double as a desk for doing work, paying bills, or writing letters while you do laundry or cook dinner in the adjacent kitchen. Some owners use a corner of their laundry rooms to store dog food or a giant-size detergent bin. You might also add open shelves for each family member's laundry and label them accordingly. Still another idea is to carve out a niche for recycling bins because more communities now demand that you sort newspapers, plastic bottles, and tin cans.

The first floor laundry/mud room can also double as a potting room, because of its proximity to the garage where tools are stored. A wet sink can be added so you can water plants—or soak stained clothing. A dry sink can be used to prune plants. A counter for potting and a greenhouse window can be installed so you can get plants started during the winter.

If the laundry room is upstairs, it typically takes up about as much space as a nice bathroom and may have a built-in ironing board, a small utility sink, cabinets for storage of laundry materials and linens, and the washer and dryer in an alcove. It's necessary to place a metal pan under a second-floor washing machine to catch any water that may leak or splash so it doesn't saturate the floor and seep into the rooms below. The pan is usually connected to a drain.

Because these rooms are usually not highly visible, save your money and don't spend a lot to decorate them. They can be painted with a bright colored semigloss, or the walls can be papered with vinyl for easy cleaning. You can cover the floor with a seamless vinyl, quarry, or ceramic tile, which all have fewer cracks to keep water spillage from filtering through. Lots of recessed lighting in the soffits and ceiling can bring the rooms to life and make the tasks at hand seem less tedious.

BASEMENTS

In the 1950s, basements were transformed into quaint English-style rathskellers, many with knotty-pine paneling. In the '60s, they became bomb shelters.

In the '70s, they were used to store fine wine. And in the '80s—when houses grew bigger and glitzier—they were all but abandoned, considered dark dank places best suited for storing old clothing and furniture.

REGINA BARRECA (Storrs, Connecticut)

Humor writer Regina Barreca has this bit of advice, culled from one of her columns in *The Hartford Courant Sunday Magazine*: "Things going a little too well at home? Not enough domestic angst? Nobody in the house living on the edge of mania and depression? Try cleaning out the basement. Try deciding what must be kept and what must be thrown away. This activity, within the first half-hour, is guaranteed to transform even the most enviably happy couple into a pair of cranky, disheveled, sullen combatants. This works not only with basements, but with attics, with garages, and with sheds."

But basements are enjoying renewed popularity in new and remodeled houses, as evidenced in Figure 11.2. They've become a catchall, a symbol of our busier, fuller lives and the higher costs of housing. Some career-minded families turn them into home offices, if space in an extra bedroom doesn't exist. And buying a three-bedroom home with a basement—instead of a four-bedroom home—can mean a savings of $50,000 to $100,000.

Other homeowners are converting their basements into workout rooms that make getting fit more convenient than traveling to a health club. When the sky's the limit, some homeowners have dug their basements deeper and constructed indoor swimming pools or built practice driving ranges. Walk-out basements are great locations for dressing rooms if you have an outdoor swimming pool or hot tub.

Currently, a popular use of a basement is an age-old one—creating attractive indoor play space for young family members, as Highland Park, Illinois, architects Richard and Nancy Becker did for their five children, ages 3 to 14. "We had a small first-floor family room and needed more space," Richard says.

But one of the indicators that basements are finally gaining respect is that at least one multiple-listing real estate service directory now allows its agents to include the basement in a home's total square footage, which was never done before in that area.

FIGURE **11.2** Percent of New Homes Completed with Full or Partial Basement

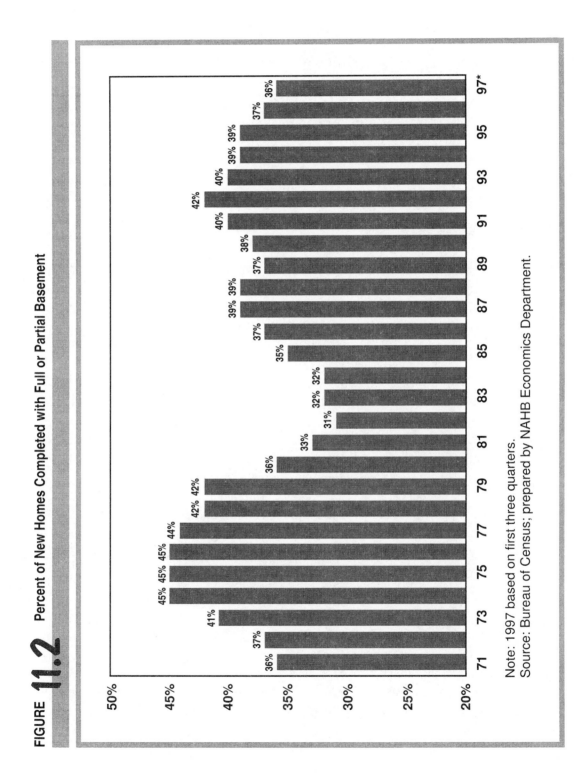

Note: 1997 based on first three quarters.
Source: Bureau of Census; prepared by NAHB Economics Department.

BOB AND RANDY COSTAS (St. Louis, Missouri)

Randy Costas and her husband Bob said in retrospect the smartest thing they did when building their home ten years ago was to dig the basement deeper than most. At the time Randy questioned why they spent so much money to do it. "We have 9' ceilings. Our basement isn't a basement, but several extra rooms: a playroom for the kids . . . there's a pool room, a ping pong table, a little basketball court and an 8' × 8' linoleum square spot where the kids can paint. There's an exercise room for us (Bob exercises every day when he's home), an extra bedroom with a full bath, and another half-bath off the playroom." Now she says she would have dug the basement even deeper. "I know people who have a squash court in their basement."

Homebuilders are taking note of the basement trend and incorporating larger, fancier, conventional or walk-out basements that have higher ceilings and brighter lighting. Square footage has grown to a more livable minimum of 1,000 square feet and is often many times that. Ceilings have been raised—sometimes from a standard 7'8" height to 9' or 10'—and walls, ceilings and floors have a nicer finish, though usually not as nice as the upstairs rooms.

Orren Pickell, a builder whose firm is based in Bannockburn, a Chicago suburb, has included basements in half the custom homes he's built over the last few years. Sometimes measuring 1,000 to 2,500 square feet of usable space, these basements can have a bedroom, a full bathroom, a family space with fireplace and small-scale kitchen appliances, and perhaps an exercise area or home theater. Most also are also accessed through dramatic entryways and staircases.

Basements are more *de rigueur* in homes that sell for $150,000 and up, according to the National Association of Home Builders. Hombuyers seeking less expensive or moderately priced houses often forgo a basement so they won't be priced out of the housing market. It can be the difference between affording a house or not.

REMODELED BASEMENTS

But savvy owners, agents, and design professionals know that existing basements shouldn't be improved to the same degree as rooms on the main level, such as the living and dining rooms. In other words, owners shouldn't spend the same money and use the same quality materials because they may not get a full payback.

"If you want to fix up a basement because you want the additional room, that's fine. Do what makes you happy. But if you spend a lot, you can't be certain you'll get it back, particularly if the basement doesn't have windows or a high ceiling," advises Elizabeth Ballis, a Chicago area real estate agent. Another agent says most of his clients view basement space as a valuable bonus but aren't willing to pay a premium for it.

Because the amount you spend on a new or remodeled basement should depend on the value of your home, there's no hard-and-fast rule regarding what amount achieves a good return. Keeping costs between 5 and 10 percent of your home's value is one rule-of-thumb, but not a guarantee. At the same time, spending less than $10,000 to remodel a basement is difficult, unless you only make cursory cosmetic changes such as painting the concrete and gluing down indoor-outdoor carpeting to warm up the space. For an 800-square-foot room finished in mid- to high-end quality, you'd have to spend at least $12,000 to $20,000.

It may make better sense economically to tackle such work at the same time you undertake another significant home remodeling project. Whenever you bring in workers, you usually have lag time during which smaller projects can be done. This way you also cut down the number of times you bring dirt and dust into the house.

The following are things to consider when making your basement habitable and organized so it doesn't look and feel like an old musty storage room. Many of these points also apply when building a basement in a new house. You can sketch a floor plan and plot the permanent fixtures such as the hot-water heater and furnace.

- Make it dry. Before you remodel and/or decorate, have an expert determine if the basement is dry enough. Some are so wet that the dampness will not only affect your enjoyment of the lower level but could also harm the home's foundation. Experts estimate that almost 80 percent of all basements are somewhat wet, as evidenced by the mold and mildew that grows on walls and stored items. How you eliminate the dampness depends on its cause and pervasiveness.

    If the foundation is cracking because there is too much water in the house or underneath it, the water needs to be redirected. To do so, you may need to open up the earth on the outside, repair damaged drainage tiles—installing more if necessary—and fix the foundation walls.

    If seepage occurs at the point where the floor and wall come together—known as the cove—there's too much water underneath and the inside floor needs to be opened along the perimeter to add more drainage. Paints that promise to seal walls and ceilings are risky because they usually just redirect the water to another area instead of eliminating the problem.

- Give it height. The next biggest potential problem is the height of the ceiling. Many older homes have low basement ceilings, sometimes only 7 feet. Such spaces may be fine for tots to play in but don't warrant extensive work because most adults won't want to spend much time there. If you insist on adding height, you can excavate the ground, which is labor intensive and very expensive. It's heavy construction, which involves removing concrete and soil. But if the space is sought after and you have no other room for an addition, it's an option.
- Bring in light. The brightness of the basement affects the occupants' enjoyment as well as resale. If natural light is available, consider using glass or acrylic blocks to allow in light but still provide security.

  If the basement doesn't have a window well, don't automatically forsake fixing it up. Some architects and contractors often use recessed incandescent light if there's sufficient joist space, or put halogen bulbs on tracks or in wall sconces. They also suggest staying away from fluorescent lights because the color is too harsh. Some also advise steering clear of torchère lights if children use the space because they can be easily knocked over.
- Add coziness. You'll definitely want your basement to be cozy and inviting, which means having a floor that's nicer than the typical bare-bones concrete. Laying ceramic tile can be expensive. And installing wool carpet isn't practical in an area where water seepage is possible. Safer bets are vinyl tile squares or industrial-grade, low-loop, or indoor-outdoor carpeting. Vinyl and carpet are similarly priced, under $10 a square foot. If you have young children who like to ride bikes, choose vinyl. If you want a look that's softer and quieter, pick carpet. Glue either down so that if a water problem occurs they're easier to remove and clean.

  Finishing a basement also means having nice walls and ceilings. You can put up a wall covering topped with brightly colored vinyl wallboard. Exposed brick provides a nice homey backdrop. Or you can frame the wall with studs, then add insulation, a vapor barrier, and drywall. For the ceilings consider suspended acoustic tiles, which are inexpensive and allow access to plumbing shutoff valves and mechanical equipment. There are a lot of good looking styles available now, so the room doesn't have to resemble an inexpensive ugly office.

- Consider a bathroom. Having a half or full bathroom makes sense if you want to accommodate a guest or nanny overnight. (Also, be sure to find out if your local ordinances permit a bedroom on the lower level.) If stacks don't exist, adding them can be costly. On average, a half bath is about half the cost of a full bathroom. A full bath can be done for $15,000 if not overly fancy.

- Furnish the area. Furnishings needn't be expensive to make the room pleasurable. Consider using your old living room furniture or buying new futons, hanging posters, and installing inexpensive wire shelves. Depending on how you plan to use the room, you may also want to add a pool table or ping-pong table, bookshelves, and entertainment equipment. The benefit of adding a fireplace doesn't usually justify the cost, which can run $5,000. Also, not crowding the room with furniture will make it appear more spacious.

- Check electrical wiring, heating, and air conditioning. Be sure an electrician checks to be certain that the home's wiring can accommodate any electrical equipment you use in the basement—TVs, sound systems, computers, small kitchen appliances, etc. Don't tap into the home's heating and air conditioning system, which will redirect some of the air away from the upper levels, unless your units are large enough to service the additional space.

- Provide access. If possible, try to be sure you have access to the outdoors from the basement beside the interior stairway. This can include having windows large enough to use as emergency exits. These may also be required by your local building codes.

THE BASEMENT OF THE FUTURE: FROM SQUASH COURT TO MEDIA CENTER

Not every homeowner asks his builder for a basement like this one: it has a children's play area; a dance floor; a billiards area; a family room; a saltwater fish tank; a media room with fiber optic lights in the ceiling that resemble stars; a bar, small kitchen, and a bathroom with lockers that guests can use after swimming in the backyard pool.

But including a basement in your construction plans has its rewards. For one, it can cost less than it would if the contractor were asked to build it later. In addition, it's less expensive to finish a basement that already exists than to build an addition above ground. Orren Pickell, whose company built 27 high-end houses last year, pegged the basement cost at between $30 and $100 a square foot, versus $120 to $200 for the rest of the house. "If you do it from the start you can save $5,000 to $10,000," he said. This is more true in the city where tight lots put space at a premium.

The degree to which your basement is finished varies dramatically according to the pricepoint of your house, and whether you have a production, semicustom, or custom home. The majority of builders today include an unfinished basement as a standard feature in the base price of their mid- to high-priced homes rather than incorporating a finished basement that would increase the selling price.

But what exactly does unfinished mean? Typically, it's an open space with concrete walls and floors, exposed ceiling joists, and sometimes roughed-in bathroom plumbing. Finished translates as nice surfaces such as drywall, tile, carpet, and wood. It may be worthwhile to consider paying extra to have the builder finish the basement because the cost can be built into your mortgage so you won't need to get additional financing later for remodeling.

One couple paid their builder $25,000 to turn their lower-level foundation into a finished basement with a full bathroom, drywalled ceiling and walls, and carpeted floor. One side has a desk, bookcases, console, and TV; the other side has a sofa bed and a second TV for the children and grandchildren.

In addition to price, another reason that builders generally don't finish basements is because of the variety of homeowners' needs. Some may want a fitness room, while others desire a home office. And some homeowners don't have any idea how they're going to finish their basements until long after they've settled in, or squirreled away additional funds. Still others never do anything to the basement because they lose interest after they realize that nobody in the family ever ventures downstairs.

Will the trend to build home offices or fitness rooms continue and should you consider having a basement to house them? Yes, say experts, because basements help sell a home faster even in markets where they're not as common. Homeowners have started to view them as a necessity, which makes it harder for builders not to offer them.

Experts warn, however, that you may not recoup all your expenses if you finish your basement to the same degree as the rest of your house. Remember it's not the living room. Avoid using fancy moldings, cabinets, and granite. Adding in a nice staircase, opening up the access, and lighting the area well so that you don't feel like you're in a dark hole, however, can be money well spent. But in the end, it all depends on the next buyers' tastes, lifestyle, and what part of the country they're from—and there's no predicting those factors.

GREENHOUSES: A YEAR-ROUND HOME FOR YOUR PLANTS

The first thing you notice about a greenhouse, sunroom, solarium—a windowed room for people—or conservatory, is that it looks gorgeous rising inconspicuously at one end of the house. The shape and configuration should complement the home's architecture and lines. Whatever the design, these additions look powerful with their patterned extrusions and plastic or glass glazing.

Styles

Today, these structures come in a number of designs, many of which are quite affordable, says Janice L. Hale, editor of *Hobby Greenhouse,* a publication of the Hobby Greenhouse Association. They come in conventional or contemporary designs—box-like English styles with straight side walls, pitched roof, and glass all the way to the floor or raised footing; curved-eave style made of contoured glass or plastic; Dutch-style with walls that slope from the eave to the foundation, angled to get more sunlight; hoop houses that use a metal or plastic pipeframe covered with heavy plastic film or flexible fiberglass; gothic arch design glazed with the same material as hoop houses; geodesic or small portable domes that offer maximum light but limit the size and height of plants due to the shape; circular gazebo style with a flaring top; or a Quonset hut of molded fiberglass.

Types

There are only a few basic types of greenhouses: an even-span structure which receives the most light and can be freestanding—the most expensive to build and to heat—or abut one wall of the house; a lean-to—the most popular—which leans against the house, is easy to construct, and is cheaper because it requires less glazing (and the shared wall reduces heat loss); and window or pit greenhouses that are constructed so half the house is below the ground.

The type of greenhouse you choose should be dictated by what you plan to grow, how you want to enter the greenhouse—from inside your home or outside, how you want to access utilities, the climate where you live, and your area's building codes, neighborhood covenants, and local zoning laws.

It's What's Inside That Counts

Greenhouses can have many different features. You can include a foundation or footing; a structure; side, ceiling/roof, and floor vents; heating (for cold climates), cooling and humidification (swamp coolers are popular in the South); exhaust fans; electricity (because of the moisture, be sure to protect electrical connections with a ground fault circuit interrupter); growing benches; lighting (many use a vapor proof fluorescent fixture that can handle moisture and humidity); and grow lights (which come in various shapes, sizes and strengths). In addition, many have hot and cold running water, a storage area for pots, wire closet shelves, hoses, fertilizers, and pruners.

Then there are the extras. These include automatic misting or sprinkling systems, shades, spigots, and an alarm. If you live in the north where it gets cold, you can hook the greenhouse alarm into your home alarm. If the temperature drops too low, the alarm sounds.

SIZE

Greenhouses range in size from tiny—6' × 8', to the larger more popular sizes—10' × 12' or 9' × 12'. Some are modular and allow additions later on. The larger the house, the easier it is to control heating and cooling.

Furnishings

Growing benches should be placed strategically in relation to the heat source, walkways, thermostat, and watersource. These benches are along the inside of the glass walls. Some plants require low light levels and should be placed away from direct light.

The Plants

Consider a variety of pots in various sizes to make it more visually interesting. Move the plants outside in summer, then repot and return them to the greenhouse in winter.

Cost

Prices can range from about $400 for a tiny house to $20,000 for a custom-built structure. The cost, however, is basically contingent on the size of the greenhouse and the materials used to construct it.

Getting Started

First read everything from horticulture books and periodicals to catalogs, brochures, and ads. Talk to other greenhouse owners. Call the Hobby Greenhouse Association. Then decide how often you'll use the greenhouse, if you should build it yourself or have it built, and where it should be located. Ideally, one long side of the structure should face south, southeast or southwest, and one end should catch the morning sun.

WINE CELLARS

Many homeowners enjoy having specially built wine cellars in their basements so they can select a bottle to enjoy with dinner, take to a tasting, serve at a party, or give as a gift.

A wine cellar provides the optimum storage conditions and an ideal environment for your vintage treasures, and can organize your collection so it can be enjoyed for years to come. If there's any room left in your cellar, you might think about setting up a tasting room with space for sitting, sipping wine, and perusing favorite wine magazines and books. But a temperature-controlled cellar does not have to be relegated to the basement. It can be built in any part of your house such as the kitchen, the butler's pantry, or the dining room.

For collections under 500 bottles, a wine cabinet or wine cooler will suffice. Many models are advertised in food and wine magazines. For larger collections consisting of 500 to 1,000 bottles, many connoisseurs find a cool spot under their basement stairs or in a closet and use the natural conditions.

For even larger collections of 1,200 to 1,500 bottles—and growing—a walk-in temperature-controlled wine cellar may be the smartest ticket. You can transform a mundane dark cavernous space in your basement into the perfect secret underground room, that has a practical as well as aesthetic side.

Rooms for wine storage have evolved into appealing, elaborate structures with their own furnishings and style. The degree of decorating is strictly a matter of your taste and budget. Cellars can be complex and dressed up like a first growth Bordeaux with a great deal of character, ornamentation, and accoutrements like ultra-premium redwood racks, expensive tile or flagstone floors, etched glass paneled doors, recessed incandescent lighting, artwork, furniture, and even a PC for you to inventory your wines on a database.

Some cellars are less embellished, dressed down like a plain California red table wine in a simple sturdy space lined with prefabricated racks, with an inexpensive cooling system and a painted concrete floor. Yet, these, too, can keep your wine drinkable for decades.

The most challenging part of converting a space into a wine cellar may be finding the right place. Because your basement might be filled with boxes, extra furniture, and old clothes, consider a spot in your kitchen or family room. Once you find the spot, however, the conversion is well within the realm of an amateur carpenter. If you're not comfortable doing the work, take your ideas to a local carpenter or someone who specializes in building wine cellars.

Develop a plan, establish a budget, and decide on the ideal size. As a rule, calculate how much room is needed for new wine and how quickly you consume the wine you already own. Double the number of bottles you currently have to be safe, because an attractive cellar will lead to more collecting. Also decide on the kind of racks, cooling system, flooring, and lighting you desire. Get some books on wine collecting from your local library or glance through wine magazines for ideas.

When you begin, focus on the basics. First, lay a new floor or paint the existing one. Appropriate flooring can be a sturdy kitchen vinyl or imported tiles. Wall-to-wall carpeting is verboten because it tends to breed mold. Next comes the vapor seal, build out, insulation, and cooling—either a self-contained unit or a spilt system. A cooling system keeps cellar temperatures between 50 and 65 degrees Fahrenheit with a 60 to 70 percent humidity level. Have an electrician install lighting. It can be fluorescent or low voltage halogen—a type of incandescent.

Racking is needed to cradle your bottles. Racks can be built in various depths to store one, two, or three bottles per opening. Racking comes in various styles, woods, and grades. Redwood is the rack of choice because it has the best track record for resisting mold and mildew. There are also pine, Honduran mahogany, red oak, metal, and glass racks. The bins can be in different configurations: diamonds, lattice, waterfalls, triangles, or trellised slots. Other accessories for your cellar might include bottle tables, bin tables, bottle tags, cork bulletin boards, cork trivets, rolling ladders, adjustable shelves, display cabinets, and built-in tables.

Building a cellar can take up to six months. Costs can spiral if you add special doors, glass, various styles of racking, and fancy flooring.

After the cellar is built, organize your wine as you would books in a library. You might group your imported and domestic selections separately. When finished, close the door to guard the secret of what's inside, unless you allow guests to peruse your assortment, or hang glass doors on the front to offer a tantalizing peek.

COMING HOME TO THE OFFICE

Where do family and work meet? In the home office. More than 52 million people do some type of work from home—including 3.6 million who work at home full-time—according to a 1997 America Internet User Survey. In architecture and design today, it would be remiss not to plan space for a home office or a computer workstation, whether designating a separate room or tiny alcove in a larger room such as a deep closet in a bedroom or kitchen.

Again, builders are designing and prewiring homes to handle the additional equipment needed by those who work at home, such as extra telephone or modem lines, and outlets for fax machines, personal computers, multipurpose machines, and other electronic accessories.

Paul Edwards, who coauthored the book *Working from Home: Everything You Need to Know about Living and Working under the Same Roof* (Tarcher/Putnam) with his wife Sarah, is a pioneer in the field of home business. He points out that there are common ingredients, detailed below, that go into all well-designed home offices.

Equipment

You need a phone system, computer, modem, and accompanying hardware. This means planning and allowing for enough power in the house to handle the additional needs of this technology. Ideally, if you're buying a new home and you're uncertain as to who your Internet service provider will be, have a fiber optic or cable connection put in the area designated as an office. If you need multiple phone lines and modems, consider having an integrated service data network (ISDN)—interim technology that generates faster access to the Internet, comparable to two or more phone lines. ISDN routers pare the costs of having to install multiple phone lines, according to *Home Office Computing* magazine.

Multipurpose Machines

You might consider a multipurpose machine, which requires less space and fewer outlets. More of these are being sold today than the traditional stand-alone versions. You can now purchase a copier, printer, scanner, telephone, fax, and answering machine all in one. Many fax machines also have phone and copying capabilities. Office machines are getting smaller and more affordable each year.

Natural Light

Try to have some natural light whenever possible. For artificial lighting, you will need soft, subdued light for doing computer work and brighter light for reading and writing.

Sound-Proofing

Make sure there's an extra layer of insulation in the walls to keep out noise coming from other family members and block the noise that comes from your office.

Flooring Choices

If you have a desk chair that rolls or any filing cabinets or bookshelves on wheels, you might not want to have carpeting in your office. Consider installing a vinyl or rubber surface instead. You can get a masonite piece to place under your chair, however, if there is carpeting.

Comfortable Chairs

One ergonomic chair doesn't fit all types of bodies. Comfortable chairs with good back support are mandatory. The rest of the furnishings should also accommodate your body movement, to promote mental alertness and productivity. You might want to build some filing cabinet drawers in your desk or workstation. Have storage space with bookshelves and/or filing cabinets on wheels close at hand.

Computer Placement

There should be ten inches between you and the keyboard. The keyboard should be two to three inches lower than the standard 30-inch-high desk. The screen should be 10 to 15 inches from your eyes.

Desks

It's important to have enough counter space on each side of your computer to place documents. Computers haven't eliminated paper; in many cases, they've generated more. Be sure and have plenty of bookshelves, as well as space for miscellaneous supplies such as pencils, revolving card files, dictionaries, disks, and paper.

Plumbing

Have a bathroom nearby, especially if you have customers who come into your home or other workers working alongside you.

CONSTRUCTIVE TIPS

Keeping the Spaces Pragmatic

The following list discusses spaces that are first and foremost meant to be utilitarian. Don't make them so glitzy that you end up wasting too much money.

- Don't make the garage too large. Most families only need enough space to house three cars, bikes, garden equipment, snow removal supplies, and sporting goods. Build in some shelves to stash odds and ends; and consider hooks on the walls for bicycles and lawn equipment. But anything more may be unnecessary.
- Don't add more than one bedroom or playroom and one bathroom to the attic. Most future owners won't ever venture up there. Be sure you air condition the attic in some way or have a good ceiling fan because attics get very hot in summer.
- Don't forget to add in a large closet or two in the mudroom for stashing winter coats, hats, boots, and gloves, a place to organize miscellaneous sporting gear including a rack for tennis racquets, and a bin for basketballs.
- In your basement, don't make the ceiling too low, and don't forget to add in both natural and artificial light, a good foundation, and an air conditioning system because the area may experience wide temperature swings. A half bathroom and a practical floor that will wear well and resist water stains—or worse, flooding—should also be included. Don't forget to make sure that the basement is dry. Also consider adapting part of the basement to your favorite activity or need, such as a wine cellar, darkroom, or suitcase storage area.

12

Finalizing Decisions on Building Components

Don't leave any stone unturned. After spending so much time and money to plan and finance your new home or remodeling project, you should be certain that the structure is sturdy, long-lasting, and constructed according to all the right building codes.

To do so you need to understand all the major components that go into putting a house together. However, be forewarned that your geographic location, the lot's terrain, and your community's rules and regulations will dictate some decisions.

Before you make any choices, do your homework thoroughly. Just because your best friend swears by his vinyl siding, don't take his word for it. Look at it yourself, find out all the advantages and disadvantages, and get several bids. Don't forget to check the Internet for information and resources, as well as shelter and industry publications, videos, home shows, model houses, showhouses, and giant home centers. One fancy Chicago designer recently marveled at how inexpensive knobs were at one giant home center chain store. He had paid much more for them at an independent specialty retailer. "When you're buying 100 knobs, it's worthwhile to shop around," he says in retrospect.

Finally, secure copies of all codes from your local city hall or comparable group, including the Uniform Building Code, the Uniform Plumbing Code, the National Electric Code, and the Uniform Mechanical Code. The following sections detail the major building categories in the order you should consider them.

FOUNDATION

As stated earlier, before the first shovelful of dirt is dug, your builder should have had the soil tested to determine the strength of your pad—the ground the house sits on. (See Chapter 3.) Certain soils such as wet clay or loose sand require support by driving expensive pilings down to more stable soil. The foundation consists of a footing, which is the wide base that spreads the home's weight over a large area, and the wall, which helps elevate the house off the ground and keep it dry and free from pests. The footing's base must be below the frostline to avoid cracking when cold weather comes.

Most new houses will have a foundation constructed of concrete block, brick, poured concrete, or treated wood. The James Company in Northbrook, Illinois, just outside Chicago, uses only poured concrete because it considers this the quickest and most cost effective material for the cold Chicago climate. The foundation can be built atop a slab or grade, with a crawl space or a partial or full basement—this decision again will be based on your soil type and your budget.

One disadvantage of building atop a slab or grade is that this foundation makes it harder to heat your first floor. If you do use this, plan to put in some kind of baseboard or radiant heating and add carpeting or another material to warm up the floor. When the foundation is finished, be sure your builder dampproofs it from the elements and adds perimeter drains around the foundation for further protection.

FRAMING

During the framing stage, the builder puts up the walls and floors with temporary, and then with permanent bracing—sort of like when the dentist puts on a temporary cap before the permanent one.

The type of framing material varies. Some builders use galvanized aluminum framing; others use wood—which is less expensive and quicker. The floors will be further supported by beams and the doors and windows by headers. Be sure that the space between the wall studs is consistent with what was specified on the plans. Certain materials needed for framing will be labeled "PT"—which means they've been pressure treated.

It's also good to know that houses have two main types of walls: a bearing wall, which helps support the house, and a nonbearing wall, which separates two rooms but has no structural purpose.

ROOFS

For both aesthetic and maintenance reasons, it's important not to discount the shape of your roof—whether gabled, hipped, gambrel, A-frame, or mansard to name a few—and the roofing material—asphalt shingles, cedar shingles, cedar shakes, tile, fiberglass, heavy textured fiberglass, slate, or simulated variations of slate that are less costly. The shape of the roof will be influenced by climate. In colder areas, for example, it's still best to avoid a flat roof, unless a slightly sloping framing structure is used. Heavy snow can pile up on a flat roof and damage the structure.

Although you may believe a roof is a single layer, it actually consists of overlapping rows of whatever material you choose. The material choice will again be based in part on your climate. A seasoned builder would never construct a roof of asphalt in a hot climate like Arizona because the sun would soften it too much. A clay tile roof would be a smarter choice. In cold climates, asphalt and cedar are much smarter choices. Slate, however, can be used anywhere, though it's very costly.

A roof can be built with an engineered truss—consisting of preassembled framing lumber with vertical, horizontal, and diagonal members—a factory-built truss, or a frame constructed on the site—a construction method known as stick building. The advantage of the last method is the flexibility to work in a very small custom area or with an unusual roof shape. Engineered systems give you the ability to work with large roof spans.

CHIMNEYS

Chimneys can also add character to a roof—alone or flanking either side—and there are many ways to lay the stone or brick to create interesting patterns. Some builders are getting away from using them, however, by installing direct-vent or gas fired fireplaces—which cost less money, but still create the look of a fire within through fake logs.

GUTTERS

Your roof's gutters, which now are almost always made of aluminum, vinyl, or copper, will be installed before the roof is completed. Your builder may also suggest gutter screens to protect them from leaf build-up, debris, and animals—like birds that build nests. Gutters send water to downspouts, which are vertical pipes that carry water to the ground. Concrete blocks or downspout extensions can be added to keep the runoff water away from the foundation, or the gutters can be tied directly to a storm sewer so the water is taken away and recycled to a sprinkler system.

EXTERIOR FINISH

The outer layer of the house can be covered in a variety of materials, including brick, stone, stucco, a manmade version of stucco called Dryvet®, asphalt shingles, wood (cedar or redwood), vinyl, or aluminum siding. In certain parts of the country, your choices may be based on the readily available supply—fieldstone in Philadelphia, brick in Washington, D.C., and adobe in New Mexico.

Today, many new materials are also available. The James Company has recently been using a new vinyl siding that closely resembles cedar but is maintenance-free, comes in a variety of colors, and is easy to repair. Dryvet® is also gaining proponents. It is a cement-based, less-expensive version of stucco that offers the benefits of less cracking and easier cleaning. It can also be painted easier than stucco, and it is a good insulator. Another new acrylic-based manmade stucco variation is called Sto. Do your homework before you consider any of these new materials. It's also important to take into account what surface you're covering.

Today some communities, particularly those in older neighborhoods or in historic districts, still favor one material over another despite the fact that most building materials are available throughout the country. Your homeowner's insurance must also be considered when choosing a material. Wood or clapboard is more flammable than brick, for example, and more costly to insure.

MECHANICAL SYSTEMS

Mechanical systems consist of the plumbing, electrical and heating, ventilation and air conditioning—also known as HVAC.

JOHN HIMMEL (Chicago, Illinois)

In many new houses, plumbers put the shower controls too high so that owners need the reach of Michael Jordan to turn the faucet on and off. "With a little forethought, you could have them placed more conveniently—outside the wet space or on an opposite wall—so you turn it on without getting a hernia," says Chicago designer John Himmel.

Plumbing

The first part of the rough-in involves the plumbing subcontractor adding the main water system to the house and installing a hot water heater, sump pump, and all the plumbing for the home's sinks, toilets, showers, bathtubs, hot tubs, and other water sources. You'll want to be sure your plumber avoids too many bends and turns in your pipe system because they decrease the speed water can travel. You also want him to add shut-off valves where water comes into the house, and at each fixture and appliance in the bathrooms, kitchen, and laundry room.

The plumbing subcontractor is followed by the heating subcontractor who installs all the ductwork and pipes for the heating and air conditioning systems. This work should be done in a way that minimizes heat-loss, maximizes insulation, and distributes heat evenly.

Electricity

The electrician then installs the main service panel that distributes power to the home's outlets, lights, appliances, furnace, alarm system, and every mechanical need such as cable TV wiring, telephone lines, or in-house vacuum cleaner. If a humidification system is incorporated into the HVAC work, be sure the electrician provides a panel with enough circuit breakers and protects all the bathroom, kitchen, garage, and outdoor outlets with a ground fault interrupting device (GFI). Don't forget to include enough outlets for small countertop appliances.

Insulation

After the mechanical systems are complete, the insulation contractor installs insulation as dictated by your building code, your geographic location, and the level of energy efficiency you choose. The two most popular types are loose insulation blown through the attic—which can be filled to different degrees—and batt insulation, which comes in a roll and is installed between the wall studs, floor and ceiling joists, and the roof trusses or rafters. Both are 100 percent fiberglass. Some builders also like paperback insulation in walls, which is fiberglass covered by paper.

When you choose insulation, you'll need to consider the R-value, which is the material's resistance to heat flow. The higher the value—such as R-60—the better the insulation. Can you use too much insulation? Yes, you can make your house so airtight the house can't breathe and condensation will build up, causing your wood windows to stick and freeze.

It's best to make choices about all of these systems during construction so you don't have to rip through walls and ruin nice paint jobs later to make changes.

DRYWALL

Wallboard thickness varies between 1½-inch and ⅝-inch, and the thicknesses may vary in different parts of a house. Drywalling involves several steps: hanging it, applying a first coat of tape, sanding that coat, and then applying a second or finish coat, often called mud. Different builders apply their drywall differently. Some screw it in—except on the ceiling where workers both glue it and screw it to be sure it remains firmly in place—and some only use nails—which may pop as the house settles. After the drywall is up, holes will be cut for switches, receptacles, and HVAC registers. Rooms will then be ready for painting and flooring.

JOHN CHALLENGER (Winnetka, Illinois)

John Challenger, executive vice president of Challenger, Gray & Christmas, an outplacement firm in Chicago, said he would never again neglect putting in sufficient soundproofing when remodeling. The three-story addition he and his wife Nancy put on their Winnetka house lacks adequate noise control. "We can hear through all our walls. I don't know why it occurred. We used a good architect. Perhaps the essential internal soundproofing wasn't added. We've thought about going back and adding in foam for better noise proofing, but it would be expensive. Be sure you ask your architect and contractor whether walls are solid enough so each room is quiet and you don't have sound travel."

FLOORING

The floor of the house has a heavy responsibility—to support people and furniture. To do so, the floor joists must be spaced at certain even distances and there should be a minimum ½-inch-thick tongue-and-groove plywood subfloor. If the main floor will consist of oak strips that are glued and nailed to the joists, the subfloor should be a minimum of ¾-inch. There may also be an underlayment above the subfloor to build up the floor and add stability. Homeowners may want to be sure there's acoustic or thermal insulation between the joists for good sound insulation.

STEPHANIE AND LARRY SAMUELS (St. Louis, Missouri)

Stephanie and her husband Larry, a doctor in St. Louis, remodeled their kitchen. Stephanie wanted wash-and-wear flooring in the kitchen, sun porch, and laundry room because of her dogs. Basically she ended up with the opposite. "I spent extra money to have epoxy grouting between ceramic tiles. The light-color grouting is a new product that isn't supposed to show the dirt. Well, within one week the grouting was dark. The grouting company came out and said that the floor was laid incorrectly. They dug it up, which took one week to saw the grout in three rooms. They redid the floor and again within one week the grout was dirty. The grout company refused at that point to take any responsibility, but they told me it was cleanable with a certain product that's ultra strong. It comes with instructions like don't get it on your hands, on baseboards, or anything but the floor. Well, one Sunday I'm on my hands and knees. I'm wearing rubber gloves, a t-shirt, biker shorts, and socks squirting this on the lines and scrubbing it with a toothbrush. I wipe it up and when I'm done, I take off my socks. I had just had a pedicure and all the polish on my toenails was gone. This easy maintenance floor has become a horror story."

There are numerous options today for the visible flooring surface, from rubber to cork to hardwood—which can be unfinished, prefinished, or solid which includes strip, plank or parquet, engineered, laminate, or acrylic impregnated—according to the National Wood Flooring Association. Then there is also ceramic, terrazzo, marble, slate, stone, and carpeting.

Your selection should depend in part on price, but also on your lifestyle. Limestone can run $15 to $50 a square foot while similar looking ceramic tiles can be found for $5 a square foot. Wood generally ranges from $8 to $15 a square foot, depending on the type of wood you select. Each choice requires other decisions. With wood, for example, you'll need to decide how you want to protect it. Most often the choice is two coats of polyurethane. Slate, on the other hand, requires a sealer. Granite and marble—which can be very pricey—may require a penetrating sealer, but be aware that some marbles, especially white, may yellow. The use of a sealer often depends on how porous the material is and how heavy the traffic will be, but in almost all cases marble will demand it more often than granite. In addition, both of those materials require careful cleaning. Many acidic cleansers can mar marble; granite is a bit more forgiving. (When these cleaners are used on countertops be extra careful not to use any that are toxic.)

JO ELLEN AND SANDY SCHONWALD (St. Louis, Missouri)

When they remodeled an older home in St. Louis, interior designer Jo Ellen Schonwald and her husband Sandy, a businessman, removed some radiators and needed to match the wood floor underneath. They knew it would be impossible. Jo Ellen had a brainstorm. She told the contractor to rip out the wood floors from the closets. Voilà, the wood matched perfectly.

But don't let price be your only guideline. Also consider wear and tear. Wood scratches easily, especially if small children will be riding bikes on it; a tough linoleum might be a smarter choice. Ceramic floors are beautiful in kitchens, but can be tough on your feet, if you stand a lot and cook. The same is true of brick or quarry tile. It's sort of like choosing a new mattress: see, touch, and walk on any potential choices and ask about maintenance. You may not want to wash that white ceramic floor daily.

LESLIE STERN (Chicago, Illinois)

After a heated floor installed in her master bathroom malfunctioned, Leslie Stern had to remove all the floor tiles to get to the wiring. She learned that whenever you put in a heated floor, have a backup plan so you can easily get to the electrical source without tearing out all the tiles.

Once your floor is installed, don't forget to protect it when moving appliances and furniture by covering it with cardboard or another protective surface. Finally, know that because houses expand and contract and can take a full year to dry, your floors, too, will shift.

CEILINGS

Do you want wallboard, plaster or another material? Smooth, textured, or a finish? Exposed beams? These are all choices to consider when installing a ceiling, in addition to determining its height. The low ceilings that were associated with early American houses are rarely used today and the push is on for two-story vaulted spaces. Know, however, that these cost more to heat, cool, and paint, and they also take longer to drywall because scaffolding must be used. Such large expanses also require larger furniture, lights, and artwork. A nice alternative that offers some architectural panache on a smaller scale is a cove ceiling that rims a room.

INTERIOR TRIM

The trim—doors, windows, baseboards, crown moldings, and any finished staircase risers, treads, and spindles—will be added next. When you select windows, consider energy efficiency. For doors—both exterior and interior—you need to consider material, style, and finish. Skylights? Decide where, how many, what shape and size, and if they will be fixed or opening. Interior choices should be dictated by the style of your house and budget. You won't want to add a stark contemporary staircase in a traditional English Georgian house.

CABINETS

When choosing cabinets you need to select material, style, finish, color, hardware—knobs and pulls—and the number and location of the doors, drawers, and storage accessories.

Prices of cabinetry—including vanities for bathrooms—vary dramatically based on whether the cabinet is custom or a readily available stock design, how much paneling and detail decorates the outside, how it is held together at its corners—dovetailed or screwed—the type of material selected, and the accessories used such as the hinges and knobs. A well-made cabinet will last a long time. If cost is a factor, forgo the fancy exterior trappings and spend more money on the inside material, the construction technique, and quality because those affect alignment.

You should also consider buying furnishings rather than building them in if you don't plan to stay long in the house. You can then take that bookcase, desk, or hutch with you. Even kitchen cabinet companies are making movable pieces—some on wheels—which has long been a proven favorite in England.

COUNTERTOPS

Again, choose from different materials, styles, and colors. There are numerous choices of laminates, butcherblock, and tile at the low end; and glass blocks, stainless steel, granite, Corian, slate, marble, and soapstone at the high end. You'll also have to choose the shape of your countertop edge. With Corian alone, there are more than ten choices, including a double-beveled edge.

APPLIANCES

It's easy to be swayed by name brands, especially the status models for each type of appliance such as Sub-Zero refrigerators, Viking ranges, Franke sinks, Bosch dishwashers. Yes, sometimes status does mean better quality, but not always. How do you decide? Review several good consumer guides such as *Consumer Reports* or *Consumer Digest,* and compare each brand in the same way you would if you were buying an automobile. You can also find information on the Net. Ask for guidance from friends who cook often or professionals you know—

but make sure they don't make money from selling appliances. Also ask your sources about special requirements.

KAREN AND MARK ZORENSKY (Clayton, Missouri)

Don't go for glamour, because the glamour wears off. It may look beautiful, but it has to be functional for you as well as for the next person. Consider resale. That's why Karen Zorensky was very hands-on in doing the remodeling of her Clayton, Mo., home. "I didn't have anyone choose items for me. I had to see, touch, and feel everything. For example, when the oven company tells you the cavity size, it doesn't mean anything. When I went to look at ovens, I brought the largest roasting pan I have and made sure it could fit in the oven I chose. Also make sure on the cooktop that the knobs are comfortable to your fingers. Don't just buy a brand," says Karen. "You touch those buttons all the time and I felt they had to be something I could get my fingers on."

Ovens should not be placed in a high traffic area, and allow enough space for installation. Make sure you have the correct gas lines for a gas oven, or the right voltage for an electric one. Cooktops or ranges need proper ventilation, no matter what type you select—freestanding, drop-in or slide-in, microwave, induction, or convection. If you incorporate a restaurant-style range, you need to pay special attention to proper insulation between the range and any cabinets, and you need to have a hood that has a high enough BTU rating to rid your kitchen of strong odors. Ventilation types include the standard updraft—with a hood, or down draft—a standard down draft, or back down draft where the ventilation system is part of the unit.

Decide also the number of sinks you want in the kitchen and bath, and faucets in the kitchen—including spray attachments—style and finish, and kitchen exotica—trash-mashers, disposers, soap dispensers, etc. The adage about kitchen triangles is true—they reduce your legwork and increase your efficiency in the kitchen. Almost any kitchen can boast a working triangle layout, if planned in advance. Figure 12.1 displays a common triangle layout.

Develop a realistic budget and prioritize your wants. If you love to bake, you may need a second oven—and a convection one at that. If you love to cook Chinese food, you may prefer a gas cooktop with a built-in wok ring.

Don't forget to also allow space for your refrigerator, cautions Lon Langille in "Refrigerator Issues," an article in the November 1995 issue of *Building and Remodeling News.* Consider more than just height and width and don't forget to

FIGURE **12.1** Kitchen Triangle

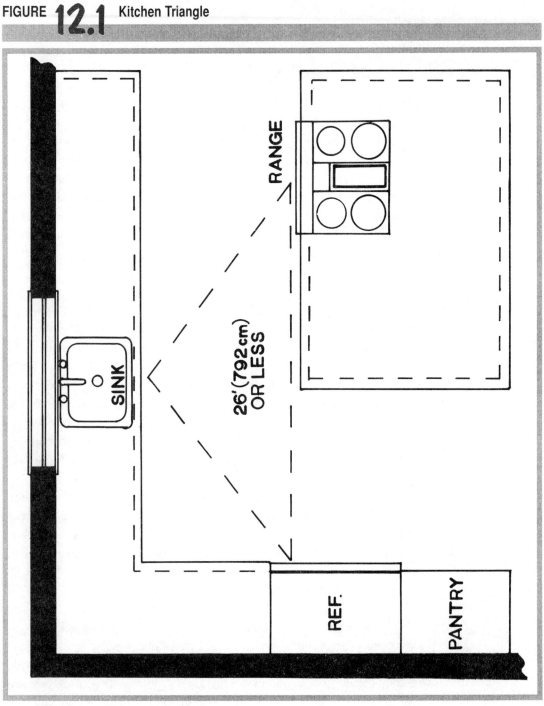

Source: National Kitchen & Bath Association

allow room for air to circulate. Various depth measurements are important as well: "Depth of the unit without the door, the depth to the front of the door, the depth to the front of the handle, and finally the depth with the door swung 90 degrees from its closed position." Stresses Langille, "Never take dimensional information over the phone or from an appliance sales person at a retail store unless it is in writing and each dimension is defined."

REGINA BARRECA (Storrs, Connecticut)

Regina Barreca, professor, Department of English, University of Connecticut at Storrs, and author of *Sweet Revenge* (Crown Books), wrote about her kitchen remodeling in *The Hartford Courant Sunday Magazine:* "...there are no walls, no ceiling, no appliances. There's no water; and even if there was water it wouldn't help because there's no sink for it to go into. I doubt that there's a floor, but at this point I'm afraid to look down for fear I'm walking on air or steel grating...So this I say to you: appreciate your sinks, the view from your window as you wash the dishes; clean your refrigerator and wash out the little egg holders; offer praise to the idols and goddesses of the kitchen and hearth. The kitchen is an important place, never as important as in its absence. When mine is finished, I promise I'll never complain about cooking again. At least, not for a whole week."

Refrigerators are very important because they are opened an average of 35 times a day, so it doesn't pay to cut corners and buy a poorly designed model with doors that don't open and close easily. Don't overlook miscellaneous accessories such as ice makers and door panels.

One good new Internet source for kitchen decorating assistance—as well as help in other rooms—is Home Portfolio's Web site at www.homeportfolio.com. Eventually, the site will offer 100,000 products such as faucets, sinks, ranges, sofas, and doors—with retail rather than wholesale prices. When you visit the site you can create your own swatch boards of favorite selections so you can see how they look together, and if you can afford them.

KAREN AND MARK ZORENSKY (Clayton, Missouri)

Don't get too grandiose with appliances, warns Karen Zorensky who, with her husband Mark, remodeled several rooms in their home. "Make sure that what you get can be serviced. You can get talked into a certain dishwasher by your contractor and find out that only one place in town can service it. It's not like one of the big commercial operations like GE who will come out immediately."

Figure 12.2 shows a before and after kitchen layout for your inspiration. As you can see, there is a lot to be said for thoughtful planning the first time around!

PAINT

Before you paint, be sure all the mechanical trades have returned to make their final installations. The heating contractor will put in grills and floor vents, the plumber will install toilets, sinks, and faucets, and the electrician will hook up your appliances, and add finish plates and switches. The painter is then ready for his preparation work. He will sand, fill nail holes, and caulk the trim to the drywall—if the carpenter hasn't already done that. A good painter always primes, then paints a minimum of two coats. Whether you opt for flat, enamel, or a glaze will hinge on your budget and lifestyle. Be careful with semigloss—except for trim—because it shows all flaws. Instead, choose a flat coat, a glaze, or a faux finish. If you opt for glazing, be sure you've seen the painter's workmanship because this highly shiny surface will definitely show all imperfections in plastering and priming. Faux finishes do a good job of hiding fingerprints.

LESLIE RICHMOND SIMMONS (Milton, Massachusetts)

Leslie Richmond Simmons, a greeting card and stuffed animal designer, found that her painter made a tremendous mistake when doing the walls of her kitchen. "He was a sweet guy but not a good painter and didn't understand quality. He put latex over oil so there are always chips coming off the walls. He's willing to redo it, but all our cabinets are finished and it would make a mess," she says.

COLOR

Color may be the most important decorating tool available to bring your rooms to life. In a flash, you can create a mood or illusion. Certain colors will make a room look larger or smaller, and ceilings seem higher or lower. Certain colors are also better for resale. The majority of homeowners still favor white for an exterior, with gray as their second choice. Popular colors can also vary by region. Green is popular in the Midwest, and pink a favorite in warmer zones. While there's tech-

FIGURE 12.2 Before and After Kitchen Layout

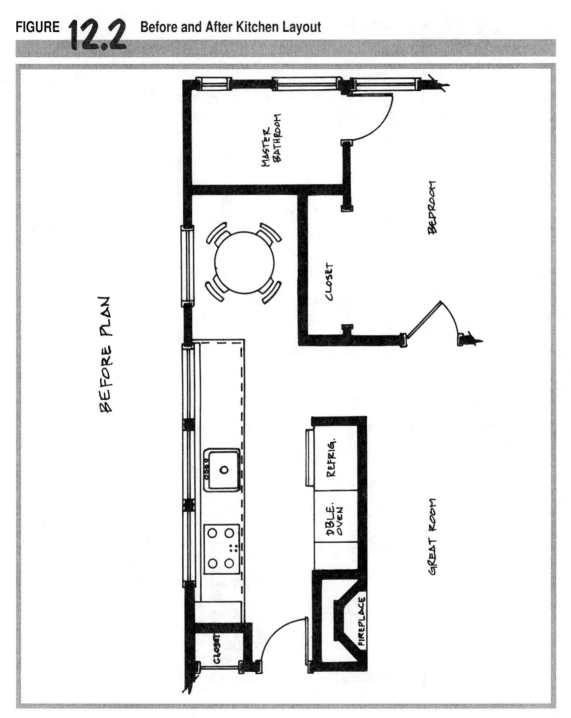

Source: de Giulio Kitchen Design, illustration by Brian Connor

FIGURE 12.2 Before and After Kitchen Layout (Continued)

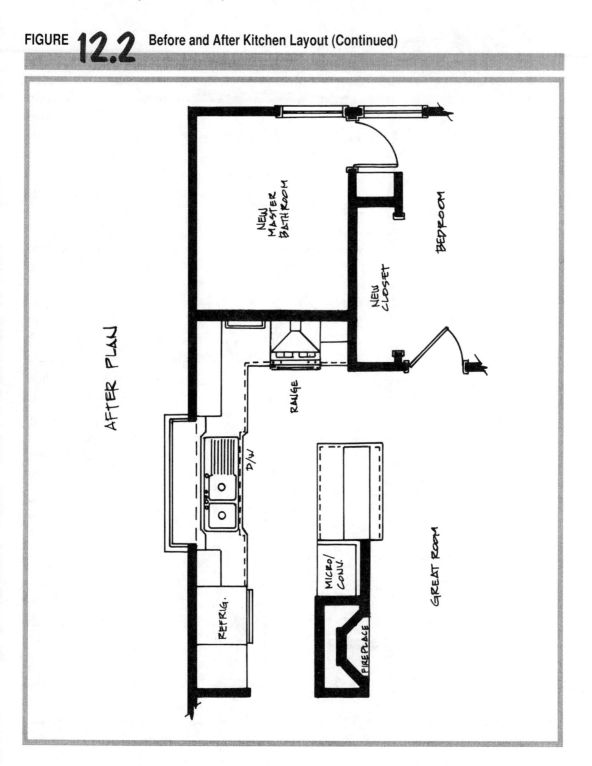

nically no right or wrong color or scheme, some choices are smarter than others. And it is best to have an overall color scheme throughout the house.

What you want a color to do architecturally may influence your choice. If you have a room with a large high ceiling and you want it to appear cozier, paint or paper the ceilings a darker color than your walls. If you want to rejuvenate your home and loosen it up, add some quirky colors that you mix and match—perhaps yellows and oranges.

Also consider how the palette suits your surroundings. If your home is in New Mexico or you're attempting to simulate a Southwestern feeling, gear your choices toward brighter, hotter hues. If you work all day surrounded by color—perhaps in a paint or department store—you might be ready for a more neutral, calming setting at night. Finally, you might be influenced by the colors you wear. Chicago designer Eva Quateman tends to favor black and white clothing and her Chicago apartment also reflects that palette, with a few dollops of color for accent.

Before you take the plunge and make color choices, try them out. Take some paint chips from a local paint or hardware store and tape them to a wall to get a feel for what the color might look like in that room. Or consider painting one wall so that you can really see what the wall color looks like at various times of the day and in both natural and artificial light. Add some other colors and see how you feel. Still another way to test your selection is to get some pillows, mugs, or placemats in a few of your favorite hues. Live with them for a while—perhaps over several seasons. Add other colors, take some away. Over time, you'll notice that you favor some colors over others. Remember two good things about using color: (1) it's one of the easiest choices to change, and (2) there are always new colors surfacing—often with different textures.

ODDS AND ENDS

After the painting is done, your contractor will add closet shelving, mirrors, shower doors, medicine cabinets, knobs, and wall-to-wall carpeting. The painter will come back for a final touch-up after you move in, and the electrician will add the switch plates and the light fixtures. You may even want to paint or wallpaper the switch plates to match the walls in the room.

BUILDING AND REMODELING FOR HANDICAPPED ACCESSIBILITY

When you build or remodel, don't forget to plan ahead. Homeowners are living longer, and it's never too early to make your house accessible to older people, or people with physical disabilities. Universal Designs mean space and products that can be used easily by those of varying abilities—short, tall, wheelchair bound. Specifically, doorways may have to be wider, ramps may be necessary, cabinets and sinks should be at waist level to allow a wheelchair to roll up to them, showers should be free of doors so that wheelchairs can also roll into them, and bathroom fixtures and hardware should be designed for any physical disability, including arthritic wrists. (For more information see Chapter 21.)

FINISHING AND CLEANING UP

Any remodeling project will involve some degree of mess, and it's critical to know early on what the level of cleanup will be. Once again, you might want to spell this out in your contract. Will your general contractor (GC) haul away debris daily? He should, but be sure you clarify this, as well as specifying that workers bring their own garbage bags, vacuum cleaners, and other equipment instead of using your residential supplies, which may not be strong enough for endless bags of sawdust. When your house or remodeling is completed, the builder, architect, or GC should provide a cleaning crew before you take your final walk-through, and then another cleaning after you're closed on new construction. Be sure the house is broom clean and that dust in the duct system has been removed.

SUSAN AND NORMAN PAPPAS (Bloomfield Hills, Michigan)

The Pappases, who live in a Detroit suburb, found that a good housekeeper was invaluable when they did their remodeling, which included an addition. "She was there daily to be sure that everything was cleaned up and put back together, particularly when the workmen didn't do so," says Susan.

PUNCH LIST

If it's new construction, carefully inspect your house during the seven days prior to your closing. Bring along a pad of paper, sharpened pencils, and your eagle eye—or someone with a good eye. Now is the time to find any area that is incomplete or unsatisfactory—what's termed the punch list. Hopefully, you've been able to withhold a percentage of your total payment until you are totally pleased.

CONSTRUCTIVE TIPS

Good, Better, Best

When choosing materials, learn what's good, better, best, but be prepared to pay accordingly for quality. Here are some tips to get you started.

- Exterior Facing

  good: vinyl or aluminum siding
  better: wood siding
  best: brick or stone

- Wood flooring

  good: prefinished wood parquet tiles
  better: strip oak flooring
  best: large-scale, ¾-inch thick, custom-finished parquet flooring

- Walls

  good: painted drywall
  better: plaster
  best: surfaced with a permanent hard material such as ceramic tile or marble

- Lighting

  good: lamp lighting
  better: lamps and surface mounted sconces or chandeliers
  best: combination of lamps, surface, and specific recessed lighting

- Roofing

  good: heavy textured fiberglass shingles
  better: wood shingles
  best: clay tile or slate

CHAPTER 13

Exterior Thoughts

Creating Curb Appeal

You've been busy for months thinking about the layout of your house and you probably have a rough idea about the exterior you envision building or the way you want to remodel your existing home to make it more attractive on the outside. Real estate agents speak all the time about the importance of putting the best face on your home—particularly when it's time to sell, so that potential buyers will want to cross the threshold.

You'll also want to make the exterior attractive for yourself when you're building or remodeling, because the facade is the first part of the house you'll see every morning when you leave and every night when you come home. Don't short-shrift yourself by choosing a shape or silhouette, style, materials, or elements that aren't exactly what you want. There are many to choose from so something you like is sure to exist.

In some cases, you may have a vague idea about the exterior style you desire—a vertical row house for a narrow city lot with a center front door and shuttered windows on either side; a tall Victorian with lots of quirky peaked gabled roofs and porches all around; or a sprawling contemporary for a large suburban tract which suits its hilly site.

If you don't have a clue or want to firm up your vague ideas, look at other homes and snap photographs for ideas. Think about houses in movies and on television that you liked and jot them down. Maybe you fondly remember the white picket fence from the remake of *Father of the Bride* or the lakeside setting of the vacation house in *What about Bob?* Scan old photographs at your local historical society or library; skim current-day shelter and plans magazines.

Another good resource is architecture books that detail housing styles and the distinguishing features that comprise them such as the proper window, door, column, sheathing material, porch, roof, and gutters. You needn't be 100 percent accurate, but you also don't want a hodgepodge of disparate parts.

MICHAEL AND BENITA ROMANO (River Forest, Illinois)

Michael Romano, a Chicago businessman, and his wife Benita built their first house and learned the hard way that it doesn't pay to be naive and trusting. "The first time you build you do rely on the expertise of the tradespeople so you trust them. I trusted our architect that everything would be right, however when we started building the house, the roof lines were wrong. We fired the architect and refused to pay him."

Two good books to study for ideas are *What Style Is It? A Guide to American Architecture* by John C. Poppeliers, S. Allen Chambers Jr. and Nancy B. Schwartz (The Preservation Press) and *A Field Guide to American Houses* by Virginia & Lee McAlester (Alfred A. Knopf). Both are still in print and can be found in many libraries.

The following sections detail the key features to consider for your exterior.

FRONT DOOR

Beside the shape and scale of your house, its front door is probably the most important element, and what you and others will first notice. Consider its height, length, and width, whether you want solid or paneled—and how many panels—if you want sidelights and a transom or fanlight above, if you need a canopy or other overhang for protection from inclement weather—and to provide a gracious welcome—and if you want detailing such as a pediment or columns. Most doors on new houses are built of wood or metal and with dimensions of 3′ wide × 6′8″ high × 1¾″ thick. Don't forget an appropriate doorknob, knocker, kickplate, set of house numbers, and mailbox to give your entryway its fully finished look.

FRONT STEPS

Topography will limit your choices, but if you don't have to climb up to your front door at least make a nice pathway to it to create a sense of grace. The stairs and path should be fairly straight rather than circuitous. You might make the path brick, cobblestone, concrete, flagstone, or slate.

WINDOWS

The type of window you choose—a casement with muntins, a muntinless window, a protruding bay, or a high-up dormer (which itself can vary from gable to eyebrow to hipped)—will depend to a large degree on the style and size of your home. Windows can be embellished with pilasters, fanlights, lintels, pediments (in triangular, ogee, or broken design forms), sills, balconies, grilles, and shutters. Keep any of these extras appropriate to the window and to each other. You'll also have some choice when it comes to the framing material. Vinyl is the most cost effective on both the inside and outside because it requires less maintenance than aluminum. Some builders like to use windows clad in aluminum on the outside with wood inside. This gives the window a quality appearance, and allows you to paint the interior surfaces any color.

SALLY QUINN AND BEN BRADLEE (Washington, D.C.)

Sally Quinn, author of *The Party*, and her husband Ben Bradlee, former executive editor of the *Washington Post*, have built and/or remodeled several homes. She offers this warning: "Beware of architects who want to make their statement with your house. Once I was building a country house in West Virginia and the architect and I came to blows over the windows. He wanted round windows and I didn't want our simple country house to look like an A-frame in Vail. It's my home and I have to live in it long after the architect leaves."

Because of the escalating cost of heating and cooling a home, choose energy-efficient designs if you're replacing old windows or building from scratch. The newest innovation, according to a spokesperson from Pella Corporation, based in Pella, Iowa, is high-performance glazing. Also known as low E-glass, it significantly increases the R-value—the thermal rating of the window. When it was first developed, it was expensive, provided poor clarity, and had a heavy tinting. But improvements have brought down its costs, and given it a high shading coefficient that blocks the sun's heat-gain rays and a high shading coefficient that also blocks ultraviolet rays. It comes in two forms—with a coating that goes on the glass or an argon gas—and they can be used in tandem. When utilizing a low E coating with argon gas, it's not uncommon for the R-value to increase 50 percent. Finally, don't forget about storms and screens, if the windows you purchase don't automatically include them in the design.

PORCHES

The front porch has witnessed a resurgence in popularity and not just in warm-weather climates or on summer houses. It's viewed as a pleasant place to sit or welcome guests. Decide whether you want a full-height porch with a cover above, one that spans the entire front—if your house has two stories and the porch can span both levels reminiscent of New Orleans style galleries—one that stands only along one side, or one that wraps around the entire house. A screened-in porch in back is also an amenity you might consider for those cool summer nights.

EXTERIOR COLOR

Color is the easiest way to give your facade instant personality and update your home, but do so judiciously. While Victorian "Painted Ladies" cry out for a variety of hues—often vibrant ones—most houses look best if their palette is kept to only a few choices—one color for the facade, one for the shutters (if any), and possibly a third for the front door and other detailing. Test out any colors on a small outdoor area to see how it looks on cloudy and sunny days, and try not to make the tones too harsh. Many architects prefer darker grays, blues and greens to black. Remember that neutral tones such as white or gray appeal to a wider audience than sharp reds and blues. You can always add additional color through your landscaping and flower choices.

CARL J. CIRCO (Overland Park, Kansas)

Real estate attorney Carl J. Circo, who had to rebuild a burned-down barn on his 11 acres outside the Kansas City metropolitan area, discovered the importance of studying specifications and asking questions when it came time to sign the contract. "We had maintenance-free cedar before and that's what we wanted again. When I started asking questions and looked at the builder's specifications list, I saw that he proposed other paneling. It would have been cheaper, but would have needed to be primed and regularly painted."

And remember, whatever you do on the exterior, don't overdo it for the size of your house and the neighborhood.

CONSTRUCTIVE TIPS

Thrifty Thoughts

Be prudent with your dollars. You can refine rough edges, apply explosive colors, and experiment with materials without spending thousands of dollars. Roger Mandekick, executive vice president of sales and marketing for Concord Homes in Palatine, Illinois, offers some excellent ideas for imitating more expensive looks.

- Vinyl side your woodframe house. You don't have to paint it and you can use aluminum soffits and facia board. Before you put the gutters over aluminum, cover in cedar, paint, and attach the gutter to the cedar facia board to make it look like you have cedar soffits—a more expensive look.
- Put in a premade firebox, which is one-third to one-half the cost of a conventional one. For a conventional fireplace, you have to pour the foundation and lay the chimney outside the building all the way down to the basement on a concrete block up to the ground level, then brick it the rest of the way up. With a prefab, you're saving manhours of digging and doing the brickwork. The prefab chase can be made of siding, cedar, or aluminum and it nails on to the house. It operates the same as a conventional fireplace.
- Call in a landscape company to draw you a design and ask to keep the prints. Then, do the planting yourself and save about 40 percent.
- Go hogwild with outside lighting. There are kits you can use to have external ground lighting behind shrubs. You can hire an electrician at $45 to $50 an hour to dig a cable, or you can use a kit and cover the wires with mulch or bark to achieve the same effect. Buy yourself a plug, put it by the sidewalk, and just plug in the lights. A kit costs about $150 plus extras that may run about $300 compared to $6,000 to have ground lighting done by an electrician.

14

Completing the Picture with Landscaping

It pains you to spend money on grass, trees, and plants when you don't even own dining room furniture. Is landscaping that important? you muse. If only money grew on trees.

According to the article "Looks Aren't Everything" in the March 1997 issue of *Lawn and Landscape,* writer Bob West refers to Gary Moll and Stanley Young's book *Growing Green Cities—A Free-Planting Handbook* when he cites an American Forestry Association study that illustrates how one tree provides the following annual savings: "$73 on air conditioning, $75 in controlling erosion and storm water, $75 as a wildlife shelter, $50 in controlling air pollution. If those costs are compounded over the 50-year lifespan of that tree with normal cost adjustments factored in, the tree's worth to its owner becomes $57,151." Multiply that figure by your number of trees, and you amass quite a savings.

THE IMPORTANCE OF LANDSCAPING

Landscaping is no longer the neglected stepchild of homebuilding or remodeling. It has become a vital element in completing the package. With building and renovating at an all-time high, there are also swelling numbers who want beautiful outdoor environments. Whether it's for aesthetics, pragmatics, energy efficiency, or to preserve the environment, as much attention and detail should go into planning your outside living areas as your inside ones.

A lawn is a statement. It not only reveals something about the people who live there, but it immediately establishes a certain relationship with your neighbors. In some communities, there's a high degree of pride in well-kept lawns and gardens that are as noticeable as the tiny colored lights framing doorways and windows at holiday time.

But a landscape offers much greater pleasures than just curb appeal. It offers the sounds of birds or cascading water, the aroma of flowers or a freshly mowed lawn, the taste of grapes picked from a vine, or the feel of cool grass underfoot. It has economic and environmental cachet as well.

Economically it adds value. If you sell a home, the real estate agent will tell you to put mulch down, plant flowers, seal the driveway, do some pruning, and replace dead plants. "It's amazing how this enhances the overall effect of a home. People have a tendency to walk into it with a more positive way of thinking," says Faye Levey, real estate agent in Coldwell Banker's Ladue office in St. Louis. Figure 14.1 demonstrates landscaping's added value.

Scott Byron, landscape architect and president of Scott Byron & Company, a design/build landscaping firm in Lake Bluff, Illinois, concurs. He's been told by real estate agents that the value of the front of a house is one of salability. "If there are two houses for sale with similar size and appeal, the one that will be sold quickest will be the one that looks the best landscapewise."

You can't expect an outdoor environment to add measurable dollars to the value of your home, however. "Gardens by their very nature are personal. If you're doing a garden and adding a trellis, a pergola, or patio, you are doing it for yourself and to improve the quality of your life. It's not really a dollar for dollar investment value," explains Byron.

On the other hand, a garden can save you money by reducing energy bills. According to the Wisconsin Energy Bureau:

- Evergreens planted on the northwest corner of your lot can block winter winds and save you up to 25 percent on heating bills.
- Certain trees provide shade on the west and south sides of your house, and in summer can block 70 to 80 percent of the sun's rays.
- Trees without their leaves let in the sun to warm your home in winter.
- Shrubs planted on all sides of the house help reduce wall and soil temperatures.

In addition, the Environmental Protection Agency (EPA) estimates that shading an air conditioner can save up to 10 to 15 percent in annual cooling/energy costs.

FIGURE **14.1** Budget Worksheet

BUDGET WORKSHEET

A landscaping investment of 5 percent on a $100,000 home ($5,000) can actually increase the value of the home by $10,000 based on the 200 percent recovery value. This brings the home's "new" value to $110,000. To determine what dollar amount you should invest and what dollar amount you will gain, apply the following formulas to your own circumstances.

$_____ × _____ = $_____
(Current market value of   (Percentage you choose   (Your landscaping
your home)   to invest)   investment in dollars)

$_____ × _____2_____ = $_____
(Your landscaping   (Reported recovery   (Potential value added to
investment in dollars)   value = 200%)   home after landscaping)

$_____ + _____ = $_____
(Current market value of   (Value added to your home   (New value of your home
your home)   after landscaping)   after landscaping)

SAMPLE

$_____100,000_____ × _____.05_____ = $_____5,000_____
(Current market value of   (Percentage chosen to   (Your landscaping
home)   invest = 5%)   investment in dollars)

$_____5,000_____ × _____2_____ = $_____10,000_____
(The landscaping   (Reported recovery   (Potential value added to
investment in dollars)   value = 200%)   home after landscaping)

$_____100,000_____ + _____10,000_____ = $_____110,000_____
(Current market value of   (Value added to your   (New value of your home
your home)   home after landscaping)   after landscaping)

Source: ©1991 Garden Council

The value to the environment is palpable, too. Trees, bushes, and plants help absorb outdoor noise in the same way that indoor carpeting does inside. Plantings also freshen the atmosphere.

Whether you want to sink money into creating a splendid landscape or something simple and functional depends on your value system. How much you want to embellish your property and the way in which you do it may be related to where you've put down roots. Have you chosen a seaside location or a place in the desert? Did you find a cool homesite in the mountains or one by a lake rich in wildlife? Are you in the middle of the boonies where the land has been leveled by bulldozers to make way for your abode? Did you add on a room with a wall of windows to get a better vista of the outside only to find there's not much to look at? The answers to these questions will help you select the appropriate landscaping.

INFORMAL AND FORMAL LANDSCAPING

Beauty can occur naturally or it can be planned. If it's already there, try to preserve nature. Trees make a home look more finished. But you can enhance intrinsic beauty. If it's not there, it can be created in an informal or formal style whether your lawn is expansive or the size of a shoebox.

If informal, the design usually reflects a plan that combines man and nature. "The site is usually meant to look natural or less planned, more random, and to mimic what actually grows in the area. You look at plant associations that grow in nature next to each other," Byron says.

If formal, the garden represents man's dominance over nature. It's probably more balanced and strongly geometric with circles, ovals, angles, paths, borders, fence lines, or linear rows of clipped hedges. It's more precise and requires more care. The plants chosen are forced into compliance, possibly against their nature.

Whether casual or prim, those who create a landscape strive to play up the positives of a site. It's like one of those makeovers on the Oprah Winfrey show where a makeup artist hides unattractive features and stresses those that enhance appearance.

A site makeover is especially important if you have a subdivision home. Most production and semiproduction builders provide almost no landscaping except a little bit of sod or seed here and there. In many cases the ground has been leveled to get equipment in and out leaving few—if any—trees intact, as well as removing the existing topsoil that benefits plants. If your home sits in a development with existing trees, the homes typically will sell for more money than homes in a barren area. However, in almost all new building cases, you start with a blank canvas.

THE LANDSCAPING PLAN (HERE YOU GO AGAIN)

All this foment can be managed if you plan your landscape systematically. Here are some clear-cut steps.

Wish List

Before you begin, compile a wish list of everything you've ever wanted in an outdoor environment—and more. Leaf through shelter magazines and home and garden books, and visit retail garden centers/nurseries to pick the brains of the landscape architect and designers on staff, attend garden shows, join a garden club, and surf the Net for garden-related items. Go to a local botanical garden, look for the genus and species you like and find out if they will grow in your soil and climate. Also, determine if your dream plan will fit your time schedule and needs in terms of maintenance. One homeowner always dreamed of an English wildflower garden, but her garden designer told her that her busy schedule eliminated the possibility of properly tending to it. One option she had was to hire a maintenance firm for the time-consuming and back-breaking chores, but it was too pricey.

Include a focal point in your plan. It might be a bark-mulched path with a series of beds radiating from it, an elaborate birdbath, raised beds filled with flowers or herbs, a gazebo or colorful trellis covered with creeping vines, a hot tub, a flagstone patio, or an ornamental wrought iron gate. You might even envision a soft spring green lawn framed by flowering trees and shrubs. Figure 14.2 provides a wish list you can use to prioritize your ideas.

Mission Statement

Critical mass, vertical and horizontal integration, synergy, balance. These are grand concepts often used in business circles. However, these ideas apply to your landscape plan as well and should be incorporated into the design.

If you can, state your plan in 25 words or less. Define the size and scope of the project. Have a schedule and budget. A landscape plan should reflect your lifestyle, what you want to get from the landscaping, your priorities, and how much maintenance you can afford in terms of time and money.

FIGURE **14.2** Wish List

WISH LIST

Rate the following ideas in order of importance.

1 = Least Important

5 = Most Important

_____ A vegetable garden

_____ Flower beds with a variety of plants

_____ A big deck or terrace for entertaining

_____ A water feature (i.e., water pond, swimming pool)

_____ Protected play space for children

_____ Storage for sports and garden equipment

_____ A tennis court

_____ Privacy from neighbors or a busy street

_____ Protection from frigid winter weather or scorching summer sun

_____ Increased parking for family and guests

_____ A greenhouse

_____ A shady area

_____ A landscape conducive to year-round use

_____ A landscape that invites wildlife visitation

_____ Low maintenance

_____ A particular element, theme, or style you would like to see repeated (i.e., formal, natural) _____

Additional wishes:

_____

_____

_____

_____

_____

Source: © 1991 Garden Council

DOING IT YOURSELF

For some, doing it yourself is akin to putting a child's toy together. There's a knack to doing it. Either you're mechanically inclined or you're not; either it comes easy or it doesn't. If you can't even screw in a light bulb, this job probably isn't for you. And if it is, it helps to have the right tools and resources on hand.

Gardening is much the same. Some people just have a green thumb and an affinity for nature. They find any type of landscape work therapeutic. Daily watering and weekly sessions with grass, shrubs, and flowers offer a sense of order.

If you are a serious gardener or want to be, and you loved geometry in high school, there are books, aids, computer programs, and stock plans to help you get the job done.

Risks

Be aware there are potential risks. Going at it alone opens you up to the possibility of poor design and plant selection and incorrect installation. Landscaping requires a great deal of effort, high maintenance, and a certain visual imagination. Any outside design should have unity and a visual flow achieved through colors, forms, or textures; the types of plants; curves or straight lines; or construction materials. It's like playing a game of garden chess. If you follow the rules and use good strategy, you're more likely to make the right moves.

Plan

Begin with a plan that takes into consideration your site. Have your soil tested to see what will grow. Some sites may have several different soil types and conditions. Call your county government office to find out how to test the soil or who to contact to test it for you for a minimal fee.

Drainage

One of the biggest hurdles in landscaping lies in the geography of your site. Drainage can be the biggest headache, even for the best gardener. After a strong rain, see if water drains off your lot properly. Joel P. Albizo, spokesman for the American Nursery and Landscape Association (ANLA), was hit with a nasty surprise on his site—poor drainage. "My backyard was wet and muddy. I couldn't grow anything. I had to find a professional to come in and fix it with grading and drainage."

Design Choices

Design is another aspect of landscaping where ignorance can be costly. When you do the design, sketch ideas that embody your wish list and your needs. Start with what you are trying to accomplish aesthetically, what you can do on a technical basis, what unique features you want to incorporate, what you have to spend, and tie it all together into a neat package. Use the shape and size of your lot as the launching pad.

Because structures in your yard cannot be moved as easily as chess pieces, work around permanent structures such as walkways, a swimming pool, pond, or gazebo. Choose the construction materials first, then the plants. And don't forget the grading of the lot, the planting of seed or sod for the lawn, and the lighting—which is important for safety as well as aesthetics and the irrigation.

Dividing the Space

In plotting your lot, the parts are worth as much—or more—than the whole. Divvy up the space carefully. Make a rough sketch of where everything will go—a public area, a service area for garbage cans, air conditioner, and wood pile—a private living area, and a place for cars. Carve out a space for each family member—a garden for you, a pool and lawn for your husband, a play area for the kids. Next decide how much space you'll allot for each area and where it will go. And pay attention to neighborhood covenants and setbacks. You may not be able to have a fence or a circular driveway in front.

What comes next? Select how you want to design and landscape these specially carved out areas. Much like the rooms in your house, your garden should have dividers such as bushes, fencing, bricks, rocks, or changes in color or plant types to designate the division of these areas.

Pets in Your Outdoor Environment

Don't forget to make room for pets. A dog roaming the site may trample plants, so some types of landscaping may need to be put on hold. There are also many decorative fencing choices—such as New Orleans-style iron or a more rustic basket-weave border—that can keep pets out. And, find out if your dog likes to dig. You may have to set aside a special place outdoors for your pet to play.

Designing Spaces to Complement Your Home

You've plotted your grand strategy, but keep in mind that landscape design should complement your home. Ideally, your home and the site design should be inseparable. Even if you build a house from a stock set of plans, the view is there. Take advantage of the best views when you plant. In addition, be consistent with the colors and materials used on the outside of your home, such as wood trim, siding, or brick, and don't forget the architecture of your abode. If it's a cottage-style home, you don't want a formal garden. You might want to plant wildflowers and make the environs as natural and unplanned-looking as possible.

TIPPI HEDREN (Acton, California)

Actress Tippi Hedren's story isn't for the birds. Rather, it's about animals. Hedren, who lives one hour northeast of Los Angeles, is an animal enthusiast who built her home to accommodate her large family of animals. Her 65-acre backyard is a wild animal preserve with 62 wild cats and two elephants, designed by her son-in-law Joel Marshall. "I planted more than 800 trees 26 years ago and have in each of the animal compounds either a river, a pond, or a lake. I have entertainment centers with trees and telephone poles for the animals to climb on as well. Inside the house, I put up shelves in what I call my 'tree room' so that my eight house cats can jump from one to another. The tree room is built around two trees which are there for the cats."

It's fine to get bold, but don't get too lofty. Simplicity is crucial. Like too much copy on a page, your design should be spread out by limiting the number of plants to make good use of green space. Just because there's a space in the center doesn't mean you have to plant in it. But don't oversimplify and make it lifeless either. Plant in groupings and add other lone plants for diversity. Use some big patterns. Have a theme or specialty garden—English, cottage-style, rose, water, butterfly, bird/wildlife, herb, or fragrance garden. Stick to one theme because too many tend to make it look tangled and wild.

Landscaping Computer Programs and Kits

To keep you on the right track, you can buy computer CD-ROM programs about garden planning that allow you to design and "plant" your site. For example, there's Garden Companion Deluxe put out by Lifestyle Software (about $35), 3D Garden Designer and Encyclopedia by Burpee Software ($50), or Great

Home Garden by Homeart ($25–$30). You can even purchase stock garden plans from shelter magazines or find them on the Net.

When doing your own planting, experts recommend following these five steps:

1. Do lawn and groundcover first.
2. Put in trees.
3. Add foundation, corner, and entrance plantings.
4. Do borders and screens next to create spaces and privacy.
5. Make refinements: add flower beds, ponds, lighting, specimen plants, etc.

If it's a small project, you may design it by using a kit such as *The Garden Planning Kit* by The Gardeners' Guide which is available at bookstores. Other project planners can be purchased at garden stores, nurseries, and landscape or horticultural firms.

These kits will help you analyze your needs and preferences. Some require measurements and photos of the area so you can map it out on graph paper, says Richard B. Campbell of Campbell's Nurseries and Garden Centers in Lincoln, Nebraska. Make a rough sketch of the house and other structures and do the plan according to scale, he suggests. In addition, Campbell says a design must include:

- The boundary or point on the property that is north so you can plot sun and wind direction
- The location of utilities (before you dig)
- Existing plants (measure or estimate how much space they occupy)
- The functional areas
- The traffic areas
- The characteristics of the soil (clay or sand, wet or dry, fertile or infertile)
- The topography of your property (how it slopes, and how many ravines or ridges and rocks or outcroppings there are)
- An indication of views (on or off the property, good or bad, and any need for screening or framing)

When it's time to plant, you don't have to go out on a limb to make your choices. Take your plan to a local garden center or nursery. Ask what full shade plants work with your climate, soil type, and drainage to achieve your desired effect. Consider what you expect from a plant, a bush, or a tree. Do you need tips on how to reduce pesticide use or maintenance such as pruning? Do you want plants that grow in a certain shape or fit in a certain spot—under a window or by a fence? Do you want plantings that have different textures, forms, and colors?

Experts at Auburn University in Auburn, Alabama, also suggest these other considerations:

- The plant's tolerance to cold and heat
- Amount of light needed
- Amount of water needed (group plants with similar water needs)
- The Ph of the soil
- The plant's susceptibility to insect and disease problems
- The plant's rate of growth and mature size.

Plants are like kittens, don't underestimate how large they may get. Find out. Some cypress trees can grow 40 feet tall, while others only 6 feet tall. A spruce planted in front of the house can grow up past the windows, blocking the view or preventing you from washing the windows. If you have a window in the dining room that provides light, don't allow a plant to grow in front of it and create a dark, foreboding room.

Match what you want to what you can afford. If you plan to install the plants yourself, you can save up to 40 percent and many nurseries guarantee the plants even if you put them in. But make sure to get good maintenance instructions.

YOUR SITE'S PUBLIC AREAS

Corner plantings, like an exclamation point, are used to accentuate the corners of the house. Foundation plants are the anchors and direct the eye to your home's entrance, say experts. Entrance plants beckon visitors. You want them to be inviting with lots of color and ground cover. This is where you need to bring the architecture of house and the garden together, which helps carry the eye to the front door. Walks also lead guests to the home's front door. Border plants are like scenery in a play. They provide the backdrop for your site and often are used for screening and privacy. Here you can use a subtle mixture of color in the spring and fall, if you choose, or go simple with evergreens such as boxwoods and easy-to-grow ground cover such as English ivy.

YOUR SITE'S PRIVATE SPACES

The private areas of your site are usually your sanctuary and are located in the back. You can have a fence, border, or gate to delineate this. The private area may have a pool, patio, greenhouse, kids' area, and gardens for favorite shrubs, flowers, vegetables, and herbs. Don't forget your side plot, an often neglected spot. You can do interesting plantings that screen views, add color, or just plant a vigorous ground cover so you don't have to worry about maintaining it.

WHAT TO PLANT AND WHERE

There is no need to rush to plant everything at once. Some ideas can wait. If you are watching your pennies (or peonies), start with slower growing plants. Plant shade trees and major evergreens first. They break the wind and add privacy. Then, start filling in. It's much like adding adjectives to a simple sentence.

Your gardens are the best place for you to state your theme and show your true colors because they're where you'll get the most variety. In them you can plant cuttings, bulbs, or seeds. The flower beds involve preparing the site, choosing the right time to plant, and postplanting maintenance. Flower beds should be mulched to inhibit grass and weeds from growing in the beds, which lessens weeding time. Beds should be placed around the main plants along with ground cover to create interesting lines and shapes, says Campbell. Talk to your garden center about potting soils and which plants do best in which mixtures.

There are no absolutes—which trees, flowers, shrubs, or ground cover you should plant and where. What works in one climate, may not work in another. It's up to you to confer with local experts.

If you're completely worn out at this point, you might hire a professional to do the hard labor such as planting big trees, preparing beds, and removing old plants.

WORKING WITH A LANDSCAPE PROFESSIONAL

The landscape professional works on two levels. One is personal. He will listen to the homeowner's ideas, goals, and considerations. On a professional level he must consider the conditions of the site: drainage, sunlight, and views of the property from different rooms. He will also try to bring the inside and outside together. He'll attempt to come up with a plan that works on both levels.

One of his first jobs will be to tell you what can be salvaged and what cannot. He'll peruse your site for identifying features. A low area can become a pond with plantings. If it's flat, tall trees can give it dimension, and raised beds can create a step effect like shelves. If the lawn slopes or there's a big muddy berm, the area can be transformed into a terrace, steps, or a retaining wall. Sometimes the slope determines the site's theme. The trick is to get the slope to blend in with the rest of the surroundings.

An experienced pro will map a variety of spaces and come up with some creative ideas—a spa garden close to a master bedroom area separated by terraces, steps, or flower beds; an arbor; a wall fountain, and small sitting deck; or ponds with fish and flowering water plants with a humpbacked bridge.

When designing the landscape, the professional considers the owner's lifestyle. People spend time in their outdoor sites for different reasons. Some people want a water garden because they love the sound of gurgling water. Some love to entertain outside, especially if they live in a warm climate. Some people want privacy. Some want to conceal the sight of something unpleasant such as an ugly new house across the street.

The good news about using a landscaper is that you don't have to have the lifestyle that Robin Leach fawns over in *Lifestyles of the Rich and Famous*. Albizo spent about $5,000 to a professional to completely design and plant his backyard and do a front yard design for his $165,000 home. Campbell estimates that professional planning usually amounts to 1 percent of the total project cost; supervision of installation about 15 percent.

How much of your total home budget should go to landscaping? Simple landscaping to clean up the look of the house and make it more attractive is typically 10 to 15 percent of the cost of the house. If patios, fencing, and gardens are included it can cost 20 percent or more.

How long does it take? Depending on how intricate the decision is, a landscape done by a professional can take anywhere from three days to a year to design and plant.

Even if you seem totally uninterested in your landscape, a professional landscaper needs to involve you on some level. A garden is most successful when you are engaged in the planning and continue to upgrade, nurture, and change the landscape.

WHOM DO YOU HIRE TO DO WHAT?

How good do you feel on a sunny day when you look outside? The views you have of the outside of your home play an important part in maintaining your emotional health.

You might be inclined to think that the most important aspect of your landscaping is, say, oh, the plants. But the talented people who quickly transform your lot into a landscape are just as important. Choose people who have been around long enough to earn a few stripes, such as a landscape architect.

Landscape Architect

These experts work to create light wonderful views of the outdoors from your house, and play up the elements you feel good about. A landscape architect has earned a degree from an accredited college for completing a four or five year program in landscape architecture, must apprentice under a licensed professional, and must be certified by passing the Landscape Architect Registration Examination administered by the Council of Landscape Architectural Registration Boards—if the state so dictates. Call your state capitol to verify.

The American Society of Landscape Architects, a group of some 12,000 members and 46 chapters, works for legislation to have practice laws in each state. Practice laws mean the architect has to be licensed. According to research prepared by Stan L. Bowman, ASLA Manager of Government Affairs, some 45 states have a licensing law; 26 have a practice law; and 19 a title law—which means that a license is required before the professional can call himself a landscape architect. The states without a law (as of February 24, 1998) are Alaska (trying to enforce a law), Colorado, Nevada, North Dakota, and Vermont, as well as the District of Columbia. California was the first state to enact a law in 1953.

Typically a member of your homebuilding team, a landscape architect will work with your builder, architect, urban planner, ecologist, and engineer, according to the Michigan Occupational Information System on Landscape Architects. He compiles and analyzes data on site conditions such as geographic location, drainage, irrigation, and soil type. Then he plans the placement of all plantings, outdoor structures, and lighting.

Once this is accomplished, he prepares working drawings, specifications, and cost estimates for land developments showing ground contours and vegetation. The design ideas are presented to the client in writing and can include all costs, plant materials to be used, a time-table, and terms of payment. If satisfactory, the work begins.

If the professional is strictly a landscape architect, he may charge by the hour or by a percentage of the project cost—or he may charge a combination of both. He may charge design time, plus a percentage of the project cost for supervision, or he may only charge a percentage of the cost of project. Ask in advance and get the method in writing with a specific dollar amount.

Design/Build Landscaping Group

If you hire a design/build group, part of its service includes the design and installation of landscaping. A design/build group feels the best way to approach a project is to have a landscape architect on staff. You may also find it convenient to have the designer-contractor link because so many decisions that are made involve both design and installation.

Architectural Landscape Contract

Whether working with a design/build group or single practitioner, the contract is a crucial element that will help prevent bad vibes and a lot of aggravation. Without a contract, the buyer could get into a situation where the plan isn't finalized, he's stuck with slew of extras, and he doesn't have a leg to stand on. Because competition in the landscaping business is fierce and business volume is at an all-time high, the entire industry has become more professionalized, however.

The landscape architect's contract should detail the plan, the time involved, the materials to be used—plants, grasses, trees, shrubs, structures—the order in which the work will be done, the guarantees or warranties, any bonding and insurance information, the plan's sign-off agreement, and the stipulation that the proposal and the plan match.

Fees

How much do you pay upfront and how much do you hold back? Some people fear that a project will not be completed correctly and they want to hold back 10 percent of the project cost. Byron says his company's guarantee is only enforced if full payment is received. "Our guarantee is our safety net. We require a deposit of 30 percent, but it can range from 10 to 50 percent in Chicago."

Landscape Designer

Some designers are architects and some aren't, but a designer may be more in tune with the specifics of gardening and planting than an architect. They can design a plan that pinpoints the right location for plants. The designer who's also an architect looks at an entire lot and how each space interacts. The designer may charge a percentage of the total project cost.

Landscape Contractor

Landscape contractors are the builders of your outdoor sites. Some oversee grading, drainage, or irrigation. Some may have a design skill, but they profit from their construction expertise. They install the structures—patios, decks, irrigation systems, and retaining walls—and plantings and maintain them, says Bonnie Van Fleet of the Associated Landscape Contractors of America, a trade association representing about 1,500 landscape contracting firms throughout the United States, Canada, and abroad. Members do landscape construction, design-build contracting, landscape maintenance, reclamation and erosion control, irrigation, lawn care, and interior landscaping.

They generally charge a fee plus a maintenance cost. Many firms have designers and architects on staff to create a master plan that will match your time frame and budget.

Employees of these firms should have either a secondary education in ornamental horticulture or several years of experience. Many are also members of national or state landscape groups. If required by state law, the firm should be licensed or certified. You can verify certification to be sure that the professional is on the level and has knowledge and experience.

Landscape Contractor's Contract

There are various standard contracts prepared by the Associated Landscape Contractors of America. There is one for landscaping and maintenance with such provisions as the designer's and owner's responsibilities, ownership, and use of documents (who owns what), insurance, licenses, permits and taxes, exclusions, payment terms, disclaimers, owner's or designer's default and the consequences, claims, indemnity, assignment, and owner's right to cancel. The design services contract is similar.

The form for installation has such clauses as time, scope of work, payment terms, contract documents and owner's right to cancel, contractor's and owner's responsibilities orders, concealed conditions, insurance, licenses, permits and taxes, exclusions, completion and acceptance, owner's or contractor's default, claims, indemnity, warranties, and more.

There's also a landscape design services addendum for the design, bidding, construction documents, and construction phases.

How Do You Find the Best Practitioner?

Let's start with the same steps you used to find your architect, builder, interior decorator, or designer. The best way is word of mouth. Talk to your friends. If you see a site that you admire, get out and ask the owner who was responsible. Call any local associations connected to landscape contractors or landscape architects. Check references. Call the better business bureau.

How to Find a Good Landscape Professional

Recommendations from the American Nursery & Landscape Association (ANLA) and the Associated Landscape Contractors of America:

- Is your prospect a licensed business? Ask to see if they have a federal identification number that designates them as a real business, whether they have completed any certification program offered in your state, and if they are insured. Their qualification statement should list references, licensing information, and association membership. Some states require licensing or certification.
- Do they appear professional? The professional landscaper arrives on time, takes pictures or draws sketches of your property while there, and uses uniformed workers and clean equipment.
- What kind of services do they offer? Professional firms usually offer a variety of services, from design and installation to maintenance programs that include color rotations, insect disease control, and irrigation.
- How are their communication skills? It is important that you establish a good working relationship at the onset of the project. A positive approach to customer communications begins with a written estimate that explains the services, materials, and plant sizes that will be provided, the cost, and the necessary details of weed control, edging, mulching, and cleanup. Be sure to find out their anticipated work schedule and any warranties for plants that die as a result of conditions within their control.
- Do they give you a contract? A reputable firm provides you with a contract specifying start and completion dates. If a deposit is required, the contract could show that the money is held in escrow at a specific bank.
- Can they supply customer references and referrals? Referrals can provide an independent source for the answers to such questions as: How many years has the company has been in business? Do they use trained installers? Are they competent? It is best that you visit a few sites they've worked on before committing to any company.

How to Find a Good Landscape Professional (cont.)

- What is covered and for how long? What's not? Ask for proof of adequate insurance coverage for worker's compensation, liability, and vehicles. Find out whether the firm is trained and licensed for the application of fertilizers or insect and disease controls.
- Ask if you can visit a job in progress. Ask to see one similar to the work you are planning.
- Ask what services are provided for ongoing maintenance. Ongoing professional maintenance is necessary in order to protect your investment. This service usually includes mowing, fertilizing, and pest control.

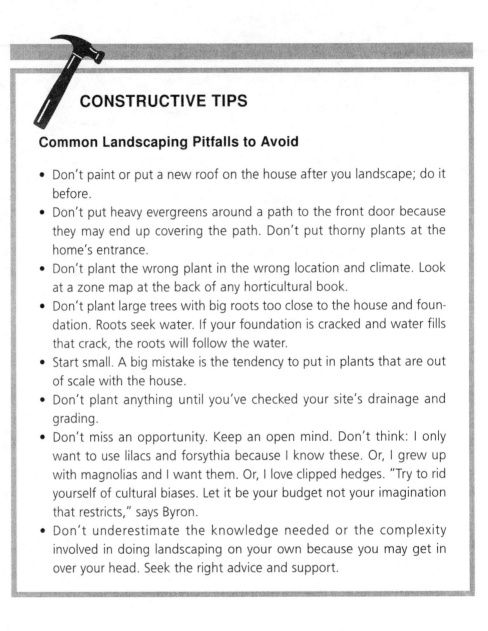

CONSTRUCTIVE TIPS

Common Landscaping Pitfalls to Avoid

- Don't paint or put a new roof on the house after you landscape; do it before.
- Don't put heavy evergreens around a path to the front door because they may end up covering the path. Don't put thorny plants at the home's entrance.
- Don't plant the wrong plant in the wrong location and climate. Look at a zone map at the back of any horticultural book.
- Don't plant large trees with big roots too close to the house and foundation. Roots seek water. If your foundation is cracked and water fills that crack, the roots will follow the water.
- Start small. A big mistake is the tendency to put in plants that are out of scale with the house.
- Don't plant anything until you've checked your site's drainage and grading.
- Don't miss an opportunity. Keep an open mind. Don't think: I only want to use lilacs and forsythia because I know these. Or, I grew up with magnolias and I want them. Or, I love clipped hedges. "Try to rid yourself of cultural biases. Let it be your budget not your imagination that restricts," says Byron.
- Don't underestimate the knowledge needed or the complexity involved in doing landscaping on your own because you may get in over your head. Seek the right advice and support.

CONSTRUCTIVE TIPS (continued)

- Don't overlandscape. Don't do the two-for-one at the garden center. Don't buy it just because it's a bargain—it is not the best way to go about landscaping. You may get home and find out you bought something with roots that are too shallow, or too big, or you're fooled by the size of the cutting. Lots of plants today will reach only a certain height or form. And don't overplant. If you have good views, leave your property more open.
- Don't plant trees near underground pipelines or overhead power wires. Don't plant closer than five feet from a sidewalk or patio because the roots will tear it up.

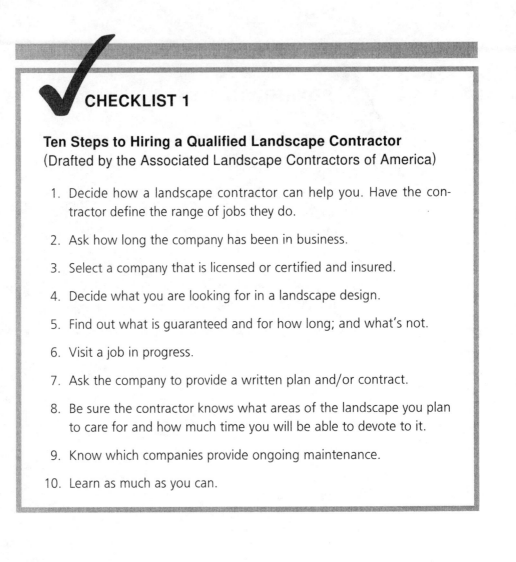

CHECKLIST 1

Ten Steps to Hiring a Qualified Landscape Contractor
(Drafted by the Associated Landscape Contractors of America)

1. Decide how a landscape contractor can help you. Have the contractor define the range of jobs they do.

2. Ask how long the company has been in business.

3. Select a company that is licensed or certified and insured.

4. Decide what you are looking for in a landscape design.

5. Find out what is guaranteed and for how long; and what's not.

6. Visit a job in progress.

7. Ask the company to provide a written plan and/or contract.

8. Be sure the contractor knows what areas of the landscape you plan to care for and how much time you will be able to devote to it.

9. Know which companies provide ongoing maintenance.

10. Learn as much as you can.

✔ CHECKLIST 2

How to Make Your Home a Stand-Out with Landscaping
(Excerpts from the newsletter of the ANLA)

❑ Design front entry planting with curving lines.

❑ Use groups of three. Take a triangular approach to color, texture, and quality of plants and group three colors, shapes, textures, or numbers within a four-season blooming schedule.

❑ Complementary color schemes like yellow, pink, and blue play off each other when they bloom in the same tonal gradations.

❑ Follow a triad method with texture. You might group a broad-leaf shrub with a blade-shaped perennial and low-leafed fuzzy plant.

❑ Plant in odd numbers rather than pairs, unless you want to draw attention to a feature in the landscape, or you do so for balance. Try not to crowd plants. Have a sequence to the flow with a focal point and make the design proportionate.

❑ Make your hardscape—the materials of your structures—blend with the landscape.

15

Illuminating Your House and Adding Music to Your Life

Lighting. We take it for granted like the oxygen we breathe. It's there. But that's shortsighted and can short-circuit your progress. Too often homeowners spend little time thinking about their lighting decisions before the construction or remodeling gets underway. How unfortunate. The sooner you decide what type of light you want and where you want it placed, the better and the cheaper it will be. It's far less costly to install wiring before walls are primed and painted.

ZELMA LONG AND PHILLIP FREESE (Northern California)

Zelma Long of Simi Winery and her husband Phillip Freese called their contractor's bluff. "We had security lights or spotlights installed around our house and a sepa-rate garage. Each light had a round base for attaching to the house and two cone-shaped lights that held the spotlights. One weekend we came to inspect the progress (we were living elsewhere, thank goodness). We saw that the lights had been installed. Phil immediately noticed that they were crooked, and while I did not find them offensive, I called the contractor's agent, who in turn, said she would call the electrician. She then called back and reported that the electrician told her, 'This is the way they are supposed to be installed.'" Zelma and Phil were deter-mined not to be duped. Because Zelma had managed construction of a new wing of Simi Winery, she was savvy in these matters and replied, "'Okay, just send us the installation diagram for the lights that verifies their proper installation, and we will not complain.' Several days later, when I returned to check progress, the lights had been properly installed."

VISIT LIGHTING SHOWROOMS OR LIGHTING LABS

Where do you start and how do you become enlightened? If you haven't been into a lighting showroom recently, do so. Most display many options in both fixtures and lamps (bulbs) in the three main types of lighting—general, accent, and task (to literally help you perform a task such as see a cutting board in a kitchen). The right lighting makes your home more pleasant, brighter, more energy efficient, and safer.

Many showrooms across the country now have lighting labs, according to the American Lighting Association (ALA), which is headquartered in Dallas. These labs are typically built as a separate section within a showroom or at a manufacturer's educational center and feature a set of furnished rooms as would be found in your home—a kitchen, living space, and even a garden. But instead of incorporating one light solution, each room vignette features a host of fixtures and lamps to demonstrate all the traditional and newest trends.

Cutting-Edge Illumination Inside and Out

One of the popular cutting-edge illuminators are low-voltage halogen MR-16 bulbs that cast crisp beams of white light onto accent art, furniture, and even food to make it look more appealing. Slender cables have popped up in many restaurants as a new fixture design. And there are fiber optic tubes available that can be run from a remote source to a wall, ceiling, or even in a swimming pool.

LESLIE STERN (Chicago, Illinois)

In a master bathroom Leslie Stern was trying to remodel, she had to deal with a waste stack that was in the middle of the room and gobbled up a lot of square footage. She made it the focal point of the room by putting glass block on either side of the toilet with a light behind to cast a glow throughout the room. She also used a similar colored light between the cove molding and the ceiling.

With so much to choose from, it can be confusing. Ask lots of questions and consider these lighting options:

- On the ceiling, use recessed cans—available in different shapes with different outside covers. They come in both standard and low-voltage current, with a choice of incandescent, tungsten-halogen, or energy-efficient compact fluorescents.

- Undercabinet and undershelf lights can be used for task or accent lighting. Energy-efficient fluorescent lights, miniature tracks, and low-voltage strips can also serve this purpose.
- Tracklights can serve as general, task, or accent lighting. They are also available in standard or low-voltage current with a choice of incandescent, tungsten-halogen, or energy-efficient compact fluorescent bulbs.
- Sconces, spotlights, lanterns, table lamps, and cables strung with light are the new generation of track lighting.

Don't forget to light your front, side, and back entrances well, not only for friendly greeting but safety. Garages can be lit with high-pressure sodium bulbs that produce more light per watt and last longer. Photocells used in outdoor fixtures turn lights on at dusk and off at dawn to reduce energy consumption.

The outdoor rooms at a lighting lab, which usually feature a variety of textures and fake plantings, show how lighting is now used for both decoration and safety.

Recent advances allow you to have a 120-volt line voltage system, a 12-volt low voltage system, or a combination for outdoor use. The 12-volt system requires a transformer, but it can be a do-it-yourself project. It is more energy efficient, with little risk or no risk of shock, minimum disturbance to your lawn, and fixtures that can be easily moved when desired. On the other hand, a 120-volt system usually lights larger areas more brightly with longer beam throws. To get the benefits of both you can install a 120-volt line and add 12-volt branches or circuits using transformers.

Many of these lighting labs will help you plan a lighting design that provides your home with the right amount and different types of light, and correct placement of outlets and switches. A lab will also help you avoid turning your house into a mini Las Vegas because overlighting is almost as easy as underlighting. You also want to be aware of automatic devices you can use to turn lights on and off such as timers, photocells, or home electronic control systems (See "Intelligent Houses" in Chapter 16). If you or your design professionals buy products at a lighting lab, the lab usually waives the design fee. If you use the lab as a resource but buy elsewhere, the lab will usually charge $50 to $75 an hour for design services. Some also make house calls and typically charge an additional fee.

To find labs and designers, surf the Web, or call the ALA for a list of certified lighting consultants (CLCs) at 1-800-Bright Ideas. The International Association of Lighting Designers in Chicago is composed of members who charge by the hour or by the project. (You can find them listed in the Appendix.)

CONSTRUCTIVE TIPS

Great Places to Put Lighting

Using light in unusual ways can give character to your home. Here are some great lighting ideas:

- Put lights outside along walkways and in trees and bushes.
- Lights in cabinets and bookshelves can highlight your collections.
- On walls, use small lights to accent art—especially in kitchens, bedrooms, and bathrooms.
- Lights dropped from ceilings bring life to countertops.
- Along interior hallways, accent lights illuminate a safe pathway at night.

OUTDOOR LIGHTING

The ALA suggests concealing the light source behind shrubs or trees whenever possible unless the fixture itself is a decorative element. Here are some outdoor lighting terms to give you ideas.

- *Accenting* highlights a focal point, perhaps an ornamental tree with an uplight placed in the ground or slightly above the ground.
- *Backlighting* creates a backdrop by uplighting a tree or object from its rear side.
- *Cross lighting* illuminates a tree or statue from more than one side to reveal its three dimensionality, usually through downlighting.
- *Grazing* shoots a beam of light close to a surface to highlight textures, shapes, and heights.
- *Moonlighting* filters soft light down through branches from a fixture placed high in a tree.

- *Path lighting* places fixtures several feet apart to create a safe, attractive walk or group of steps.
- *Shadowing* lets light filter through a tree to create shadows.
- *Uplighting* aims lights upwards, sometimes from in the ground, to create a dramatic effect similar to theatrical light. These are best used with interesting trees, statues, or textured walls.
- *Pool lighting* allows swimmers to tread water safely at night, and adds a dramatic aura to this area of your backyard.
- *Tennis court lighting,* albeit expensive, can allow you to play at night and longer into the seasons.

Don't be in the dark about the various lighting options as well as lenses, diffusers, and mounts.

SIGHT AND SOUND DESIGN

There are sound systems and then there are Sound Systems. But this is a realm of electronics known more for its technology than styling. So why should you be concerned about how it looks or fits into your home? Because you must prepare and prewire at the right point in your construction if you plan to install a system more intricate than a pair of speakers that sit on a shelf.

"Choose the system based on sound. But if you don't hear a difference in sound between a moderate and expensive system, don't spend the money," says Dwayne Boyer, manager of Music for Pleasure in St. Louis. "It's much like tasting wine. You know which wine you like better because you develop a taste for it, although you might not be able to describe the exact flavors. Similarly, you know the sound you want when you hear it."

Changing technology, however, has placed an increased emphasis on appearance. Speakers and televisions are morphing into pieces of furniture in various shapes, sizes, and sundry materials—from wood to plastic—and are fashioned with curves and angles.

Multimedia home theaters fuel this trend with enormous screens and speakers, digital satellite systems, surround sound capabilities and built-in modems for Web access. This is only the tip of the iceberg. With several emerging technologies, soon sound systems will be hooked up to computers. The screen will inflate in size and as it does, it may be tucked into walls, pieces of furniture, or hidden behind closed doors.

But back to sound basics. Taste in sound runs from elementary to high-end. You can spend a few hundred or a few thousand. And for the musical cognoscenti who covet the high-end products, you can drop $60,000 to $100,000+ for a home theater system. Some audiophiles can even manage to spend a few hundred thousand on intricate wiring and multiple zones to run separate components.

Before building or adding on a room, it's important to decide on the sound system you want. It's difficult, expensive, and sometimes unfeasible to wire a sound system after the drywall is in place. A person will build a house or a room and typically several years later realize the sound system they've chosen is not what it should be. They want to redo it. If the basement is finished with dry wall, or there is no access to the walls at all, it is difficult to go in and wire. It's ultimately more pricey than doing it right the first time.

Most dealers will come to your home and give an estimate and their input on what will work best for your room. This means what type of equipment to use, what size speakers, and what power amps.

16

Protecting Your Home

Now that you've gone to all the trouble to build your home and landscape and illuminate it, you may want to protect it better. The right plants can discourage intruders and reduce crime, says the American Nursery and Landscaping Association (ANLA). "Planting sharp-textured plants like hollies or spike barberries near your home creates a colorful barrier that will deter prowlers from entering through windows or hiding between house and foliage."

Lighting also helps and so does a dog. You can buy a good deadbolt lock and key, but you may not find any of these protections sufficient. You are not alone. At least one in five single-family houses has some sort of alarm system.

BOB AND RANDY COSTAS (St. Louis, Missouri)

Another lesson Randy learned is not to install an alarm system that is so sensitive it goes off during every thunderstorm. "It went off last night at 3 AM, but it never seems to do this when Bob is home."

Fear is one reason to install an alarm system, but not the only one. The cost of installing and maintaining a system has dropped. What was once considered a luxury item is now within the budget of many homeowners, according to the Central Station Alarm Association (CSAA) in Bethesda, Maryland, one of the country's two main member associations.

In 1998, installation costs averaged $1,200, down from about $1,500 five years earlier, says the National Burglar and Fire Alarm Association, the other prime organization representing member companies and also in Bethesda, Maryland. Due to the heightened competition among companies selling security systems, some don't even charge for installation. They recoup costs through long-term monthly monitoring agreements. These monthly monitoring fees typically average between $20 and $30, and your smoke detectors can be wired into your system for an additional but worthwhile fee.

Protecting Your Home before the Alarm System Is Installed

Even before you call a home security company, cut the potential interest of burglars by taking some precautionary steps and making your house less easy prey.

- Install good window and door locks and consider bringing out a locksmith to check them. The best are pinlocks on windows and dead bolts on doors.
- Be sure you use your locks, even when you're working in the backyard.
- Prune overgrown shrubbery because it makes an easy hiding place.
- Be sure your illumination is bright enough—indoors and outdoors—when you're home and away. Automatic timers are inexpensive and easy to install.
- When you go on a vacation—even for a day—don't let your mail or newspapers stack up. Have the post office hold them or ask a neighbor to retrieve them. Put any valuable jewelry, silverware, or papers in a bank vault.

SELECTING AN ALARM SYSTEM

When it comes to choosing an alarm system, decide whether you want a wireless, do-it-yourself system, or a hard-wired system that a professional company will install—which will cost more. If you hire a professional, get several bids, preferably from companies that belong to the NBFAA or the CSAA, which indicates the members are knowledgeable about the latest technology. And always have a fire alarm, whether battery operated or as part of your alarm system. If battery operated, have the battery checked periodically.

FINDING THE RIGHT INSTALLER AND EQUIPMENT

Make sure each potential installer explains what his bid includes and ask him the following questions:

- What devices will you install and where? Which doors and windows will have contacts?
- Will the protection come through hard wires, motion detectors, or both?
- Where will the alarm sound—at your office or at the local police or fire station?
- Will I be charged for false alarms? How many false alarms do I get at no charge?
- How many keypads—used to arm and disarm the system—will you provide?
- Will I be able to provide different codes to different members of my household and to any workers temporarily on the premises?
- Does the system come with a warranty, and what is the life expectancy of the system?

Many experts recommend protecting the perimeter of the main floor and any upper floors with contacts on every door and window. The more contacts, the heftier the price. Be sure that the keypads provide large enough numbers so they're easy to read and use. Also be sure you like the design of the "panic button," which is the key you hit in case you hear or see an intruder. (Keys to turn the alarm on and off have been pretty much eliminated with the newer numbered designs.)

HOW THE SYSTEM WORKS

In case your house is entered, understand how the alarm works. You need to know not just where it sounds—a central office is more common today than the police office—but also whether your phone line goes dead when the call is made. That could necessitate a second phone line in your house.

UPDATING THE SYSTEM

At some point you may want to update your system, possibly to include more window or door contacts, or add an entire room to your system. You may also want to take advantage of developing technologies such as systems that are activated and deactivated by the sound of your voice, your palm print, or the sight of your eyeball. Some homeowners also like to install surveillance cameras throughout their grounds or build a bulletproof safe room, but such systems are expensive and more likely to appeal only to the very rich or to homeowners who work in high-risk industries.

SAFETY CHECK

At least once a year you should have the installation company come out to clean and check the system to make sure it's fully operational. You might also want to periodically change the code number for safety.

Is an alarm system worth the expense and effort? Your chances of being burglarized are said to decrease by about 14 percent if you do so. And if you are burglarized, you will pare your losses because most thieves will grab what they can and quickly leave if an audible alarm sounds.

INTELLIGENT HOUSES

Another—and more romantic—way to protect your home is by creating your own "intelligent house." Remember in the movie *Pillow Talk* when Doris Day pushes a button in Rock Hudson's bachelor pad and the lights turn off and a record with romantic music goes on at the same time a sofa bed unfolds? Once little more than a Hollywood fantasy, homes today are being prewired to do these tasks and more.

KEITH RICH (Sugar Grove, Illinois)

Keith Rich, president of ISR, Inc., in Naperville, Illinois, which designs, sells, installs, and services TronArch—a home electronics control system, lives in an intelligent 15,000-square-foot home on a family estate of 26 buildings totalling 53,000 square feet. "My house and the other houses where my family lives are all integrated together in the same intelligent system. The intelligence is designed around our lifestyle. For example, I have an antique car museum where one button controls all the lights and makes sure the humidity stays at 62 degrees to preserve the leather and tires. My wine cellar is programmed to stay at 57 degrees. I have Navipage, a monitoring system that works through my digital pager. If it's cold in Chicago and the temperature goes down to 40 degrees in my master bedroom, I'm paged to check it and correct it."

Today you can press a mode button such as "Entertain," and several functions will be performed simultaneously. The temperature adjusts to 72 degrees, lights dim, music plays, and the security system disarms in the public areas of your estate. At the same time, the temperature is lowered, lights turned off, and security is armed in the private spaces.

In actuality, there are three levels of intelligent homes in the marketplace: automation, system integration, and intelligent integration.

Automation

Automation has been around for a long time as the ability to turn systems on and off at a scheduled time. It's the timed operation of separate subsystems—programming the sprinkler to go on at a certain time every day, scheduling the thermostat to adjust according to a fixed schedule, having your favorite CD start playing at the single press of a button.

KEITH RICH (Sugar Grove, Illinois)

Keith Rich whose company ISR designed the intelligence system in his home, touts his home theater which he says is "awesome from an intelligent point of view. We have a 'night out in our own home.' The room has a 153-inch diagonal screen, digital projector, AM-FM tuner, and DVD, all controlled by one button." He also talks about the other functions of his system: "If my daughter leaves the fan on or the lights on in her bedroom or bathroom when she goes to school, it shuts off at 9 AM. If she's home sick, my daughter presses 'sick mode' and it changes the schedule for the day. We also have a 'cleaning mode,' which turns our house into one big cleaning environment. All the lights turn on, all the drapes and motorized shades go up for washing windows. When I go into my study, I press 'work mode' and it opens up motorized doors for the computer, the computer turns on, and the motorized TV comes out of the back end of the cabinet. When I leave, I press one button and it all turns back into something out of *Architectural Digest*."

System Integration

System integration has been around for ten years or more as part of the digital revolution and is a quasi-intelligent system. It is a series of subsystems—activated by a voice or push of a button—that can communicate with each other. These subsystems might include climate (HVAC, humidity, air filtering, heated floors, driveway/walkway snow melt), indoor and outdoor lighting, security (alarm systems, security cameras, security gates, electronic door and window locks, garage doors), entertainment (distributed audio and video, authentic THX certified home theaters), communications (home office/phones, intercoms, pagers, PCs, remote access), and water management (garden irrigation, pools, spas, hot tubs, waterfalls, fountains, ponds, landscaping).

BILL AND NANCY SWANEY (Florida)

Bill Swaney, retired chairman and chief executive of Perrigo Company—the largest manufacturer of over-the-counter store brand pharmaceutical, nutritional, health, and beauty aids located in Allegan, Michigan—and his wife Nancy, built a home in Florida between Ft. Lauderdale and West Palm Beach. They put in an ISR intelligent system because of the complexity and large size of their home. They don't live in the house full-time and wanted the ability to know what is going on in the house when they're not there. Bill can access his system through his computer and find out how the house is running. "I have many different systems and modes. I make sure the air conditioning is running, security is on, all gates are closed, and the correct lights are off and on." For example, if you're leaving your home and want to arm your security, and at the same time want your shades to shut and your temperature to be lowered, the subsystems can interact with each other.

Intelligent Integration

Intelligent homes have taken the system integration a step further, says Keith Rich, president of ISR, Inc., producers of TronArch home electronics control system. "There's more intelligence in the software to make events happen the way you want them to and that can adjust to variables such as time of day or time of week. We can take any subsystem out there the client wants, program it to his lifestyle, and integrate all the systems into one unit." The systems are tied together with low-voltage wiring that feeds to the TronArch control system which is connected to touch screens and/or keypads.

BILL AND NANCY SWANEY (Florida)

Bill and Nancy carefully chose several modes when they built their intelligent home in Florida. "When Nancy works out in our exercise room, she puts in her 'exercise mode,' the lights turn on, and so does her favorite music (Elvis). I can do the same. When I get on the Stairmaster, it's the Beach Boys for me. We have a mode for going down to play tennis. If it's at night, the tennis lights go on and the alarm system in the house goes on. It's the same for our beach mode. The system is very user-friendly; everything is controlled from one panel. I'm no computer whiz, but I can get in and program the whole system. So can my wife. We have it have set up for what we want throughout the day. We can set our window treatment for what-ever time of day to go up or down. We have 13 pages of light options we can use in the house. Most people never use their living rooms, but the other night we were entertaining in the dining room and our guests wanted to see our living room. We walked in and I set 'entertainment mode.' The lights went on automat-ically and the music came on." The Swaneys' guests were awed.

Homes of the Year 2000 and Beyond

Intelligent houses, with their varying degrees of automation, are the homes of today and will be the homes of the year 2000. Known in some circles as Smart Houses, a term which has become as generic as Kleenex, Smart Houses are really a trademarked set of electronic plans which stems from a cooperative research and development project initiated in 1984 by the National Association of Home Builders, says Susan Ritter, NAHB vice president, Industry Relations. In 1990, the group was spun off into a private operation that markets the technology. Today SMART HOUSE, Inc. is a national network of home systems dealers and installers.

SMART HOUSE CEO Mark Ellis Tipton, former president of the NAHB (1991), says that "nine out of ten homes wired today are not wired properly to access the intelligent home services that are available to consumers." Allan Freedman of the NAHB feels that "smart homes are going to hit big any day now." This is contingent on getting the word out. "We are trying to educate builders and consumers to be more aware of the need to prewire new homes or new rooms in the building stage. It's more expensive to wire after the fact," Ritter says. The expense is in the labor to pull the wire through a finished wall as opposed to laying wire in a empty wall.

Builders may upgrade cabinets but stint on sophisticated wiring. But if one builder offers a prewiring package, others will do so just to compete, making new homes more intelligent in the new millennium.

However, very few builders or architects will suggest prewiring or automated homes unless the client asks. It's not unlike going to the doctor and suggesting to him what you might do or take for a particular ailment. Those who don't ask, don't get.

Now, the consumer has to say to the architect or builder, "I want to make certain my communication cable and phone lines are wired and are of the grade and quality to access interactive services." You can't utilize the technology available if you're not wired.

If it's a home office, wiring is needed to accommodate multiple phone lines, local area networks, faxes, and the Internet. If wired properly, you can do your work in your home office while your children upstairs can access the Internet and do their homework on their own computer. It's all the same wiring, it just needs to be run to locations that make sense. This can be done through either a dual-shield coaxial cable or category (level) 5 telephone wire. Levels are measured by the number of twists per inch in the wiring. The more twists the less interference and greater capacity for super-fast Internet access and other computer applications. Your builder may want to bring in someone who specializes in Smart House wiring and subsystems to supervise the installation.

As more builders make these accommodations, the prices to prewire will come down. Some predict by the turn of the century, four out of ten homes will be prewired for automation.

The extent to which a home is automated is up to you and your budget. It's also contingent upon the size of the house and the number of subsystems you choose. If the wiring is merely for points of security on the first floor, including windows, doors, and security for cameras, it can run $1,000 to $1,300 over the cost of the traditional home wiring.

A fairly inclusive home automation can run $6,000 to $20,000+, and be controlled from a single unit. Imagine a fully-automated home tied in to your security system, for example. If there's smoke detected, a control automatically shuts down heating and cooling systems, turns on all lights to illuminate an emergency passage out of the house, and flashes exterior lights so emergency vehicles can find your house at night because they can't see smoke.

Or how about every time you walk out your door you hit one switch on the wall that is programmed to turn certain lights in the house on or off at certain times of the day, arm your security system, reset your heating and cooling, and set into motion a lawn care package that waters your lawn every day at a certain time?

Or what about hitting a switch in your home theater room that automatically dims the lights, turns on your DVD player, and starts up your popcorn machine?

These prewired automated and fully-integrated intelligent homes give owners a feeling of independence and control. They can be useful for the elderly or for those with physical or mental disabilities. But mostly these homes use technology to enhance the way you live, says one homeowner who can turn on the spa heaters by phone so the spa is ready to be used when he gets home from work.

By the year 2003, home networking will be common in average homes for less than $100, without having to run wires through the walls, according to *Business Week* (Oct. 19, 1998). Technology will use DLS (digital subscriber lines) and cable-modem connections that access either phone lines or electrical wires. A wireless system is also in the works.

CONSTRUCTIVE TIPS

Locks That Could Keep Houdini Out

Key in to good locks. The locks and the doors you choose for your home's entrances are crucial. Deadbolts offer the best protection, says Brian Hildebrand, a locksmith in St. Louis. There are different types, and prices vary depending upon where you live. Here are some locks to consider:

- Key locking knobs. These are more decorative, but little protection. They can run anywhere from $21 to $500—for the more decorative solid brass sets.
- Kwik Set. This is a standard hardened steel bolt that's one inch in length.
- Schlage. Although basically standard, it is one of the better deadbolts. It's a single-cylinder that costs about $34.
- High security deadbolt. These are standard deadbolts, but the cylinder is pick resistant, drill proof, and has a restricted key. (The owner can only get the key from the locksmith who installed it.) These are about $100 and are made of solid brass and steel.
- Any lock or deadbolt is only as good as your door and door frame. Your doors should be solid wood or steel.

17

Site Unseen

Scheduling Site Visits and Time Management

The notion of the lamentable gap between intention and action haunts nearly all home buyers. Before all hell breaks loose and you hear yourself saying to your contractor one morning, "I don't care what you meant to do, it's what you did that I don't like," determine how much time you'll be spending at the site to make sure this doesn't happen. Also factor into your time management plan how often you'll meet with your builder or architect, what you'll look for, whether you'll photograph or video, and if you decide to secure notes in writing about the project's progress.

BILL AND NANCY SWANEY (Florida)

Bill and Nancy Swaney put almost a year of research and thought into planning their informal Florida beach home before they built it. They carefully selected all tradespeople. In November 1995, they hired Chuck Carter, a designer in Grand Rapids, Michigan, who had designed another of their homes. "We put a build/design team together. Chuck, Nancy, and I interviewed contractors. We selected one and he in turn recommended subs. We preselected the electrician, plumber, heating, air conditioning subs, all our engineers (electrical, structural, and mechanical), the architect to do the drawings, the interior designer, and ISR to do the automation. Our team met three days a month until October 1996, when we started building. We read articles on Hurricane Andrew to find out where most houses lost integrity in the storm. We were careful about roof lines and design; we have no overhang so there could be no lifting in a storm. We chose materials that would survive the salt air such as marble, stucco, and poured concrete for our home's exterior. We didn't want hurricane shutters because the motors burn out after a year. So we installed special Tischler windows, the only ones approved at the time by Dade and Broward counties and the only windows Chubb (insurance) would underwrite. The home was finished in 17 months; it was supposed to take 14. The travertine marble we ordered got caught between Italy and Spain in a trucker's strike in France, causing the three month delay."

MONITORING THE PROGRESS OF A PRODUCTION HOME

If you buy a production home, your builder will probably outline very specific times when you can visit the site to check on construction and discuss progress and problems. Typically, these times are scheduled at regular intervals after each construction stage—such as framing—has been finished, which may mean they occur every few weeks.

If you feel the need to visit the site more often, be sure you find out what the building company's policy is in advance because many don't allow future homeowners to pop in unannounced. It may insist that you call, schedule an appointment, and be shown around your lot or unfinished home by a company employee. Although your visit sometimes impedes progress, the builder's overriding concern is safety. A construction site is a dangerous place. Like it or not, you must heed the rules because in many cases the house still belongs to the builder or developer until you've closed.

SEMICUSTOM OR CUSTOM HOME CHECKS

If your home is a semicustom or custom home, you may have a bit more freedom in checking on work—sometimes even daily visits. You can ensure this by writing it into the contract. But don't expect your builder, contractor or architect to meet with you face-to-face that often, though some may oblige.

Most semicustom or custom builders and architects will try to meet with you face-to-face at critical junctures—when the walls are framed and it's important to check that the plumbing and electrical work are in the right spots, or when wall surfaces are up and you need to make sure moldings and trim are where you want them.

Of course, there are always exceptions and if you need to meet with them to discuss something you see during the course of the building or remodeling work that you feel is unsettling, speak up. Even if your main contact can't meet with you as often as you want, someone on staff can meet or at least have a quick conversation with you over the telephone a few times a week about progress and any problems.

BE PREPARED FOR PROGRESS MEETINGS

Whenever you do get together, be sure you have a pad of paper and a pencil to take notes and write down questions. Bring a tape recorder when you meet, if you feel that offers better backup, and consider bringing along a camera or videocamera to visually document progress and problems.

If you see something you don't like or have questions about it, ask right away, get a response, and find out when the work will be corrected or finished. Many owners who are building or remodeling, find it useful to keep a pad of paper next to their bed. They can then jot down things they think of in the middle of the night so they will remember to ask a worker the next day before construction progresses further.

KAREN AND MARK ZORENSKY (Clayton, Missouri)

Karen and Mark learned several valuable lessons while remodeling their vintage home. Karen warns about the importance of checking your tiles under various lighting to make sure that the dye lots match before the tiles are laid. "We had a floor that was partially done and had to rip it up."

Also, be sure you ask your contractor, builder, or architect to inform you when problems arise—if products can't be ordered, if materials come in wrong, or if the tilelayer gets the flu and has to be off work for an entire week. If you don't, some professionals will solve these problems on their own without your input. They feel that's why you've hired them. Establish in advance if they have the authority to make certain decisions without you or whether they need your approval. But remember, adds Chicago architect Richard Becker, "It makes it very tough for your work crew if you, the homeowner, try to micromanage the project. You supposedly hired good people to do so."

In one case of a new house being framed, there were valid reasons why the contractor moved the recessed lighting to another joist location without consulting the owner. There was simply no other option. But if the owner had felt that the original location was key, he might have been upset if he weren't consulted.

COMMUNICATION IS KEY

If you ever feel you're getting the brush-off or are unhappy, speak up, but be realistic. "Some homeowners think their job is the center of the universe. The reality is that most builders, architects, and contractors work on several projects and try to give as much service without compromising their responsibilities. But choose your words carefully," Becker adds. "Don't jump to a conclusion; try to be realistic and work out a solution. And don't throw out the idea of calling your attorney unless the situation really deteriorates and is unfixable because that changes the mood. Once you lose a positive working relationship, it's hard to get it back."

Whatever problems arise, keep revising your master time schedule, according to what you hear and see. It may delay your closing schedule and affect where you'll live if you're renting temporary housing or you've already sold your current home.

If all else fails, however, and you feel that you and your contractor are too far apart to come to a resolution, it may be necessary to end the relationship. But know what your contract says so that you end it as amicably and legally proper as possible.

MARIANNE AND RONALD SNEIDER (Palm Springs, California)

Marianne and Ronald Sneider, M.D., say their homebuilding experience was fabulous. Their gigantic two-story French chateau, however, was quite different than anything that had been built in Palm Springs. Marianne, an interior designer, fought to have higher-than-normal ceilings, an anomaly in the desert. "I designed the house and layout on paper and gave it to our architect. Once the building began, I was there every day when the workers arrived ready to discuss a change or a problem. The windows in the grand hall were too small for the 36-foot-high ceilings, but our builder made the change at no expense to us. Our pool was placed too close to the estate, so we were charged only half. Staying on top of a custom project like this is a must. As a result, our dream house turned out exactly like we wanted it to."

CONSTRUCTIVE TIPS

Are You House Obsessed?

When a woman is pregnant often all she notices are other pregnant women. Sometimes that's what happens when you build or remodel, all you see and think about are houses. How do you know when you've become too fixated on your project? Read on.

- You have a preoccupation to remodel or change things after they're done. You keep finding flaws and second guessing that someone else could have done it better. You're never content with the results.
- You begin to lie to yourself about how much money went into the home building or remodeling. You might even begin to lie to your spouse.
- Mirror, mirror on the wall. You're always looking at other houses and comparing them with yours. You experience constant disappointment with your own choices.
- You start to put the house above your relationships. You are driving your other family members nuts, arguing and bickering. You're in denial. You think to yourself that your family members just don't have the same high standards as you.
- At a cocktail party, when playing tennis, at work, or at the gym, all you talk about is the house. You've become a bit boring, haven't you?

CONSTRUCTIVE TIPS (continued)

After enough people begin to criticize you, recognize that your obsession is a problem. Analyze what's behind this. Stop and evaluate yourself. Why do you want to remodel or make changes in the first place? Are you using this house to make you happy? Are you using it to fill a void because something else is missing in your life? Are you just trying to show off? A house is a place to enjoy—a place of comfort and regeneration—and should not be a source of stress.

John Yunker, a licensed psychologist in St. Louis, suggests trying cognitive therapy, the "ABCDE" method. "A" stands for adversity or the problem: "My house looks terrible." "B" is the belief: "My house reflects who I am. Because it doesn't look the way it should, people will think ill of me." "C" is the consequence of that: "I must do something to fix it or move out." "D" is disputation—the therapeutic part of the equation— "What's so bad about our house? Who is it affecting? Do I really have to spend that much money to bring it up to speed?" "E" is energy that results from coming up with more productive, balanced, and rational strategies: "You don't have to completely gut the house to make it look good. You can fix up your house to sell and pretend it will go on the market and be inspected. This is one way to beat the need to have it perfect." Once a home is brought up to this level, you may want to stay there after all and make only some minor cosmetic changes, Yunker adds.

CHAPTER

18

A Word of Caution

Changes and Red Flags
along the Way

There's an old axiom that women are entitled to change their minds. This is fine in theory, but when building a home, changing your mind at the wrong point in the building process—regardless of your gender—can cost megabucks. So can unexpected problems along the way.

RICHARD KARN (Los Angeles, California)

Richard Karn, who plays Al Borland on the TV show *Home Improvement*, comes from a family of home builders. His grandfather was a builder, his father a builder, and if he had chosen to enter the family business, he too would have been a builder, according to his publicist John Zaring. Instead, Richard ended up playing a builder on TV. He is thinking about writing a book tentatively titled *How to Remodel Your House Just under Three Times the Original Price,* a humorous look at the process based on his remodeling experience which took 15 months. Karn, according to Zaring, bought a new house with the intention of remodeling just the master bedroom. The project escalated to include the entire home.

Changes can be anything from adding a fireplace to increasing the size of a room, changing your mind about a piece of equipment or an appliance, or switching from one material to another. Sometimes you may have no choice in making a change. The range you wanted is no longer made, so you have to make a substitution. Or, your contractor may discover a pipe or wiring that presents a structural, electrical, heating, or air conditioning problem—what's termed an "uncovered condition." He has to make a change in the design, which almost always increases the cost. And you're responsible. Sorry.

KAREN AND TOM UHLMANN (Chicago, Illinois)

Chicago writer Karen Uhlmann advises others doing remodeling to watch every remodeler's movement. At one point, she and husband Tom weren't paying attention when their city apartment was being worked on. "The workmen removed a wall that wasn't supposed to come down. Of course, we had to have it put back up."

PRIMARY REASONS FOR A CHANGE

There are various reasons you may initiate changes. Maybe you saw a product or material at a friend's home or in a magazine and felt that the tumbled marble would look so much better than the ceramic tile you already picked for your kitchen floor. Or, after setting foot in your almost completed master bathroom, you realize you forgot to include a seat and shelf. "More marble, please," you politely request. And as long as you are making that change, you decide you might as well have full-length mirrors, a wall heater, and a built-in heated towel rack.

MARILYN AND PHIL LISS (Chicago, Illinois)

Never be afraid to do something unplanned if it seems to make sense, says Marilyn Liss. "We weren't planning to redo the floors and as the workmen were in and doing work we decided we had to rip them out after we had torn down part of a wall because they looked awful. We were so happy we did. Sometimes, you can save, but in the long haul sometimes you can't."

Clients of Chicago architect Richard Becker went forward with a change order that also falls under the category of "might as well," he explains. "At one side of their house, they were adding a large two-story addition for a sunroom on the first level and a master bedroom and bathroom above. They decided to add a large 20-by-25-foot gymnasium over the garage on the other side of the house. Beside the gym with its vaulted ceiling, the new space will include a large bathroom, closets, and a refreshment bar. I'm used to change orders but they're not usually of that magnitude," he says.

While it's the homeowners' prerogative to make changes, especially if they're building a semicustom or custom home, be forewarned. In the home-building industry, such changes are known as change orders, and making them may involve increases in the time and money needed because new specifications may have to be drafted; new materials, equipment, and products ordered; and sometimes new building approvals sought.

After materials and products have been ordered and construction has begun, the cost of change orders gets much more expensive. Again you risk delaying your project, sometimes considerably. When you're buying a production house, the fast pace of construction doesn't permit many changes—some developers won't allow any—unless they are extremely minor and requested early on.

You also need to be aware that some contractors and manufacturers charge a restocking fee whether it's a toilet you're sending back or just a few rolls of wallpaper.

In the case of Becker's clients who asked for the gym, the change added $125,000. The project won't add a significant time delay, however, because both additions are being done simultaneously, the architect explains.

HOW TO AVOID COSTLY CHANGES

How can you avoid the additional costs and delays resulting from change orders? There's no guarantee that you can unless you leave the plans completely alone, and there are certain steps you can take to increase that possibility. One way is to spend an adequate—if not excessive—amount of time in the planning stage and be sure you and the architect or contractor understand your goals and can satisfy them. Also go to showrooms and look at choices—several times if necessary—if you have a hard time visualizing what you've picked.

If you also don't understand how a plan works when looking at only two dimensions on the blueprints, ask your architect to draw more elevations, or show you on one of the many computer programs mentioned earlier that can generate how any room will look in three dimensions. Or, have him take you to a completed project so you can see how a cabinet really looks in person—both on the outside and inside.

Be sure you also note the change order cutoff dates in your contract—which are the dates after which changes become more costly. If you even begin to get a sinking feeling that you want to make a change, let your architect, designer, or contractor know ASAP.

IF YOU DO MAKE A CHANGE, WHAT IS THE COST?

If you proceed with the change, ask exactly how much it will cost in terms of materials and labor. Most contractors will have you fill out a special change order form. If you have any credits from materials or products, you may not incur extra expenses. But many contractors charge extra for making a change regardless of the cost—sometimes 10 to 25 percent on top of the materials and labor. Also ask how the change order may delay the project. Get this information in writing as a proposed change order first while you decide, and then again as a final change order if you proceed.

JILL WEINBERG (Highland Park, Illinois)

Jill Weinberg, Midwest Director of the United States Holocaust Memorial Museum, says the greatest tragedy she and her husband Bernard encountered when redoing their kitchen occurred after they selected and installed the "perfect cabinets and perfect granite countertops." The granite was delivered, and it turned out to be too small. The length was okay but the width wasn't wide enough. The couple felt they had checked all the details a million times, but somehow someone messed up. "We couldn't make the granite grow on the island," Jill says, "but our cabinetmaker saved the day. He removed the cabinets, cut them back and reinstalled them so the granite fit. Of course, we had to pay him for his additional work because it wasn't his fault." Her advice to others is to check every detail, even more times than you think necessary.

But don't ever feel that you made a horrid mistake. Architects make changes in their own homes all the time, Becker says. He and his wife Nancy, also an architect, planned a powder room in their suburban home, then changed it to a full bathroom in the midst of construction, which added $4,000 to their costs. They also decided to finish their basement for their four children to use and add a lower-level half-bathroom, something they had planned to do down the road. "We figured, like everyone else often does, as long as we were doing other work in the house, we might as well do that." That "Why not?" cost the couple a hefty $20,000.

RED FLAGS THAT THROW YOU OFF TRACK

No matter how much you plan, inspect the work in progress and communicate with your architect, builder, and tradespeople. You may not make the master bedroom closets large enough because you forgot that you have a large collection of shoes. You may forget to design a large enough bathroom so you can have a separate shower and tub. Or, you may not have enough electrical outlets in your living room for lamps because you thought you had included a sufficient number of cans in the ceiling and in the built-in china cabinets. Some of these can be easily rectified for a bit more money and time. Others will have to be left as they are unless you're want to rip out what's been done and start over.

LESLIE STERN (Chicago, Illinois)

When renovating a client's home, Leslie Stern had her photographer take pictures of their home, just days before it was destroyed by a fire started in a neighbor's home. They moved out for six months, and redid the home using an insurance company. Fortunately, they had photographed everything for insurance purposes.

RHONDA SANDERSON (Highland Park, Illinois)

Rhonda Sanderson, a public relations specialist in Chicago, said while redoing her bathroom, "I was told only to sink so much money in but put three times more in, though not voluntarily. My remodelers were firemen, who on their off days, redid my bathroom. Their workmanship was fabulous, but each time they came over with a sample of what they could do, each was more beautiful. I stupidly didn't ask does this mean 'Double the money?' I also had a walk-in closet, and they extended it in the bedroom area, but when they put the pole up they didn't find the studs and my 30 suits came crashing down with two massive chunks of the wall out. Somebody else came in to finish the work."

HOW DO YOU HANDLE A PROBLEM THAT CAN'T BE CHANGED?

What can you do if something can't be changed in a timely fashion or for a reasonable amount of money? Try to brainstorm with your architect, builder, or designer about alternatives. Always approach him in a nonaccusatory manner. "It's best to say, 'I'm concerned about the following. Could we look at it together,'" suggests architect Charles Schagrin. "A little sugar will go a long way with me and others."

Why Disasters May Occur

Several professionals came up with the following reasons disasters typically occur:

- Clients fail to make detailed enough lists of what they want.
- Clients fail to make timely choices, make quick decisions without giving their selections great thought, or make choices based on what others want rather than on what they really love and need.
- Clients continue to make changes, forgetting their priorities and the overall scheme.
- Clients or their professionals are disorganized and don't order equipment, appliances, and materials in a timely fashion. As a result, they have to make new choices or settle for different products and materials.

In the case of the closet that was too small, there may be space in another part of the room to add a second closet or you may be able to find a piece of furniture such as an armoire that works. In the case of the bathroom, you may have to make do with a combination unit or perhaps squeeze a tub into another bathroom. When it comes to the lighting, outlets are fairly simple to add, though you should try to do so before you paint so you don't have to have your painter come back at additional cost. For anyone who can afford to make a correction, the cost is worth the peace of mind you gain.

If changes have become significant, your working relationship with your contractor is failing miserably, and you've spoken up repeatedly and written notes about your complaints yet you can't seem to resolve the differences, it may be time to part company. But how do you bow out of your contract ethically and legally without losing more than the shirt on your back? A breach of contract is the only way to terminate a contract or fire a contractor, builder, or architect. What constitutes a breach? When the professional has refused to perform to the contract's terms. You may be lucky, or you may be stuck. That's why it's important to try to keep talking and resolve differences through the big "C" words—Compromise and Communicate.

✓ **CHECKLIST**

Danger Signs That You're Almost over the Edge

If your voice is 100 decibels louder than everyone else's any time someone talks to you, you just might be over the edge, says Barbara Bader, licensed clinical social worker and psychotherapist in private practice in St. Louis. Some telltale signs:

1. You're yelling three times a day—at inanimate objects! If anyone looks at you crosseyed or yells, you crumble, raise an eyebrow, and say, "What do you mean by that?"   Yes ❑   No ❑   Sometimes ❑

2. You can't eat or you never stop eating. Emotional eating might lead you to gobble up all your children's Halloween candy or every Girl Scout cookie in the house.   Yes ❑   No ❑   Sometimes ❑

3. You can't sleep. When you're supposed to be sleeping, your routine imitates that of a lactating mother with a newborn. You're up doing laundry, reading a book, or cleaning at 3 AM It's time to take an Excedrin PM.   Yes ❑   No ❑   Sometimes ❑

4. You're so focused on the fact that the plumber didn't come on time that you forget you're frying an egg and the stove is in flames. Or you think you're cooking a pot roast, but you never turned the oven on.   Yes ❑   No ❑   Sometimes ❑

5. Decisions get blown out of proportion. You want a robin's egg blue sink. It can only be this exact color. White, pink, or another blue will not suffice, and you spend hours trying to find the color. You get so caught up in the process that you've lost your perspective. Minutiae becomes terribly important.   Yes ❑   No ❑   Sometimes ❑

If you answered yes to two or more of these, you need to step back and reevaluate your priorities. This doesn't mean running to a shrink. Perhaps you can turn to a mentor or good friend whose judgment you trust. Sit down with the friend, take a day off, and get this out of your system. If you have children, they are more important than building any house or room. Don't sweep them under the rug during this process.

PART THREE

You've Almost Made It

CHAPTER 19

Go Ahead and Laugh

Humor Can Get You Through

JON AND HILDE PENHALLURICK (Placitas, New Mexico)

When you build a house from scratch, you can't take it too seriously, says John Penhallurick, a health care administrator. "I found we had to be flexible. When we were building, we were constantly trying to decide what we were going to do and who would do what. Someone has to take the lead, but how do you decide who that will be. We sectioned up the house and each of us made selections in those rooms we thought would be most suited to us. I made choices in the living room and master bath and Hilde made selections in the kitchen and guest bathroom."

Homebuilding and remodeling require a sense of humor. Consider this scenario: The contractor walks into your home to begin a remodeling. He seems enthusiastic. Although he's a bit intimidating (he's the height of Michael Jordan with the body of John Goodman), you like his friendly manner. You trust him. He came highly recommended.

A few days into the job, you make a strong suggestion to him about where you want a window to be placed in the new family room. He contradicts you. You don't want that window here, you want it there, you say. You throw into the equation that you don't even like the window with its fake muntins. He shrugs and continues to do what he wants. You're quite put out. Through a tight smile, you ask him to let you explain. He half listens. You grab the blueprints and point to where the window is supposed to go. He drones on about how you're making a mistake.

Stop. Consider your options. You can recoil and give in, but that won't work because you'll have a migraine headache for a week. You can't change your opinion and he's not about to surrender to yours. At that point, you can mutter, "Put the darn window where it's supposed to go. Period. The end." Not so smart. Remember, he's bigger than you are. This is ludicrous, you think. Ever since you started building your home you haven't had any fun and you've lost your sense of humor. So, you seize the moment and parlay it into something absurd or funny. Go up to any object in the room (the family pet will suffice) and say with the comedic timing of Bob Hope, "Hey, could you please talk to this guy about where to put the window?" Both you and the contractor might end up laughing, and it's a sure bet that you'll get your way.

Keep that sense of humor firmly affixed. "Are you kidding?" said a doctor who just finished living through a remodeling. "Mine went out the window with the rest of the debris when we built our addition. Nothing was funny. All I knew was that I was spending tons of money and it took forever. I was so compulsive about everything; I felt I had to be on top of each detail. Every night when I came home, I inspected the job. I probably made myself crazy. In retrospect, if I had left it alone and relaxed more, it probably would have turned out alright anyway. Our contractor was really pretty good."

"Have a sense of humor?" another homebuyer asked rhetorically. "How do you laugh about the hot electrical current that tears down a cable and blows out four new appliances and ruins one?"

How do you laugh when you walk into your new kitchen and the lighting looks like something Mr. Spock might have used on the starship Enterprise. In addition, the lights are humming in what seems like quad stereo. You need earplugs and a cure for insomnia.

How do you laugh when your contractor calls you after six months to say that not all of the kitchen cabinets have come in yet and neither have your children's bathroom fixtures. This means you'll be eating fattening fast food in the living room for a few more weeks and keeping that plastic covering on the furniture and lamp shades like your grandparents did. While you're ruminating about this drastic turn of events, the phone rings. You run for it and trip over a 2-by-4-foot piece of lumber. By now you're ready to blast off at . . . guess who? Yes, the contractor. Catch your breath and count to ten. Look at the absurdity of the situation and laugh. It's a lot healthier than getting and staying mad. Remember, you both have the same goal—to get the job done well in the quickest amount of time.

A homebuilder can become excessively neurotic. A few of us still believe that a worldwide conspiracy exists to make homebuilding or remodeling as difficult as possible. So, before and during the process, we try to steel ourselves. We pick up a few clever tips from magazines, talk to others who've been through it multiple times, watch videotapes, read books, scan the Internet in the hopes of making the job ahead smoother. While these tips are supposed to help, they are often confusing and complicated. And rarely do you find out what to do when the going gets tough and you can't get going.

This Damn House!

Writer-editor Dennis Hinkamp, who lives in Utah, says he has come to tolerate fist fights on TV where nobody gets hurt, and the improbability of love at first sight in movies. But he cannot tolerate TV shows that outright lie. "Shows like *This Old House, Home Improvement,* and *The Jolly Carpenter,* have probably contributed to more marital disputes and bodily injury than all the sleazy soap operas put together. The illusion that you can install a new bathtub in an afternoon is about as close to reality as being able to make $1,000 a week stuffing envelopes at home. These are the shows that should come with government warnings. 'This show has been rated GC-13 (general contractor—$13,000). It contains graphic depictions of home improvement, which may not be appropriate for the mechanically impaired. Viewer discretion advised.' Just think how many bruised egos and scraped fingers could be saved with this simple warning label. Just for balance, I'm going to start my own show and call it *This Damn House!* My show will feature reality-based episodes, sort of like those live police action shows."

You could turn to eating, drinking, complaining, or even yelling, but the problems won't go away and you'll be left with a heaache, muscle ache or stomach ache.

The healthiest approach is to have a good laugh or treat yourself to a good time. You're better off buying drug stocks, learning to exercise, and eating right (yogurt instead of ice cream). However, there are many little things you can do every day to give yourself a reward without the calories, cholesterol, chin-ups, and stress. These tiny things can make a big difference in the way you feel.

The bottom line: Worry less about the house and more about yourself and your loved ones going through the war zone with you.

45 IDEAS THAT WILL MAKE YOU LAUGH OR CHEER YOU UP (WE'RE SURE YOU CAN THINK OF MORE)

1. Hug, cuddle, snuggle, laugh, hold hands with your partner. It says, "I'm here. You're not alone. We're both in the same boat—or house—or soon to be house."

2. Take the family on a camping trip (or camp out on the grounds of your new home or in your new addition) and have everyone sleep in one tent. Or camp out at home in one room—if you haven't been forced to already. It might be wise to film it for posterity's sake. Also, this might make a good video for "America's Funniest Home Videos" and you can recoup some of the funds you've spent on your project.

3. You're over budget anyway, so treat yourselves to a good expensive dinner. What's a few more dollars?

4. Get in the lotus position and say "Ommmmmmmm." Learning how to breathe can improve your emotional health and get rid of unhealthy emotional patterns that may cause you to turn into a shrieking crazy person.

5. Get into something new, splurge on a psychic or palm reader; jump from a plane; learn to belly dance; be a mensch and do a volunteer project with children, the elderly, or homeless to get outside yourself and help someone really in need. It isn't worth it to wallow in toxic thoughts.

6. Escape. Leave and go to a pampering spa to tone up, trim down, and be waited on where the clients have as much time on their hands as they do diamonds. For those whose budgets have gone through the stratosphere, go to a less expensive no-frills spa with a holistic approach or try a spa treatment at home. Add a massage, a pedicure, and a facial.

7. Try retail therapy. It's cheaper than a shrink, safer than drugs, and a boon to the economy. If you're really pressed funds-wise, go to a cheap retail outlet or go to an expensive one that is having a great sale.

8. Complain successfully to make you feel like you have control over something. Call the customer service department of a store where you bought something you don't like. Start with a sales clerk, move up to a

supervisor, then manager. Begin by being pleasant and end by being steadfast. You must get your way for this treatment to work.

9. Take the weekend off and get out of town. Forget about the project. Find the airport, train, or bus station. Board the first transport you see and don't look back until Monday morning. Most likely, no work was done over the weekend anyway.

10. Buy Tracy Kidder's book, *House,* about his experience building a home. It's well-written and lets you know other intelligent folk have suffered similarly.

11. If you're masochistic, watch funny movies about homebuilding: *Mr. Blandings Builds His Dream House* with Cary Grant and Myrna Loy; *The Money Pit* with Tom Hanks and Shelly Long, *Father of the Bride* with Steve Martin and Diane Keaton, or *Miss Grant Takes Richmond* with Lucille Ball and William Holden.

12. Write down positive moments during your construction in a journal, and draw on them when you experience the inevitable gut-wrenching problems that occur.

13. If remodeling, take a few minutes to tidy the cramped space you've been living in. Add some fresh flowers to brighten the area. After cleaning, check your schedule and if you have time, reward yourself by going to a good movie or watching a TV program you've been anxious to see.

14. Take ten minutes to relax and listen to an inspirational tape by any of the many inspirational authors or spiritualists promoting inner peace.

15. Take a long walk, then meet someone for a latte—or better yet, a big fattening milkshake. If you're into healthy eating, try a fruit shake made with yogurt.

16. Put some music on and dance, or go two-stepping and let the child in you come out. Shop for the outfit—cowboy hat, boots, short flared skirt (or long, lean jeans), and bandanna—before you go.

17. Savor simple pleasures: the sun rising, wonderful smells from flowers or candles, and the sounds of water. Touch everything around you—feel the coolness of marble, the warmth of wool.

18. Have a good talk with a close friend—perhaps someone else going through a remodeling or home building. Or better yet, form a support group and complain to each other to your heart's content. Gather five friends and ask each to invite two others. Bring in a speaker, perhaps an architect or contractor, to present his side of the remodeling or building equation.

19. Sniff out new fast food joints/truck stops and parlay your experiences eating fast food into writing a restaurant review, because by the time your construction is finished you'll have been to them all.

20. Stay at a hotel in town for the weekend. It might be expensive, but it's worth the respite—unless you run into your contractor who's staying there on your money. Plan your outing in advance. Buy a city guide several weeks before you break ground and reserve a seat for something special such as live entertainment.

21. Make spot inspections in the new house in the evening. Bring a good flashlight and wear old shoes or boots. It might be more pleasant than visiting during the day. No one will be around and you can take good notes. Then role play what you plan to say to the contractor the next day and have your spouse or significant other back you up.

22. Evening inspections are also a good time to check out your new neighbors. For this you might need a really good sense of humor. Make sure they don't have their cars parked on the front lawn next to their barbecue pits and pink flamingos. It might be too late to do anything about it, however.

23. Eyeball the garden next door to make sure the plants don't have leaves that resemble marijuana.

24. Check the license plates in your new neighborhood and make sure there isn't a vanity plate that says, "Charles Manson."

25. Make sure the kitchen next door doesn't have a neon blinking light that says, "Eat here."

26. If you've forgotten how to laugh, buy a good book of jokes or cartoons.

27. Rent or watch some silly old TV shows such as *I Love Lucy* or *Saturday Night Live* reruns.

28. Throw out some furnishings that you've always hated and buy some new ones to replace them. You may have forgotten how bad your taste was.

29. Don't immediately demand changes from the contractor when you see something you don't like. You may be charged extra for the time and materials. Instead say: "I'm concerned about the molding in the entrance hall and here are my concerns. Walk me through it so I can be convinced that this is really what we chose." The contractor will be more agreeable and might even change the molding for free as a favor to you.

30. Don a pair of headphones, a pair of wraparound sunglasses, lay back, and close your eyes, without a mantra.

31. Try biofeedback to relax (but beware that wiring your scalp with electrodes can leave your hair sticking out like Bart Simpson's on a good day).

32. Toast your construction in stages. At the end, have a launching party. Use champagne, of course, but don't forget to wrap the bottle in cloth to prevent spectators from being hit by flying glass.

33. If that doesn't appeal, plan a housewarming party, and have everyone bring their own remodeling or building horror stories. Have them bring photographs too, if they can. If you liked your workcrew, invite some of them or hold a separate thank-you party for them. If you didn't, post invitations all over the site and be sure they know they're not invited.

34. Go skinny dipping in the new pool or hot tub. Do a little landscaping—plan your yard or mow the grass—which will improve your optimism while getting you closer to the end.

35. Read a good murder mystery and fantasize that the victim is your contractor, architect, or builder.

36. Reread a classic: *Pride and Prejudice, War and Peace,* a Shakespeare play. Make a list of difficult words, look them up, memorize their meanings, and increase your vocabulary the next time you go off on a tirade about your contractor.

37. Invest for a better future: get into the stock market, watch the financial news stations, and surf the Net. Go into a financial chat room and get different ideas on what's hot on Wall Street.

38. Bathe yourself in luxury. Buy some exotic soaps, lotions, and oils in various scents made with fresh plant and floral extracts and enriched with natural oils, or shampoos with unusual aromas such as lavender or apple.

39. Go play 18 holes of golf—which may turn out to be more frustrating than any construction. When you're through, you'll realize that frustration is relative.

40. Clip a lot of coupons. At least you'll feel like you're saving money in some way. And don't forget to bring them along when you grocery shop.

41. Talk about the expense of the new house, and the old one will look better than ever.

42. Plan a trip you will take after the remodeling's done. Once you start unpacking boxes and cleaning up, you'll need to get away again.

43. Stop your subscriptions to shelter magazines for a year so you don't get any more ideas about how to fix up your house. And be sure not to peek at them at the beauty parlor or doctor's offices either.
44. Send your spouse out of town, especially when he or she becomes so involved in the project he starts sounding like Martha Stewart.
45. Take a ride on a motorcycle, a horse, a helicopter, a hot air balloon, or a roller coaster at an amusement park—chances are you've been on one during the entire project. In either case, you'll be glad when the ride comes to an end and life returns to normal.

CONSTRUCTIVE TIPS

Five Funny Books and Videos

Books
Lilly White by Susan Isaacs (Harper Collins/paperback)
Animal Husbandry by Laura Zigman (Bantam)
Ladder of Years by Anne Tyler (Random House/paperback and hardback)
Thank You for Smoking by Christopher Buckley (Harper Collins/paperback)
I'll Take It by Paul Rudnick (Ballantine/paperback)

Videos
Mrs. Doubtfire
Heartburn
Happy Gilmore
Austin Powers—International Man of Mystery
House Sitter

20

It's Time to Make Your Move

It's time to move into your dream house. Everything is the way you want it, down to the placement of each light switch and electrical outlet. You worked closely with the builder to oversee each detail from the bay window in the dining room to the transomed French doors, beefed up moldings in the living room, and the glossy white woodwork and pale yellow walls in the family room.

You've also been arranging, organizing, and decorating your new home in your head and on paper for months, starting the day you signed your names on the bottom line after finding a lot in a small new development.

Reality hits. You have to take everything you own, pack it up, and move it to your new abode. This includes your antiques, piano, trinkets, clothing, and furnishings. Are you going to do it yourself or call a mover? Can you use one mover to do it all? Do you need a special mover to transport your 50-year-old Steinway baby grand and your 150-year-old tallcase clock?

You start to panic in the middle of the night thinking about the voluminous amounts of work ahead and whether you'll find places for all your possessions. What if something gets lost or broken?

The worst disasters are those you don't anticipate. You want the move to be simple and you don't want to antagonize your new neighbors in the process with huge moving trucks blocking the street for hours. There's no reason to pop Xanax or Valium. Once again plan ahead and the move will be smoother than your new asphalt driveway on an icy winter morning.

"Moving is a mult-task activity where many things are overlooked or forgotten and come moving day it can hit you in the face—hard," says Cliff Saxton, vice president of communications, United Van Lines Inc. in St. Louis.

There's a rhythm to moving, it takes organization, thought, and hard work. Begin with a list of what you need to do and when. Another approach is to create a moving time table calendar on your computer or use the checklist in Figure 20.1.

JO ELLEN AND SANDY SCHONWALD (Long Boat Key, Florida)

Timing is crucial when you move. Sandy and Jo Ellen Schonwald took possession of their Florida condominium in March, which was the best thing that could have happened. "We did most of our work off season, we were able to get good prices, good people, and we weren't waiting in line for tradespeople to arrive. It was a blessing."

A MOVING TIMETABLE: FOUR TO SIX WEEKS BEFORE THE MOVE

The following countdown, a compilation of suggestions from various movers, lists how and when to get your move in motion.

Solicit bids from different movers or call truck rental companies. You can either open the Yellow Pages and make cold calls or ask friends and relatives for suggestions. Also, surf the Net. For example, you can check out Microsurf Internet Services, Inc. for mover quotes and other related information. There is moving information for every state, including prices and statistics for full-service and do-it-yourself movers.

If you're moving on a weekend, you might have to start calling movers or rental companies at least two months before moving day.

If you're moving a short distance, you might use a good—but less expensive—local mover. If moving a long distance, don't be cheap. You want all your valuables to arrive at your new location intact.

If you're doing it yourself, call various truck rental companies such as Ryder, U-Haul, Budget, and Sears. They will quote prices, conditions, and insurance options for the truck, as well as quote costs for boxes, bubble paper, and tape.

FIGURE **20.1**   **Moving Inventory**

Kitchen, Bedroom, Children's Room		Living Room, Dining Room, Den	
Item	**Qty.**	**Item**	**Qty.**
Bassinet		Bookcase	
Bed, King		Breakfast Table	
Bed, Queen		Buffet	
Bed, Double		Buffet with Hutch Top	
Bed, Single		Chair, Arm	
Bed, Youth		Chair, Dining	
Bureau, Dresser, or Chest of Drawers		Chair Occasional	
Cedar Chest		Chair, Overstuffed Recliner	
Chair, Straight		Chair, Rocker	
Clothes Hamper		China Cabinet	
Crib		Corner Cabinet	
Dishwasher		Couch, Sofa	
Double Dresser		Desk	
Dresser Chair or Bench		Drapes	
Dryer, Clothes		Extension Table	
High Chair		Floor Lamp	
Ironing Board		Hide-a-Bed	
Night Table		Mirror	
Playpen		Rugs or Pads	
Range		Tables, Coffee or End	
Refrigerator		Table Lamp	
Roaster (Rotisserie)		Table Radio or Stereo	
Sewing Machine (Upright)		Television Combination	
Sewing Machine (Portable)		Television, Portable	
Toy Chest		Television, Console	
Utility Cart			
Vacuum Cleaner			
Wardrobe Chest (Armoire)			
Washing Machine			

FIGURE 20.1 Moving Inventory (Continued)

Garage, Patio, Tools, and Toys		Boxes	
Item	Qty.	Item	Qty.
Barbecue		Small Box (1.5 cu ft.)	
Bicycle		Medium Box (3 cu ft.)	
Card Table		Large Box (4.5 cu ft.)	
Chaise Lounge		Dish-Pack Box (6 cu ft.)	
Clothes Basket		Wardrobe Box (13 cu ft.)	
Cot, Folding			
Fan			
Filing Cabinet			
Foot Locker			
Garden Cart			
Garden Hose & Tools			
Golf Bag, Clubs			
Heater			
Lawn Chair			
Lawn Mower			
Lawn Swing			
Packing Barrel			
Picnic Bench			
Stepladder			
Swing Set			
Tool Chest			
Tricycle			
Wagon			
Wheelbarrow			

Source: Ryder Moving Services

ALICE AND KENNETH STARR (McLean, Virginia)

In adding a two-story addition on to their home, Alice and Kenneth Starr decided to do themselves and the builder a favor and take a two-week vacation. "That way the builders do not have to clean up every night and can work straight through to get the job done faster," says Alice. It also helped them avoid the mess. "We went to England for two weeks and came back to find a new kitchen. Of course, you have to plan it right so that all the materials and equipment are ready when you move out."

Costs and Insurance

How do the various movers charge? If you are moving locally, an hourly fee is typical. If moving far away, go for a flat rate. To determine cost, a sales rep will come to your home and do a survey of goods. This is only a ballpark guesstimate, unfortunately. Other costs, according to Saxton of United, "include materials provided, packing, shuttle or stair carry, and valuation coverage selected based on tariff provisions, unless you request a binding estimate. This estimates all transportation costs and other charges, excluding charges for valuation coverage, requested when the computation and estimates are performed. Without a binding estimate, costs cannot be pegged until after the move based on weight and distance." The load will be weighed before and after the move.

Talk to movers about what they're responsible for and what they're not—a scratch on a floor or chipped paint. If something gets broken, to whom do you direct the complaint? How long will it take for them to respond? When do you pay for the move? Upfront? After it's over? If the moving out is higher than estimated, what happens? Are personal checks accepted? Preapproved charge cards? Ask if there's a downpayment.

Also find out what else is in the contract. Read the fine print or have your lawyer do it. Most movers will not assume liability for valuables—documents, money, jewelry, vintage wine, antiques.

United has a Full-Value Coverage Plan with your choice of no deductible, or a $250 or $500 deductible. "The minimum value you declare must be at least equal to the weight of your shipment multiplied by $3.50," says Saxton. "Valuation is not insurance; it is a tariff-based level of motor carrier liability." There's a lump-sum value (how much space in the truck a shipment occupies).

Packing

Next decide whether you're going to pack—and unpack—or have the movers do it. If left to the movers, packing is usually done the day or a few days before the move.

If the job is up to you, when should you start and what types of cartons should you use? Is it okay to go to the supermarket and ask for boxes or do they tend to crush too easily? Usually you find the containers.

If you are doing it yourself, your choice of cartons should include extra-large cartons for large outdoor items and framed pictures; large cartons for pillows, sports equipment, and lamp shades; medium cartons for clothing, bedding, and toys; small cartons for books, CDs, and files; dish cartons for glasses, china, and collectibles; and specialty cartons such as a dish cell kit with dividers, mirror cartons, and wardrobe cartons. Some movers also have lamp cartons, electronics cartons, or TV/microwave cartons. The best container for appliances is the factory box with the original packing. One woman complained that her husband saved every original box and the boxes junked up their basement. However, when it came time to move, all the electronics including the family's PC went into the original cartons. Her husband kept saying, "See. I told you these boxes would come in handy some day." He was right.

Books should be placed flat in small boxes so you won't get a hernia picking them up. If you have tons, you might donate paperbacks. Try to keep each box under 30 pounds, if you move yourself. Three or four dishes should be rolled together in newspaper to form a stack that is set in the box on its side. You can put glassware—bowls, cups, goblets—on top. Glassware should be wrapped separately in bubble wrap. Nestle cups and bowls. Cushion with towels. Put cups in the box upside down. Close and seal the box with packing tape. Stack pots and pans and cushion with paper.

Appliances should be cleaned, serviced, and packed with accessories placed in plastic bags. If moving yourself, tape down movable parts, cover with pads, and tie securely.

Hanging clothing items should be placed in wardrobe boxes, but small items can be left in bureau drawers.

Wrap lamp shades in bubble wrap and place in a box. Wrap and pack bases separately. Wrap and pack small mirrors, artwork and frames. Larger versions put in plastic and cover with cardboard.

As soon as you find a mover, begin. Gather supplies in one place—the cartons, cushioning paper, tissue, tape, scissors, markers.

Pack in small doses, one room at a time. Label boxes by room and mark "fragile" and "this side up" when needed. Perhaps number the boxes and compile a master list. Write it down or type it into your computer. Take photos or a video of valuable items.

Don't let the movers pack or move valuable items. If you're doing the packing, you might set these aside and, if possible, move them yourself. Check with your insurance company to make sure you have enough coverage in case valuables are lost or damaged during a move.

Don't pack everything. Set one box aside and pack it with items you'll need that first day in your new house. Make sure to mark any boxes you'll need before the rest of your moving shipment arrives and, if need be, keep it separate.

What to Set Aside and What to Pack Last

Put together a travel kit of aspirin, band-aids, bottle opener, flashlight, keys, paper plates, plastic utensils, paper towels, disposable cups, tissue, alarm clock, toiletries, and some toys and games.

Each family member should pack a separate suitcase with a change of clothes, cosmetics, and medications—similar to what you'd put in your carry-on luggage on a plane. And don't forget to keep your pet supplies accessible.

The final box you pack should have towels, a few tools (you might need to fix something, hang a picture, or put a bed together), more toiletries, soap, canned foods, some utensils, and dishes for the first meal. Also, you might want to pack a picnic lunch or buy some sandwiches to eat either on the road or when you get to your new home.

BETWEEN WEEKS TWO TO FOUR

Draw a floorplan of your new home to see how you want to place furniture. Give away extras to charity (and get a tax deduction), have a garage sale, or put them in storage. If you don't really need certain items, why pay to move them if the move is based on weight. If your washer and dryer are getting old, sell them and buy new ones when you arrive at your new destination.

Start to clean out closets, bookshelves, and your home office. Throw away or donate junk. Tackle the kids' rooms and get rid of old toys and clothing to drop more weight. They'll want to keep more of their things than you do, so bargain and bribe.

Records for You and Your Pet

If moving out of town, get medical records for you and your pet. Make sure your pet is licensed and vaccinated properly. Find out the best way to move your pet. Should he ride in the car with you? Fly on the plane? You might need to tranquilize your pet. Call the airline to find out its policies about bringing animals on board. You might not want your pet to fly in the luggage compartment of the plane, especially during extreme temperatures.

Get all school and medical records for you and your kids too—pediatrician, eye doctor, Ob-Gyn, dentist, allergy doctor, internist. Ask these practitioners for recommendations of doctors in your new location. Do the same with your pharmacy. Get a printout of all prescription drugs. And don't forget to obtain copies of your other records from lawyers, accountants, and stock brokers.

Contact your insurance companies and banks to apprise them of your move. If you can, arrange to transfer funds and the contents of your safety deposit box to a new bank or branch. If moving to a new city, select a bank and arrange a mortgage before the move.

Issue change-of-address cards to friends, relatives, magazines, charge accounts, banks, clubs, newspapers, and the post office.

THE LAST COUPLE OF WEEKS

It's getting close to M-day, and it's time to notify utilities, cable, and telephone companies. Be sure to give them both your old and new addresses. Arrange for utility hook-ups there; disconnections here.

Make sure you have picked up all items you sent to repair shops or dry cleaners. If you've found borrowed items such as videos, Nintendo and computer games, or library books, now's the time to take them back. Conversely, get back anything you've lent.

You're now down to just days before the move. No more than a week before, cancel mail and newspapers.

Get rid of old paint, gasoline for your mower (drain the gas from the mower and other power tools). A mover won't take these. If you are packing something liquid, fasten and secure the lid with tape and place it inside a sealed plastic bag. Have a plumber detach your gas dryer.

Decide what to do with your plants. Movers won't take them. If they're precious, such as a valuable orchid collection, you might arrange to have them transported by a nursery or florist.

Before you defrost and clean out your refrigerator and freezer, eat as much as you can, especially frozen foods—though you don't have to gorge yourself all in one sitting. Seal open boxed foods, cover the holes on salt and paper shakers. Canisters should have tight-fitting lids that you may want to tape.

Have a final evening celebration in your old house. Do it by candlelight. Bring in a nice dinner and consume a bottle or two or three of wine—it's less wine to transport. Invite your closest friends, take photographs, and write down your thoughts if you're keeping a journal.

MOVING DAY

First off, make sure you have someone to watch the children. If you're moving yourself, pack the truck with the loading door as close to your home as possible, suggests Ryder Moving Services. Load your truck in quarters from floor or ceiling. Tie down each quarter and fill open spaces with small boxes to keep the load stable. Load the largest items first—appliances then furniture. Stack boxes of equal size and weight. Put long items such as mattresses, sofas, and tables on edge against truck walls, and tie down. Mirrors and frames stay upright, and can be tied to truck walls or placed between mattresses. Odd-shaped items go along walls or on top of the load. Roll rugs and place them in the center.

If you've hired a moving company, supervise the loading. Don't worry about getting in the way. You have to be on top of what the movers are doing. Be sure the driver has your new address and directions. Get the name of the driver and the van number. Coordinate time of arrival.

Place instructions for the movers (which you can type or write out) in both the old and new houses.

Make sure the movers know where to find you at all times. If you have a cell or car phone, give them the number. If you don't, keep the phone in your old house connected until the day after your move.

Check each room of your house to make sure the movers took what they were supposed to. Don't leave your old residence until the moving company is finished.

Either vacuum or sweep out your old home. Turn out the lights, leave a key with a realtor or neighbor, and place garage door openers, pool keys, or keys to the wine cellar on the kitchen counter or in the mailbox.

When you arrive at your new home, check utility hook-ups. Walk around and turn on all the lights, flush the toilets, turn on all the faucets.

Once the movers have unloaded the truck, pull out your master inventory list and make sure all items are there and the right boxes are in the right rooms. If you're doing the unpacking, this step makes it less of a chore. Inspect furniture. Jot down any missing or damaged items on the bill or receipt. Make sure the delivery papers are signed by the driver. Don't dispose of damaged goods until you've conferred with the claims office. Contact the mover ASAP to report damaged or missing items.

Once your bed is assembled, put on the sheets and blankets and fall into it. Sleep as though you don't have a care in the world. You'll need all your energy the following day for unpacking boxes and approaching the many jobs ahead. But remember: all does not have to be done at once. Didn't someone once say that Rome was not built in a day?

Taking a Break

After you move in, you may be exhausted and in great need of a vacation. Consider renting a condo or villa. The following are several good Web sites:

- www.10kvacationrentals.com
  (covers thousands of areas and offers photographs for some)
- www.nerdworld.com
  (covers great ground so enter the words "vacation rentals" in the search box)
- www.vrma.com
  (offers luxurious rentals, which may or may not be in your budget)
- www.accommodations.com
  (offers listings primarily in Florida, Arkansas, and Utah—some with photographs)

CONSTRUCTIVE TIPS

Checking Everyone's Status

Be sure that everyone in the family is ready to move. As difficult as this may be, there are ways to ease the transition.

- Get each family member an address book to list names, addresses, and phone numbers of friends, colleagues, neighborhood people, and places they don't want to forget—even the local pizza parlor or flower store they've frequented for years. Find new resources in your new neighborhood, even before you make the move, that are comparable to those you are leaving behind (i.e., Girl Scouts, bowling league).
- Get every family member a scrapbook and inexpensive throwaway camera to take pictures of favorite neighborhood haunts, including their favorite rooms in the house. You might videotape your friends as well.
- Make a video of your current home or apartment. It's another good keepsake and good for insurance purposes.
- Throw a party so you can say goodbye to your favorite neighbors and friends; ask everyone to bring a memory or souvenir.
- Make a top ten list of everything you love about the new house and area; maybe even make an additional list of the top ten things you always disliked about the house and area you're leaving.

21

100 Ways to Make Your Newly Built or Remodeled House a Home

DECORATING TIPS: WHAT A DIFFERENCE DECORATING MAKES

You've built your new home or remodeled a room or two. Now it's time to turn the structure into a liveable space with some handy decorating and finishing. The last thing most of you want is to turn over your money and your life to a designer in exchange for a heavy-handed look or something that doesn't reflect your taste or lifestyle. But your possessions are scattered all around and you need to get rid of some furnishings, add some others, light the rooms, and organize the contents. You might want to rearrange the seating, paint the walls, accessorize, or recover chairs. For success without any further frustration or a nervous breakdown—considering all the decisions you've made up to this point—a decorator may be just what you need.

As you've watched your house or remodeling near completion, you've begun to imagine what it will look like when it's furnished. Perhaps you've already worked with a decorator. If you haven't, you've most likely subscribed to some shelter magazines or picked them up at the supermarket. In addition to the usual roster—*Better Homes & Gardens, House Beautiful, Metropolitan Home,* and *House & Garden*—don't neglect the specialized issues that zero in specifically on kitchens and bathrooms, remodelings, and gardening, depending on your decorating challenge. Also remember not to discount the *arrangement* of your treasures in your new space. As you can see from the floor plans in Figures 21.1 and 21.2, there are ways to make your rooms more inviting and useable.

FIGURE **21.1** Plan A (Before)

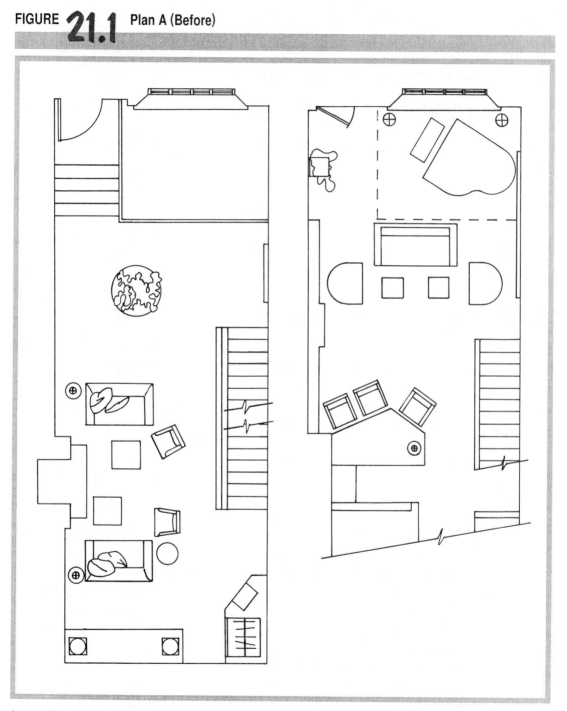

Source: Design by Cindy Christensen, illustration by Brian Connor

FIGURE **21.2** Plan B (After)

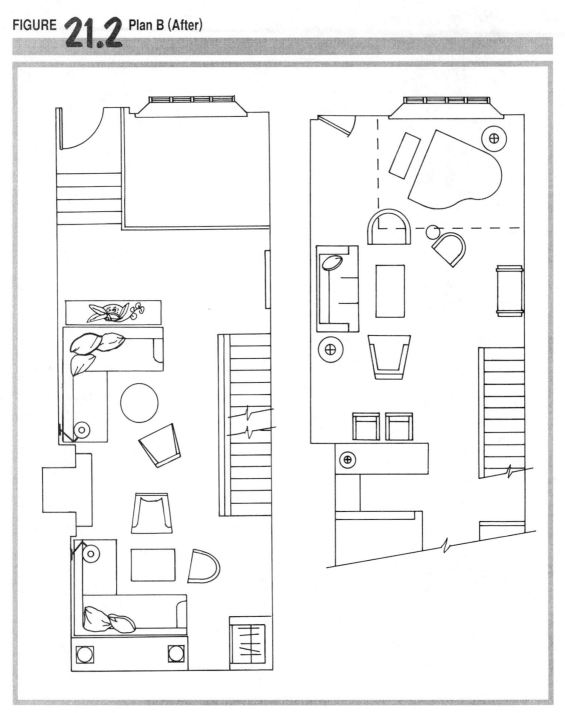

Source: Design by Cindy Christensen, illustration by Brian Connor

FIGURE **21.3** House Plans

Chicago designer Cindy Christensen makes over rooms for clients. In this case, she has transformed a typical Chicago brownstone into a more inviting and practical living space.

PLAN A (BEFORE)

Lower Level

- Piano off center to bay and jammed into corner, too hard to get to
- Sofa facing bad view
- Two small coffee tables break up space too much
- Wood floor cold for a lower level
- Two chairs too close to sofa so conversation awkward
- Sofa too constricting with long arms
- Art too long to view from above because owners can look down from first floor entry
- Long bookcase with TV in center is hard to utilize in a long, narrow room
- Awkwardly shaped bar

First Floor

- Empty feeling despite a lot of small tables and chairs cluttering the room
- Angled display cabinet next to closet is too trite and unrelated to rest of room
- Sofa too small to be comfortable, because two people are always uncomfortable sitting on these loveseat-style sofas; too many pillows, which makes it hard to sit down
- Room does not seat enough people for its size

PLAN B (AFTER)

Lower Level

- Got rid of trendy angle on bar
- Fewer seats at bar so not jammed in
- Lamp placed on inside of bar rather than outside so views are not obstructed
- Better access to all functions of the room, including piano
- Pocket doors on armoire with TV does not obstruct views of stairs
- Sofa larger and in better placement for more open views

FIGURE **21.3** House Plans (Continued)

- Coffee table placed 15 inches from chairs and sofa so almost every seat has use of the table, and small chair has a small table next to it
- Scale of furnishings varied—some with weight and upholstered and some lighter in weight—plus wing chair adds height in front of the bar and separates the two areas; more seating makes room feel more inviting

First Floor
- Less empty feeling; larger scale of furnishings in a sufficient number, plus two separate seating zones
- Eliminated angled cabinet
- Swing arm wall lights anchor and warm up each zone
- Round back on chair allows a good view behind it as you walk through the room, which is better psychologically
- Round coffee table is more conducive to breaking up shapes of rectangles
- Table behind sofa with a beautiful plant is now the first thing seen as people enter the room
- Cozy inviting room with adequate seating is achieved in a very narrow space by using the wall versus floating furniture in the room

JOHN HIMMEL (Chicago, Illinois)

Interior designer John Himmel, who recently opened John Himmel Decorative Arts, says that art, sculpture, and furnishings need to be considered before walls are installed because plywood blocking must often be added between the studs for support. Otherwise, you'll have to cut open the drywall later to add it. "A little forethought can save disaster later."

Before you even begin to look at paint, carpet, wallpaper, and fabric swatches, think about your overall goals and the look you want to evoke that fits in with your lifestyle.

Is your fantasy a spare contemporary loft space with the most cutting edge contemporary furniture from Milan, or an English antique-filled house with yards of chintz? Or, are you quite content with all the furnishings you've bought or inherited through the years and simply want to paint rooms and hang curtains to attain a homey, loved look?

Whatever your goal, you may need some help to get from point "A" to point "B" as you deliberate the incredible number of choices available.

LESLIE STERN (Chicago, Illinois)

Decorator Leslie Stern bought an old wooden mantel at a renovation store for a client's home, had it refinished and installed granite on it to match their entranceway. She also added a piece of black metal around their firebox and asked the marble man to clean it up. He did, and the blue granite was magnificent. "I struck gold. It was gorgeous, a find."

First decide whether you can tackle the project on your own. Unlike years past, you may be able to because there are so many more retail resources available today. You needn't buy from the wholesale sources that once provided most of the home furnishings through the middlepersons of decorators and architects. Today, you can find fabrics, pillows, and more at department stores with home furnishings departments like Bloomingdale's, which are often staffed by trained designers; at specialized boutiques and stores such as Pier I Imports and Pottery Barn; on TV; on the Internet; and through the mail because a slew of home furnishings catalogs such as Ballard's and Spiegel make ordering from home easy and stylish. However, you must have the interest and the time.

If you feel insecure about your taste or are simply overwhelmed by all the choices, you, of course, can choose the time-tested route and hire a decorator. Two big advantages of using one today are (1) they are much more flexible about payment arrangements, and (2) they can help you avoid costly mistakes. "Designers are trained to come up with functional spaces that may also be more aesthetically pleasing, and a good one will save you money," says Chicago designer Leslie Stern.

SPECIAL DECORATING NEEDS—UNIVERSAL DESIGN

Whether you're young, middle-aged, or elderly, you should consider adding Universal Design features to any rooms you're redecorating or remodeling. All of us hope to grow old and we may prefer to stay put rather than move to a retirement community. And in the present, we also periodically injure ourselves—

throw out our back, wrench a knee, impair vision—which makes navigating tougher. If you include certain features in your home in advance, you'll be able to get around easier and possibly avoid hiring professional caregivers, should you take ill.

For example, install light switches no higher than three feet above the floor. Make aisles wide enough and be sure there's a five-foot turning radius for wheelchairs. Doorways should be 36 inches wide to accommodate wheelchairs. If you have the space in a house or multilevel condo to accommodate it, and your budget permits, consider installing an elevator. But make it wide enough for a wheelchair to move in and out.

Many of these design features are also practical for families with young children because you want to protect them, too, from getting scalded with hot water or slipping on slick bathtub tiles, advises designer Stern, who frequently designs homes and apartments that meet the American Disabilities Act standards for Universal Design.

Flooring

Throughout the house, select appropriate flooring materials if someone is physically impaired or wheelchair-bound—hardwood or smooth stones, ceramic, or marble tiles. You don't want anything rough or slick that can cause a person to trip or slip. There are four basic types of wood flooring: (1) plank flooring that is wider, (2) strip flooring that ranges in width, (3) block flooring that is constructed from preassembled wood in different patterns such as parquet flooring made from preassembled units of small slats of wood in different patterns, and (4) end grain blocks that are solid pieces of wood that are very durable and resistant to oils, chemicals, and indentation and are used for industrial floors.

Carpeting

Room carpeting should have a firm cushion or backing, or no cushion and a level loop, textured loop, level cut pile, or level cut/uncut pile texture with a maximum pile height of ½-inch. Stair carpeting should have a tight pile or loop. Check by taking a carpet sample and bending it. If the fibers separate and "smile," the carpet is not dense enough to be installed on stairs.

Building Components

Building components should also be carefully conceived to eliminate accidents. Bookshelves should be 14 inches deep to accommodate different size books and have one-inch thick shelves properly supported so they do not bow or bend and cause books to tumble off, particularly when there is a long span. In a wet area such as a kitchen and bathroom, lighting takes on even greater importance and planning.

Kitchen

Make aisles wide enough for two people to navigate and for a wheelchair to get around. There should be a minimum of 40 inches between counters and all opposing back cabinets, appliances, or walls, except in a U-shaped kitchen, which should have a minimum of 60 inches of turning space. Consider antiscald faucets so that they won't burn the user, and opt for levers rather than pull styles. Also put levers instead of knobs on cabinet fronts. For easy opening, mount the door pulls or levels on wall cabinets as close to the bottom of the cabinet doors as possible. On the base cabinets mount them as close to the top of the doors as possible.

Counters

Have sufficient counter space to rest hot casseroles and pots, particularly next to your range or oven. If someone in the family is in a wheelchair, be sure countertops are no higher than 34 inches or consider having different counter heights, from a low of 28 inches (measured from the finished floor) to a high of 36 inches. Also, consider leaving a space open underneath the sink so a wheelchair can roll under the sink giving the person easy access.

Placement of Appliances

Allot 30 to 48 inches of clear floor space to allow a forward approach to a sink. Raise up the dishwasher so a wheelchair-bound person can empty the dishes. Consider the separate drawer-type refrigerators, which can be installed at easy-to-reach heights and an oven with controls on the front panel, which are easier to get at. Choose roll-out shelves when possible because they're also easier to reach.

Bathrooms

Be sure doors to the bathroom open out in case someone is injured and collapses. Put the vanity no higher than 34 inches from the finished floor and again leave an open area underneath the sink for easy wheelchair access. Install grab bars 33 to 36 inches above the floor. Even if nobody in the house uses a wheelchair, grab bars are useful for getting in and out of a tub and by a toilet for sitting down and standing up. Install a seat in the shower for occasional sitting while shaving, or if someone in the house uses a wheelchair, and be sure there's no threshold barrier to cross. Again, be sure you've used levers, not knobs, on cabinet fronts and faucets, and place the levers so they can be reached from a wheelchair.

Lighting

Ceiling lighting can be used for accents, task or overall illumination, and should be placed where it is needed most to illuminate dark areas. Lighting is critical for the tub and shower areas, by the mirrors and for the room overall. Lighting on both sides of the mirror is preferred over one light source mounted above the mirror as it can cast shadows on the face.

THE TRANSFORMATION FROM HOUSE TO HOME

Sometimes the smallest details and accessories can make all the difference in turning your generic all-white boxy condo or home into a personalized abode. And often these tricks needn't be terribly expensive. Following are 100 suggestions. Remember to take your time when making the transformation from house to home. And most important, have fun.

1. Buy a mailbox that says something about one of your favorite interests—a boat, a dog, a flag, a rose garden.
2. Order stationary imprinted with your name and new address.
3. Give your home a name and have a plaque made.
4. Have an indoor house-raising with your best friends each bringing part of a potluck supper or favorite tool or utensil. Eat on the floor on blankets if you don't yet have tables and chairs.
5. Line all kitchen cabinets with pretty shelf paper.
6. Buy new spices and line up the jars alphabetically.

7. Buy a new doormat/welcome mat with a great design.
8. Hang some artwork and photographs in a new arrangement.
9. Buy pretty soaps, hand towels, and potpourri for a powder room or "company" bathroom.
10. Treat yourself to fresh flowers for your front hall or a favorite table once a week or once a month.
11. Have a favorite chaise or ottoman, a good light, and an afghan where you can curl up and read.
12. Reorganize your closets and throw out anything you haven't used in the last two years. Donate items to a favorite charity.
13. Plant a tree and watch it grow as the years tick by.
14. Plant your favorite perennials and annuals.
15. Dig and plant raised vegetable beds in your backyard, then make gazpacho soup or a great salad from what you've grown.
16. Put in an underground sprinkling system to water those flowers and vegetables.
17. Put some topiary plants in large clay pots by your front door.
18. Host the family Thanksgiving, Christmas, or Passover and use all your best china, silver, and serving dishes. Try to make at least one holiday an annual tradition.
19. Throw a block party to meet your new neighbors.
20. Set out a table in the hall with a place for mail, a stand for umbrellas, and a bench or seat for putting on boots.
21. Order nice hangers with your monogram for a guest closet.
22. Have an artist do a drawing or painting of your house or a favorite room.
23. Paint one room a favorite color that you've never used before and don't forget to paint the ceiling and bookshelves as well. You may want to make them different shades.
24. Hang a border around the ceiling for a charming but inexpensive touch.
25. Get a dog to protect your new house and add some life to it. You'll explore the neighborhood more often that way.
26. Needlepoint some pillows with scenes or pictures reminiscent of your childhood home. It will add character to your rooms.
27. Change the pillows on your main sofa and chairs periodically.
28. Make it a habit to rearrange objects on your coffee and end tables.
29. Put a phone, pad, pretty jar with pencils and pens, and some books in your living room so you use the room rather than treat it as a museum or company room.

30. If you never use your dining room, consider turning it into a library or den by placing the table at one end and having some bookshelves or seating installed at the other end.
31. Put up a big bulletin board in the kitchen for everyone to leave messages and tack up mementos.
32. Try to have fresh aromas regularly emanate from your kitchen so it smells like your mother or grandmother's home.
33. Polish your family silver so it's ready to use and then put in away in Pacific cloth to keep it from tarnishing.
34. Hang a rogue's gallery of family pictures in a long hallway or place you pass daily.
35. Order new monogrammed towels and sheets.
36. Put in window seats to create a cozy nook where you can sit or stash children's toys and odds and ends.
37. Set up an area for trophies, awards, and medals and everyone in the family wins.
38. Set aside a space for a CD player and your music collection, as well as any musical instruments.
39. Put in an intercom or sound system so you can pipe your music throughout the house.
40. Organize your basement with new shelves, whitewash walls, and set up a place with emergency equipment such as a flashlight, candles, fire extinguisher, and hammer.
41. Replace doorknobs and hardware with colorful whimsical ones.
42. Restock your pantry with soup stock, beans, legumes, pastas, bouillon, canned tomatoes, hot chocolate and marshmallows, and other staples needed for emergency meals.
43. Buy new pots and pans, if you haven't done so in years.
44. Buy a new set of everyday dishes, if you haven't done so in years or if yours are broken and chipped. Try to mix and match colors and patterns.
45. Buy photo albums and catalog old pictures of your former homes.
46. Remove old carpeting if hardwood floors are underneath. Consider staining the floor a pretty, softer shade, or painting or pickling it.
47. Put in an extra large bathtub or whirlpool for those stressful moments. Add an aromatic candle and plant on one edge and be sure you have big fluffy towels and bathrobes. For a real splurge: add a heated towel rack.
48. Buy a big screen television or an extra big TV so you can host the next election night or Super Bowl party.

49. Make a wish list for your home and buy one item each year.
50. Call your parents, grandparents, siblings, or oldest friends and invite them for dinner to see your new home.
51. Recover a worn-out chair with an interesting finish or fabric rather than discarding it.
52. Erect a picket fence around the backyard where your dog may run and add to it a wire basket with flowers.
53. Build a deck; maybe add a hot tub.
54. Build a gazebo and place a table and chairs in it for outdoor dining.
55. Add a screened porch for cooling off on hot, buggy, summer evenings.
56. Buy a new self-cleaning gas grill for outdoor cooking and entertaining. Purchase new cooking tools and a grill for fish.
57. Put up wind chimes for pleasant sounds and sights.
58. Build or buy a birdhouse and/or birdbath or fountain.
59. Blacktop the driveway if it is cracking and trim the drive with pretty slate or brick.
60. Put up a hammock between two big trees.
61. Reuse a piece of indoor furniture for another purpose such as a hutch for a TV, or armoire for a bar.
62. Replace old ceiling fans with newer more attractive ones that cool rooms and save energy.
63. Replace windows with sliding glass or French doors so you use your outdoors more often.
64. Add molding to a living room or master bedroom to give it more charm.
65. Put a Franklin stove in a family room or bedroom to add warmth and a focal point.
66. To dress up breakfast room chairs, add pretty pads with floppy ties.
67. Replace the showerhead with powerful nozzles that give you a shower massage.
68. Organize the garage with the help of a plastic shoe holder and stash garden tools, sports equipment, and cleaning supplies in each pocket.
69. During warm weather, fill the fireplace with large baskets of dried flowers.
70. Start a collection and group items together such as baskets, inexpensive vintage pitchers, or childhood marbles.
71. Put out jars of your favorite candies or nuts in pretty glass bowls so people tend to congregate in the rooms where they're located.

72. Light up your home with a greenhouse window in the kitchen and grow herbs and spices there.
73. Put in a skylight in a kitchen or breakfast room. (Avoid it in a bedroom unless you don't mind sunlight streaming in at 5 AM on a summer morning.)
74. Put reminders of the past throughout the house such as some vintage crockery on shelves or handpainted plates on the walls.
75. Spray paint white kitchen cabinets a color, perhaps a soft green, or spray paint dingy whites a crisp, clean white. Change can be a boon.
76. Sharpen your knives and purchase a new one.
77. Buy one great new appliance such as a potato ricer to make great mashed potatoes.
78. Freshen your kitchen with new countertops, possibly a pretty new laminate color, granite, or stainless if you want to splurge.
79. Remove stair carpeting, stain the floorboards underneath, and add a runner.
80. Buy a pedestal for the entrance hall on which you place artwork, a small tray for letters, or a vase for flowers.
81. Replace a standard bathroom window with glass block to create a charming '50s look and gain more privacy at the same time.
82. Take out a shower curtain and replace it with an all-glass door for a contemporary look.
83. Convert one room of the basement into a playroom, home office, or exercise room.
84. Transform the space under the basement stairs into a wine closet.
85. Add a greenhouse and learn to garden year-round. Start with something simple, work up to orchids.
86. Build a treehouse for the kids—or for you and your spouse.
87. Keep a journal in which you document your move or remodeling with good notes, diagrams, and photos. You might even videotape any renovation or building showing it before and after.
88. If you have a large lot, buy a riding lawnmower; and if your garage can't accommodate it, buy a small shed.
89. Plant the wonderful garden you've always wanted—as long as it will work in your climate—such as a rose garden or wildflower garden.
90. Set up an area for good, organized files. Buy new file cabinets, folders, and tabs, and throw out any old paperwork you no longer need.

91. Organize the books on your bookshelf so you can find them easily— group cookbooks, travel books, fiction, and nonfiction. Categorize them on your computer. Then, buy one new book for every family member.

92. Have a good friend or family member to lunch on a Saturday or Sunday once a month or every other month. In nice weather, eat outdoors.

93. Take a walk in your neighborhood daily by yourself or with a family member. Make it a routine, no matter what.

94. Buy a new vacuum cleaner, if you haven't done so for years. Use it and your new your house will look cleaner.

95. Have all the windows in your house washed at least twice a year—in the fall and in the spring. You'll enjoy your rooms and outdoors more.

96. Have a nice family dinner once a month, using your best china, silverware, and crystal.

97. Replace the blinds in at least one room each year, switch from old-fashioned skinny metal blinds to newer, fatter wood blinds.

98. Put up an oversized blackboard in your kitchen on which you'll keep track of everyone's schedule, eliminating a lot of confusion and the perennial question, "What's for dinner?"

99. Stay home for a vacation and do all the things you never typically do— sleep late, don't make your bed, watch a movie in the morning, start a wonderful book, finish the book, go for a walk or bike ride in your area, play Scrabble or Monopoly with everyone in the family, and cook dinner together with everyone making a course.

100. Go away for a vacation. You'll be excited to come home again.

CONSTRUCTIVE TIPS

Questions to Ask to Ferret Out the Right Designer

Chicago designer Leslie Stern recommends interviewing several designers and asking each the following questions—preferably before your decorating project gets off the ground.

- How long have you been in business? What was your training?
- Do you have a portfolio and can you show me pictures of rooms?
- Can you define quality, in terms of upholstery, paint treatments, wallpaper hanging, and floor laying? I want to be sure we're on the same wavelength.
- Can you take me to see some projects you've done? Can you also provide me with the names and phone numbers of prior clients I can call for references?
- Where have you gained most of your experience—decorating new homes or older ones? Have you been involved with the intricacies of remodeling and building codes? Is there a particular style in which you specialize?
- Are you willing to work as part of a team with my architect, contractor, or builder from the get-go?
- Are you willing to reuse my existing furniture? Or, am I expected to buy almost everything new? (Go through your home with the designer and see how he reacts to what you already have. If he says you'll have to dispose of everything, rather than work around what you already have, that designer may not be for you.)
- Will you share your trade sources, including your painter, floor layer, paperhanger, electrician, and contractor? Or do you expect me to furnish my own work crew? Will you supervise them or simply provide their names and phone numbers? How often will you show up to supervise the project and can we put this into the contract?

CONSTRUCTIVE TIPS (continued)

- Do you limit the number of trips we can make to decorating show-rooms or the number of samples you'll show me if I don't like any of your selections?
- How do you feel if I find some furnishings or samples on my own and want to buy them without you?
- How do you deal with any problems that arise—upholstery that's not tight enough, wallpaper that comes in damaged, painting that's not smooth and professional looking?
- How do you charge and when do you expect payments to be made? All up front or a percentage at the beginning and the rest at the end?
- Do you have a minimum dollar amount I'm expected to pay for my room(s) or project? (Some tony New York designers are said not to take on jobs below $20,000 per room.)
- What is your policy about returning my phone calls?
- Will you have me sign a contract or will we work with a verbal agreement?

Payment arrangements are probably the stickiest part of the decorator-client relationship because many designers have traditionally worked in secretive ways—charging an undisclosed percentage over their markup and not revealing the wholesale price. But many are now much more open and flexible because they have to be for competitive reasons and because of the increasing number of retail options available. The following are a number of common arrangements:

- A percentage over the net price from the supplier or vendor. That percentage may run from 10 percent at the low end to 40 percent at the upper end.
- An hourly rate, which can range anywhere from $50 to $300. Usually, the client then buys the furnishings.

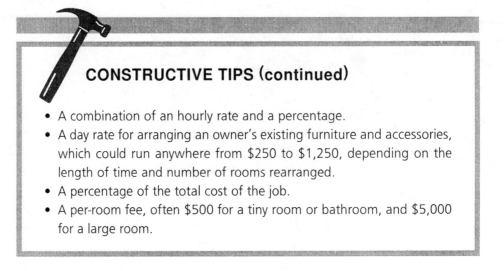

CONSTRUCTIVE TIPS (continued)

- A combination of an hourly rate and a percentage.
- A day rate for arranging an owner's existing furniture and accessories, which could run anywhere from $250 to $1,250, depending on the length of time and number of rooms rearranged.
- A percentage of the total cost of the job.
- A per-room fee, often $500 for a tiny room or bathroom, and $5,000 for a large room.

Appendix: Smart Resources to Tap

Note: Addresses, phone numbers, and Web sites may occasionally change. Not all associations have Web sites or e-mail addresses.

Adhesives and Sealants

Adhesive and Sealant Council
1627 K Street, NW, Suite 1000
Washington, DC 20006
202-452-1500
Web site: www.ascouncil.org

Sealant, Waterproofing, and
  Restoration Institute
2841 Main
Kansas City, MO 64108
816-472-7974
Web site: www.swrionline.org

Appliances

Manufacturers, Engineers, Contractors

American Society of Heating,
  Refrigerating, and Air
  Conditioning Engineers
1791 Tullie Circle, NE
Atlanta, GA 30329
800-5-ASHRAE
E-mail: ashrae@ashrae.org
Web site: www.ashrae.org

Association of Home Appliance
  Manufacturers
20 N. Wacker Drive, Suite 1231
Chicago, IL 60606
312-984-5800
Web site: www.aham.org

International Refrigeration
  Service Engineers Society
1666 Rand Road
Des Plaines, IL 60016
800-809-0389
E-mail: rses@starnetimc.com

National Refrigeration Contractors
  Association
1900 Arch Street
Philadelphia, PA 19103
215-564-3484
E-mail: assnhqt@netass.com

Refrigerating Engineers and
    Technicians Association
401 N. Michigan Avenue
Chicago, IL 60611
312-527-6763
Web site: www.reta.com

Arbitration and Mediation

American Arbitration Association
140 W. 51st Street
New York, NY 10020
212-484-4000
Web site: www.adr.org

American Bar Association
750 N. Lake Shore Drive
Chicago, IL 60611
800-285-2221
Web site: www. abanet.org

American Bar Association
    Section of Dispute Resolution
740 15th Street NW
Washington, DC 20005
202-331-2258
E-mail: dispute@net.org
Web site:
    www.uba.net.org/dispute

American College of Construction
    Lawyers
1200 G Street, NW, Suite 760
Washington, DC 20005
202-638-3906

National Institute for Dispute
    Resolution
1726 M Street NW, #500
Washington, DC 20036
202-466-4764
E-mail: nidr@igc.apc.org

Society of Professionals in Dispute
    Resolution
815 15th Street NW, Suite 530
Washington, DC 20005
202-783-7277
Web site: www.spidr.org

Architecture

American Architectural
    Foundation
1735 New York Avenue NW
Washington, DC 20006
202-626-7318
Web site: www.aafpages.org

American Architectural
    Manufacturers Association
1827 Walden Office Square,
    Suite 104
Schaumburg, IL 60173
847-303-5664
E-mail: webmaster@aamanet.org
Web site: www.aamanet.org

American Institute of Architects
1735 New York Avenue NW
Washington, DC 20006
202-626-7300
Web site: www.aiaonline.com

Architectural Spraycoaters
   Association
230 Wells, Suite 311
Milwaukee, WI 53203
609-848-6120
E-mail: ascaassoc@erols.com

National Architectural Accrediting
   Board
1735 New York Avenue NW
Washington, DC 20006
202-783-2007
Web site: www.naab.org

Architects/Engineers

National Society of Architectural
   Engineers
700 SW Jackson Street, Suite 702
Topeka, KS 66603
913-232-5707
Web site:
   www.energy.arce.ukans.edu/
   nsae/main.htm.

Automated (Prewired) Houses

Home Automatiion Association
1444 I Street NW, Suite 700
Washington, DC 20005
202-712-9050
E-mail: haa@bostromdc.com
Web site:
   creator.cometeam.com/haa

SMART HOUSE, Inc.
4630 Tarragon Park Road
Raleigh, NC 27616
919-872-8553
Web site: www.smart-house.com

Banking

Conference of State Bank
   Supervisors
1015 18th Street NW, Suite 1100
Washington, DC 20036
202-296-2840
Web site: www.csbs.org

Consumer Bankers Association
1000 Wilson Boulevard,
   Suite 3012
Arlington, Va. 22209
703-276-1750
Web site: www.cbanet.org

Federal Insurance Administration
500 C Street SW
Washington, DC 20472
202-646-2780 (flood information)
Web site: www.fema.gov

Mortgage Bankers Association of
America
1125 15th Street, NW
Washington, DC 20005
202-861-6500
Web site: www.mbaa.org

National Home Equity Mortgage
Association
3833 Schaefer Avenue
Chino, CA 91710
800-342-1121
Web site: www.nhema.org

Building Codes

Building Officials & Code
Administrators International
Inc.
4051 West Flossmoor Road
Country Club Hills, IL 60478
708-799-2300
Web site: www.bocai.org

International Conference of
Building Officials
5360 Workman Mill Road
Whittier, CA 90601
800-284-4406
800-252-3602 in Austin, TX
800-321-4226 in Kansas City, MO
800-231-4776 in Seattle, WA
800-243-5736 in Indianapolis, IN
800-336-1963 in Northern
California
Web site: www.icbo.org

National Conference of States on
Building Codes and Standards
(Association of Major City
Building Officials)
505 Huntmar Park Drive,
Suite 210
Herndon, VA 22070
800-DOC-CODE
Web site: www.ncsbcs.org

Southern Building Code Congress
International
900 Montclair Road
Birmingham, AL 35213
203-591-1853
Web site: www.sbcci.org

Building Industries
Trade, Business, and Commercial Organizations

Building Industry Association
1330 South Valley Vista Drive
Diamond Bar, CA 91765
909-396-9993
Web site: www.bisc.com

Building Research Council
(Videos and brochures about
remodeling available.)
University of Illinois
One East St. Mary's Road
Champaign, IL 61820
800-336-0616
E-mail: kgallghr@uiuc.edu
Web site: www.arch.uiuc.edu/brc

Design-Build Institute of America
1010 Massachusetts Avenue NW,
Suite 350
Washington, DC 20001
202-682-0110
Web site: www.dbia.org

National Association of Home
Builders of the United States
(Operates National Commercial
Builders Council, National
Council of the Multifamily
Housing Industry, National
Remodelers Council, and
National Sales and Marketing
Council.)
1201 15th Street NW
Washington, DC 20005
202-861-2104
800-368-5242
Web site: www.nahb.com

North American Building Material
Distribution
401 N. Michigan Avenue
Chicago, IL 60611
312-321-6845
E-mail: nbmda@sba.com
Web site: www.nbmda.org

Bricks/Masonry

Brick Institute of America
11490 Commerce Park Drive
Reston, VA 22091
703-620-0010
E-mail:
76446.2075@compuserve.com
Web site: www.brickinst.org

Brick Institute and National
Association of Brick
Distributors
11490 Commerce Park Drive
Reston, VA 20191
703-620-0010
Web site: www.bia.org

International Masonry Institute
823 15th Street NW
Washington DC 20005
800-803-0295
E-mail:
7112.2120@compuserve.com
Web site: www.imiweb.org

Mason Contractors Association
of America
1910 South Highland Avenue,
Suite 101
Lombard, IL 60148
630-705-4200
Web site:
www.masoncontractors.com

Masonry Society
2619 Spruce Street
Boulder, CO 80302
303-939-9700
Web site:
   www.masonrysociety.org

Ceilings and Walls

Association of the Wall and
   Ceiling Industries International
307 E. Annandale Road, Suite 200
Falls Church, VA 22042
703-534-8300
Web site: www.awci.org

Ceilings and Walls/Acoustics

Acoustical Society of America
500 Sunnyside Boulevard
Woodbury, NY 11797
516-576-2360
Web site: asa.aip.org

Concrete

American Concrete Institute
PO Box 9094
Farmington Hills, MI 48333
248-848-3700
Web site: aci-int.org

American Concrete Pavement
   Association
3800 North Wilke Road, Suite 490
Arlington Heights, IL 60004
847-966-2272
Web site: www.pavement.com

National Association of Brick
   Distributors
1600 Spring Hill Road, #305
Vienna, VA 22182
703-749-6223
E-mail: nabd@brickvalue.org
Web site: www.brickvalue.org

Ceilings and Interior Systems
   Construction Association
1500 Lincoln Highway, #202
Street Charles, IL 60174
847-584-1919
E-mail: cisca@juno.com
Web site: www.cisca.org

National Council of Acoustical
   Consultants
66 Morris Avenue, Suite 1A
Springfield, NJ 07081
973-564-5859
Web site: www.ncac.com *or*
   www.i2000.com

Concrete Foundations Association
107 First Street West
PO Box 204
Mount Vernon, IA 52314
319-895-6940
Web site:
   www.concreteworld.com/cfa

Concrete Reinforcing Steel
   Institute
933 Plum Grove Road
Schaumburg, IL 60173
847-517-1200
Web site: www.crsi.org

Expanded Shale, Clay, and Slate
Institute
2225 E. Murray Holladay Road,
Suite 102
Salt Lake City, UT 84117
801-272-7070
Web site:
www.concreteworld. com/escsi

National Concrete Masonry
Association
2302 Horse Pen Road
Herndon, VA 20171
703-713-1900
Web site: www.ncma.org

National Ready-Mixed Concrete
Association
900 Spring Street
Silver Spring, MD 20910
301-587-1400
Web site: www.nrmca.org

Prestressed Concrete Institute
175 West Jackson Boulevard
Chicago, IL 60604
312-786-0300
Web site: www.pci.org

Tilt-Up Concrete Association
107 First Street West
PO Box 204
Mount Vernon, IA 52314
319-895-6911
E-mail: esauter@tilt-up.org
Web site: www.tilt-up.org

Construction/Contractors

American Council for
Construction Education
1300 Hudson Lane, Suite 3
Monroe, LA 71201
318-323-2413

Associated Construction
Distributors International
1201 Roberts Boulevard, #219
Kennesaw, GA 30144
770-422-5218
Web site: www.acdi.net

Construction Net
Web site:
www.constructionnet.net

Contractor Network
E-mail: info@contactornet.com
Web site: www.contractornet.com

Construction Owners Association
of America
1200 Peachtree Street, NE
Atlanta, GA 30303
800-255-8325
Web site: www.coaa.org

Construction Specifications
Institute
601 Madison Street
Alexandria, VA 22314
800-689-2900 x742
E-mail: csimail@csinet.org
Web site: www.csinet.org

Professional Construction
  Estimators Association of
  America
PO Box 11626
Charlotte, NC 28220
704-522-6376
Web site: www.pcea.org

Contractors

American Building Contractors
  Association
12123 Woodruff Avenue
Downey, CA 90241
310-803-5520

American Institute of Constructors
466 94th Avenue
St. Petersburg, FL 33702
813-578-0317
Web site: www.aicnet.org

Associated Builders and
  Contractors
1300 N. 17th Street
Rosslyn, VA 22209
703-812-2000
Web site: www.abc.org

Associated General Contractors of
  America
1957 E. Street NW
Washington DC 20006
202-393-2040
Web site: www.agc.org

Independent Electrical Contractors
507 Wythe Street
Alexandria, VA 22314
800-456-4324
E-mail: ieccasey@aol.com
Web site: www.ieci.org

Mechanical Contractors
  Association of America
1385 Piccard Drive
Rockville, MD 20850
301-869-5800
Web site: www.mcaa.org

National Association of
  Demolition Contractors
16 N. Franklin Street
Doylestown, PA 18901
800-541-2412
Web site:
  www.demolitionassn.com

National Association of Elevator
  Contractors
1298 Wellbrook Circle
Conyers, GA 30207
770-760-9660
E-mail: naec@minspring.com

National Association of the
  Remodeling Industry
4900 Seminary Road, Suite 320
Alexandria, VA 22311
703-575-1100
800-440-NARI (Remodeling
  hotline)
Web site: www.nari.org

National Association of
  Waterproofing Contractors
2550 Shagrin, Suite 403
Cleveland, OH 44122
800-245-NAWC
E-mail: nawc@apk.net
Web site: www.apk.net/nawc

National Electrical Contractors
  Association
3 Bethesda Metro Center, #1100
Bethesda, MD 20814
301-657-3110
E-mail: neca@necanet.org
Web site: www.necanet.org

National Electrical Contractors
  Council
Associated Builders and
  Contractors
1300 N. 17th Street
Rosslyn, VA 22209
703-812-2000
703-812-2006
Web site: www.abc.org

National Mechanical Contractors
  Council
Associated Builders and
  Contractors
1300 N. 17th Street
Rosslyn, VA 22209
703-812-2000
703-812-2006

Remodeling Contractors
  Association
17 S. Main Street
East Granby, CT 06026
860-653-6751
Web site: www.remodeling
  assocation.com

United American Contractors
  Association
85 Central Street
Boston, MA 02109
617-357-4470

Homebuilders

National Association of Home
  Builders Research Center
400 Prince George Boulevard
Upper Marlboro, MD 20774
800-638-8556
Web site: www.nahbrc.org

Home Builders Institute
  (Educational arm of NAHB)
1090 Vermont Avenue NW,
  Suite 600
Washington, DC 20005
202-371-0600
Web site: www.hbi.org

Home Improvement Research
  Institute (Do-it-yourself aids)
400 Knightsbridge Parkway
Lincolnshire, IL 60069
847-634-4368
847-634-4375 (Fax)

National Association of Home
  Builders of the United States/
  Remodelers Council
c/o NAHB
1201 15th Street NW
Washington, DC 20005
800-368-5242
Web site: www.nahb.com

Subcontractors

American Subcontractors
   Association
1004 Duke Street
Alexandria, VA 22314
703-684-3450
E-mail: asa@asaonline.com
Web site: www.asaonline.com

Doors and Windows

American Association of
   Automatic Door Manufacturers
1300 Summer Avenue
Cleveland, OH 44115
216-241-7333
E-mail: aaadm@taol.com
Web site: www.taol.com/aaadm

Door and Hardware Institute
14170 Newbrook Drive
Chantilly, VA 22021
703-222-2010
Web site: www.dhi.org

International Window Film
   Association
PO Box 42033-383
Phoenix, AZ 85080
602-595-9758
Web site: www.iwfa.com

National Association of Garage
   Door Manufacturers
1300 Sumner Avenue
Cleveland, OH 44115
216-241-7333
Web site: www.taol.com/dasma

National Fenestration Rating
   Council
1300 Spring Street, Suite 120
Silver Spring, MD 20910
301-589-6372
E-mail: nfrcusa@aol.com
Web site: www.nfrc.org

National Sash and Door Jobbers
   Association
2400 E. Devon Avenue
Des Plaines, IL 60018
708-299-3402
800-786-SASH (7274)
E-mail: info@nsdja.com
Web site: www.nsdja.com

National Wood, Window, and
   Door Association
1400 E. Touhy Avenue, #470
Des Plaines, IL 60018
800-223-2301
Web site: www.nwwda.org

Pet Doors

America's Pet Door Outlet, Patio
  Pacific
Department ZZ
1931 North Gaffey Street, Suite C
San Pedro, CA 90731
800-826-2871
Web site: www.petdoors.com

Pet Doors USA
Department NW-96
4523 30th Street West
Bradenton, FL 34207
800-749-9609
Web site: www.petdoor.com

Electronics/Electricity

American Electronics Association
5201 Great America Parkway,
  Suite 520
Santa Clara, CA 95054
408-987-4200
Web site: www.aeanet.org

The Consumer Electronics
  Manufacturers Association
2500 Wilson Boulevard
Arlington, VA 22201
703-907-7600
Web site: www.cemacity.org

Electricity Consumers Resource
  Council
1222 H Street NW, West Tower 8th
  Floor
Washington, DC 20005
202-682-1390
Web site: www.elcon.org

The Electrification Council
Web site: www.eei.org/CSM/tec

Electronic Industries Association
2500 Wilson Boulevard
Arlington, VA 22201
703-907-7500
Web site: www.eia.org

Electronics Representatives
  Association
444 N. Michigan Avenue,
  Suite 1960
Chicago, IL 60611
800-776-7377
Web site: www.era.org

Electronics Technicians
  Association, International
602 N. Jackson
Greencastle, IN 46135
800-288-3824
Web site: www.eta-sda.com

International Association of
  Electrical Inspectors
PO Box 830848
Richardson, TX 75083
800-786-4234
E-mail: 76226.563@
  compuserve.com
Web site: www.iaei.com

International Society of Certified
  Electronics Technicians
2708 W. Berry, Suite 3
Forth Worth, TX 76109
817-921-9101
Web site: www.iscnet.org

National Association of Electrical
    Distributors
45 Danbury Road
Wilton, CT 06897
203-761-4900
Web site: www.electricnet.com

National Electronics Service
    Dealers Association
2708 W. Berry Street, Suite 3
Fort Worth, TX 76109
800-797-9197
E-mail: clydenesda@aol.com
Web site: www.nesda.com

Environment: Soils and Foundations

Foundations

ASFE: Professional Firms
    Practicing in the Geosciences
8811 Colesville Road, Suite G106
Silver Springs, MD 20910
301-565-2733
Web site: www@asfe.org

Deep Foundations Institute
120 Charlotte Place, 3rd Floor
Englewood Cliffs, NJ 07632
201-567-4232
E-mail: dfihq@sohi.ios.com
Web site: www.dfi.org

The International Association of
    Foundation Drilling
9696 Skillman, Suite 280
PO Box 280379
Dallas, TX 75243
214-343-2091

Pile Driving Contractors
    Association (International
    Association of Foundation
    Drilling)
PO Box 410260
St. Louis, MO 63141
314-275-7453
Web site: www.piledrivers.org

Environment

National Association of
    Environmental Professionals
6524 Ramoth Drive
Jacksonville, FL 30006
904-251-9900
Web site: www.naep.org

National Society of Environmental
    Consultants
PO Box 12528
San Antonio, TX 78212
210-271-0781

The Nature Conservancy
1815 North Lynn Street
Arlington, VA 22209
703-841-5300
Web site: www.tnc.org

Society for Ecological Restoration
1207 Seminole Highway
Madison, WI 53711
608-262-9547
Web site: nabalu.flas.ufl.edu/ser/
    SERhome.html

Soil and Water Conservation
  Society
7515 NE Ankeny Road
Ankeny, IA 50021
515-289-2331
Web site: www.infonet.net/
  showcase/swcs/

Soil Science Society of America
677 S. Segoe Road
Madison, WI 53711
608-273-8080
Web site: www.soils.org

The Urban Land Institute
1025 Thomas Jefferson Street NW,
  Suite 500 West
Washington, DC 20007
202-624-7000
Web site: www.uli.org

Expansion Joints

Expansion Joint Manufacturers
  Association
25 N. Broadway

Tarrytown, NY 10591
914-332-0040
Web site: www.ejma.org

Fences

American Fence Association
5300 Memorial Drive, Suite 116
Stone Mountain, GA 30083
800-822-4342
E-mail: afa@minspring.com
Web site:
  www.americanfenceassoc.org

Chain Link Fence Manufacturers
  Institute
9891 Broken Land Parkway, #300
Columbia, MD 21046
301-596-2583
Web site: www.fenceusa.com

Finishers

Metal Finishing Suppliers
  Association
801 Cass Avenue, Suite 300
Westmont, IL 60559
630-887-0797
E-mail: rcrain211@aol.com
Web site: www.mfsa.org

North American Refinisher's
  Association
6778 Edmonton Avenue
San Diego, CA 92122
619-558-0095
Web site:
  www.tclsystems.com/nara

Frame Builders

Framing/Metal

Metal Framing Manufacturers
 Association
401 N. Michigan
Chicago, IL 60611
312-644-6610

Framing/Wood

National Frame Builders
 Association
4840 W. 15th Street, Suite 1000
Lawrence, KS 66049
800-557-6957
E-mail: nfba@postframe.org
Web site: www.postframe.org

Hardware

American Hardware
 Manufacturers Association
801 N. Plaza Drive
Schaumburg, IL 60173
847-605-1025
Web site: www.ahma.org

Builders Hardware Manufacturers
 Association
60 East 42nd Street, Suite 511
New York, NY 10165
212-661-4261
E-mail: assocmgmt@aol.com

International Hardware
 Distributors Association
401 N. Michigan Avenue,
 Suite 2400
Chicago, IL 60611
312-644-6610

Heating, Cooling, and Ventilation (HVAC); Plumbing

HVAC

Air Conditioning Contractors of
America
1712 New Hampshire Avenue NW
Washington, DC 20009
202-484-9370
E-mail: accainfo@acca.org
Web site: www.acca.org

Air Conditioning and
Refrigeration Institute
4301 N. Fairfax Drive, Suite 425
Arlington, VA 22203
703-524-8800
E-mail: ari@dgsys.com
Web site: www.ari.org

Air Distribution Institute
4415 W. Harrison Street,
Suite 242-C
Hillside, IL 60162
708-449-2933

Air Movement and Control
Association
30 W. University Drive
Arlington, Heights, IL 60004
847-394-0150
E-mail: amca@amca.org
Web site: www.amca.org

American Society of Heating,
Refrigerating and Air
Conditioning Engineers, Inc.
1719 Tullie Circle NE
Atlanta, GA 30329
404-636-8400
E-mail: orders@ashrae.org
Web site: www.ashrae.org

Better Heating Cooling Council
35 Russo Place
PO Box 218
Berkeley Heights, NJ 07922
908-464-8200
908-464-7818 (Fax)

Home Ventilating Institute
(Division of the Air Movement
Control Association)
30 W. University Drive
Arlington Heights, IL 60004
847-394-0150
E-mail: hviramm@aol.com

The International District Heating
and Cooling Association
1200 19th Street NW, Suite 300
Washington, DC 20036
202-429-5111
Web site:
www.energy.rochester.edu/idea

International Ground Source Heat
Pump Association
Oklahoma State University
490 Cordell South
Stillwater, OK 74078
800-626-4747
E-mail: jbose@master.ceat.
okstate.edu
Web site: www.igshpa.okstate.edu

Masonry Heater Association of
North America
11490 Commerce Park Drive
Reston, VA 20191
703-620-3171
Web site: www.mha-net.org

Sheet Metal and Air Conditioning
 Contractors National
 Association
4201 Lafayette Center Drive
Chantilly, VA 20151
703-803-2980
E-mail: smacna@erds.com
Web site: www.smacna.org

Plumbing

American Supply Association
222 Merchandise Mart, Suite 1360
Chicago, IL 60654
312-464-0090
E-mail: asaemail@interserve.com
Web site: www.asanet.com

International Association of
 Plumbing and Mechanical
 Officials
20001 Walnut Drive
Walnut, CA 97789
909-595-8449
E-mail: iapmo@earthlink.net
Web site: www.iapmo.org

National Association of Plumbing,
 Heating, and Cooling
 Contractors
PO Box 6808
Falls Church, VA 22040
703-237-8100
Web site: www.naphcc.org

National Standard Plumbing Code
 Committee
180 S. Washington Street
PO Box 6808
Falls Church, VA 22040
703-237-8100
Web site: www.nspcc.org

Plumbing and Drainage Institute
45 Bristol Drive, Suite 101
South Easton, MA 02375
E-mail: pdi-ww@worldnet.att.net

Plumbing, Heating and Cooling
 Information Bureau
800-342-8594
Web site: www.phcib.org

Plumbing Manufacturers Institute
Building C, Suite 20
800 Roosevelt Road
Glen Ellyn, IL 60137
630-858-9172
Web site: www.pmihome.org

Sump and Sewage Pumps

Sump and Sewage Pump
    Manufacturers Association
PO Box 647
Northbrook, IL 60065
847-559-9233
E-mail: 102061.1063
    @compuserve.com
Web site: www.homearts.com/pm

Insulation

Insulation Contractors Association
    of America
PO Box 26237
Alexandria, VA 22313
703-739-0356
Web site: www.insulate.org

Insulation Contractors Association
2210 K Street
Sacramento, CA 95816
916-444-2950
E-mail: bob.burt@bbs.
    macnexus.org

National Insulation Association
99 Canal Center Plaza, Suite 222
Alexandria, VA 22314
703-683-6422
E-mail: niainfo@insulation.org
Web site: www.insulation.org

North American Insulation
    Manufacturers Association
44 Canal Center Plaza, Suite 310
Alexandria, VA 22314
703-684-0084
Web site: www.naima.org

Kitchens and Baths

Kitchen Cabinet Manufacturers
    Association
1899 Preston White Drive
Reston, VA 20191
703-264-1690
Web site: www.kcma.org

The National Kitchen and Bath
    Association
687 Willow Grove Street
Hackettstown, NJ 07840
800-843-6522
Web site: www.nkba.org

Society of Certified Kitchen
    Designers
687 Willow Grove Street
Hackettstown, NJ 07840
908-852-0033
Web site: www.nkba.org

Coatings

Laminating Materials Association
116 Lawrence Street
Hillsdale, NJ 07642
201-664-2700
E-mail: 1mainfo@soho.ios.com
Web site: www.lma.org

Porcelain Enamel Institute
4004 Hillsborough Pike,
  Suite 224B
Nashville, TN 37215
615-385-0758
Web site: www.porcelain
  enamel.com

Glass/Mirrors

Glass Association of North
  America
3310 SW Harrison Street
Topeka, KS 66611
913-266-7014
Web site: www.glasswebsite.
  com/gana

Sealed Insulating Glass
  Manufacturers Association
401 N. Michigan Avenue
Chicago, IL 60611
312-644-6610
Web site: www.sigmaonline.
  org/sigma

National Glass Association
8200 Greensboro Drive, Suite 302
McLean, VA 22101
703-442-4890
Web site: www.glass.org

Lighting

American Lighting Association
PO Box 420288
Dallas, TX 75342
800-274-4484
Web site:
  www.americanlightingassoc.com

Illuminating Engineering Society
  of North America
120 Wall Street, 17th Floor
New York NY 10005
212-248-5000
Web site: www.iesna.org

Home Fashions Products
  Association
355 Lexington Avenue, 17th Floor
New York, NY 10017
212-661-4261
E-mail: assocmgmt@aol.com

International Association of
  Lighting Designers
1133 Broadway, Suite 520
New York, NY 10010
212-206-1281
E-mail: iald@iald.org
Web site: www.aecnet.com/iald/
  iald.html

National Lighting Bureau
8811 Colesville Road, Suite G106
Silver Spring, MD 20919
202-457-8437
Web site: www.nlb.org

Locks and Keys

Associated Locksmiths of
  America
3003 Live Oak Street
Dallas, TX 75204
214-827-1701
E-mail: aloa@aloa.org
Web site: www.aloa.org

Metal and Steel

American Institute of Steel
  Construction
One East Wacker Drive,
  Suite 3100
Chicago, IL 60601
312-670-2400
Web site: www.aisc.org

American Iron and Steel Institute
1000 16th Street, NW
Washington, DC 20036
202-452-7100
Web site: www.steel.org

Insulated Steel Door Institute
30200 Detroit Road
Cleveland, OH 44145-1967
216-899-0010
Web site: www.isdi.org

Metal Building Manufacturers
  Association/Metal Roofing
  Systems Association
1300 Sumner Avenue
Cleveland, OH 44115
216-241-7333
Web site: mbma.com *or*
  www.tool.com/mbma

National Association of
  Aluminum Distributors
1900 Arch Street
Philadelphia, PA 19103
215-564-3484
Web site: www.naad.org

National Association of Metal
  Finishers
112-J Elden Street
Herndon, VA 20170
703-709-8299
Web site: www.namf.org

National Ornamental and
    Miscellaneous Metals
    Association
804 10 Main Street, Suite E
Forest Park, GA 30050
404-363-4009
Web site:
    www.nomma.org/nomma/

Steel Deck Institute
PO Box 9506
Canton, OH 44711
330-493-7886
E-mail:
    bcromi.sdi.off@worldnet.att.net
Web site: www.sdi.org

Steel Door Institute
30200 Detroit Road
Cleveland, OH 44145
216-899-0010
Web site: www.steeldoor.org

Steel Window Institute
30200 Detroit Road
Cleveland, OH 44145
216-899-0010
E-mail: swi@taol.com
Web site: www.taol.com/swi

Paint

Aluminum Extruders Council
1000 N. Rand Road, Suite 214
Wauconda, IL 60084
847-526-2010
E-mail: aec@mc.net
Web site: www.aec.org

National Paint and Coatings
    Association
1500 Rhode Island Avenue NW
Washington, DC 20005
202-462-6272
E-mail: npca@paint.org
Web site: www.paint.org

Painting and Decorating
    Contractors of America
3913 Old Lee Highway, Suite 33B
Fairfax, VA 22030
800-332-7322
Web site: www.pdca.com

Screen Printing and Graphic
    Imaging Association
    International
10015 Main Street
Fairfax, VA 22031
703-385-1335
Web site: www.sgia.org

Steel Structures Painting Council
40 24th Street, Suite 600
Pittsburgh, PA 15213
412-281-2331
E-mail: research@sspc.org

Paperhangers

National Guild of Professional
  Paperhangers
10521 Street Charles Rock Road
Street Ann, MO 63074
800-254-6477 (hotline)
Web site: www.ngpp.org

Patios

National Patio Enclosure
  Association
12625 Frederick Street 1-5, 315
Moreno Valley, CA 92553
909-485-8881

Pavement/Asphalt

National Asphalt Pavement
  Association
NAPA Building
5100 Forbes Building
Lanham, MD 20706
888-468-6499
E-mail: napa@hotmix.org
Web site: www.hotmix.org

Plastics

International Cast Polymer
  Association
8203 Greensboro Drive, Suite 300
McLean, VA 22102
703-610-9034
E-mail: icpa@icpa-hq.com
Web site: www.icpa-hq.com

Polyurethane Division, Society of
  the Plastics Industry
355 Lexington Avenue
New York, NY 10017
212-351-5425
Web site: www.socplas.org

Pools and Spas

National Spa and Pool Institute
2111 Eisenhower Avenue
Alexandria, VA 22314
703-838-0083
Web site: www.poolspaworld.com

Roofing

Asphalt Roofing Manufacturers
Association
4041 Powder Mill Road
Centerpark, Suite 404
Calverton, MD 20705
Web site: www.asphaltroofing.org

Chicago Roofing Contractors
Assocation
4415 W. Harrison Street,
Suite 242-C
Hillside, IL 60162
708-449-3340
E-mail: crcainfo@crca.org
Web site: www.crca.org

Institute of Roofing &
Waterproofing Consultants
401 North Michigan Avenue,
Suite 1120
Chicago, IL 60611
312-321-6864
Web site: www.irwc.org

National Roofing Contractors
Association
O'Hare International Center
10255 W. Higgins Road, Suite 600
Rosemont, IL 60018
708-299-9070
Web site: www.roofonline.org

Roofing Metal & Heating
Association, Inc.
PO Box 21187
Philadelphia, PA 19114
215-927-5262

Roof Consultants Institute
7424 Chapel Hill Road
Raleigh, NC 27607
919-859-0742
Web site: www.rci-online.org

Roofing Industry Educational
Institute
Building H, Suite 110
14 Inverness Drive E
Englewood, CO 80112
303-790-7200
E-mail: rieiroof@aol.com
Web site: www.members.aol.com/
rieiroof

Roof Coatings Manufacturers
Association
6000 Executive Boulevard, #201
Rockville, MD 20851
301-230-2501
Web site: www.roofcoatings.org

Truss Plate Institute
583 D'Onofrio Drive, Suite 200
Madison, WI 53719
608-833-5900
608-833-4360 (Fax)

Wood Truss Council of America
5937 Meadowood Drive, Suite 14
Madison, WI 53711
608-274-4849
E-mail: qualtim@msn.com

Rubber

Rubber Manufacturers
   Association, Inc.
1400 K Street, NW, Suite 900
Washington, DC 20005
202-682-4800
Web site: www.rma.org

Shelving

Material Handling Industry
Shelving Manufacturers
   Association
8720 Red Oak Boulevard,
   Suite 201
Charlotte, NC 28217
704-676-1190
Web site: www.mhi.org

Stone

Cast Stone Institute
2299 Brockett Road
Tucker, GA 30084
404-270-2353
Web site: www.caststone.org

Marble Institute of America
33505 State Street
Farmington, MI 48335
810-476-5558
Web site: marble-institute.com

National Stone Association
1415 Elliot Place, NW
Washington, DC 20007
202-342-1100
Web site: www.aggregates.org

National Terrazzo and Mosaic
   Association
3166 Des Plaines Avenue,
   Suite 121
Des Plaines, IL 60018
800-323-9736
Web site: www.ntma.com

Tile

American Ceramic Society
735 Ceramic Place
Westerville, OH 43081
614-890-4700
Web site: www.acers.org

Ceramic Tile Distributions
  Association
800 Roosevelt Road
Building C, Suite 20
Glen Ellyn, IL 60137
800-938-CTDA (2832)
Web site: www.ctdahome.org

Ceramic Tile Institute of America,
  Inc.
12061 Jefferson Boulevard
Culver City, CA 90230
310-574-7800
310-821-4655 (Fax)

Facing Tile Institute
PO Box 8880
Canton, OH 44418
330-488-1211
E-mail: starkcer@sssnet.com

National Tile Contractors
  Association
PO Box 13629
Jackson, MS 39236
601-939-2071
Web site: www.tile-assn.com

Tile Contractors Association of
  America
11501 Georgia Avenue, Suite 203
Wheaton, MD 20902
301-949-5995
Web site: www.tcaainc.org

Tile Council of America
PO Box 1787
Clemson, SC 29633
803-646-TILE (8453)
Web site: www.tileusa.com

Tile Promotion Board
900 East Indiantown Road,
  Suite 211
Jupiter, FL 33477
561-743-3150
Web sites: www.coverings.com
  www.floor-expo.com
  www.itse.com
  www.iwce.com
  www.stone-expo.com
  www.stoneexpo.com
  www.tile-expo.com
  www.tileexpo.com
  www.tilenet.com
  www.tilexpo.com
  www.wall-expo.com

Wood

American Fiberboard Association
1210 West Northwest Highway
Palatine, IL 60067-3609
847-934-8394

American Hardboard Association
520 N. Hicks Road
Palatine, IL 60067
847-934-8800

American Plywood Association
PO Box 11700
Tacoma, WA 98411
206-565-6600
Web site: www.apa.org

American Wood Council
(American Forest and Paper
Association)
1111 19th Street, NW, #800
Washington, DC 20036
202-463-2700
Web site: www.afandpa.org

Architectural Woodwork Institute
1952 Isaac Newton Square
Reston, VA 20190
703-733-0600
Web site: www.awinet.org

Cedar Bureau/Cedar Shake &
Shingle Bureau
515 116th Avenue NE, Suite 275
Bellevue, WA 98004
425-453-1323
Web site: www.cedarbureau.org

The Engineered Wood Association
7011 South 19th Street W
PO Box 11700
Tacoma, WA 98411
253-565-6600
Web site: www.apawood.org

Fine Hardwoods Veneer
Association
260 South First Street, #2
Zionsville, IN 46077
317-873-8780
E-mail: fhvaawmawc
@compuserve.com

Hardwood Manufacturers
Association
400 Penn Center Boulevard,
Suite 530
Pittsburgh, PA 15235
412-829-0770
Web site: www.hpva.org

Hardwood Plywood and Veneer
Association
PO Box 2789
Reston, VA 20195
703-435-2900
Web site: www.hpva.org

National Hardwood Lumber
Association
PO Box 34518
Memphis, TN 38184
901-377-1818
Web site: www.natlhardwood.org

National Lumber and Building
Material Dealers Association
40 Ivy Street, SE
Washington, DC 20003
202-547-2230
Web site: www.nlbmda.org

Composite Panel Association
18928 Premiere Court
Gaithersburg, MD 20879
301-670-0604
Web site: www.pbmdf.com

APA—The Engineered Wood
  Association
PO Box 11700
Tacoma, WA 98411
253-565-6600
Web site: www.apawood.org

Wood Molding and Millwork
  Producers Association
507 1st Street
Woodland, CA 95695
800-550-7889
Web site: www.wmmpa.com

Timber Products Manufacturers
  Association, Inc.
951 E. Third Avenue
Spokane, WA 99202
509-535-4646
E-mail: tpmspok@aol.com

Wood/Flooring

Maple Flooring Manufacturers
  Association
60 Revere Drive, Suite 500
Northbrook, IL 60062
847-480-9138
E-mail: mfma@maplefloor.com
Web site: www.maplefloor.com

National Oak Flooring
  Manufacturers Association/
  Oak Flooring Institute
PO Box 3009
Memphis, TN 38173
901-526-5016
Web site: www.nofma.org

National Wood Flooring
  Association
233 Old Meramec Station Road
Manchester, MO 63021
800-422-4556
E-mail: natlwood@aol.com
Web site: www.woodfloors.org

Wood/Paneling

Structural Insulated Panel
  Association
1511 K Street, NW, Suite 600
Washington, DC 20005
202-347-7800
E-mail: sip@xtn.net
Web site: www.natraweb.com

Consumer Guides and Hotlines

Asbestos Information Association
1745 Jefferson Davis Highway,
    Suite 406
Arlington, VA 22202
703-412-1150
E-mail: aiabjppigg@aol.com

*Consumer Guide to Home Energy
    Savings,* (Published by the
    American Council for an
    Energy-Efficient Economy)
202-429-0063

Consumer's Digest
800-272-0246

Consumer Information Center
18th and F Street, NW,
    Room G-142
Washington, DC 20405
202-501-1794
Web site: www.pueblo.gsa.gov

Consumer Product Safety
    Commission
Washington, DC 20207
800-638-2772

Consumer Reports
800-915-3377

800-Directory (to order)
800-426-8686

Environmental Information
    Association
3050 Presidential Drive, #101
Atlanta, GA 30340
888-343-4342
E-mail: nahhhcom@aol.com

Environmental Protection Agency
    (Headquarters)
401 M Street, SW
Washington, DC 20460
800-368-5888
202-457-4900
Web site: www.epa.gov

Environmental Protection—
    Agency Safe Drinking Water
    Hotline
800-426-4791

Radon Hotline
800-SOS-RADO

U.S. Consumer Products Safety
    Commission—Hearing
    Impaired Hotline
800-638-8270

U.S. Consumer Products Safety
    Commission Hotline
800-638-2772

Energy

American Council for an Energy-
    Efficient Economy
1001 Connecticut Avenue NW,
    Suite 801
Washington, DC 20036
202-429-8873
Web site: www.aceee.org

Development Center for
    Appropriate Technology
2105 East 32nd Street
Tuscon, AZ 85713
520-624-6628
Web site: www.netchaos.com

Energy Conservation and Services
Department
Pacific Gas and Electric Company
111 Alameda Boulevard
San Jose, CA 95115
800-933-9555
Web site: www.pge.com

Energy Efficient Building
Association
2950 Metro Drive, Suite 108
Minneapolis, MN 55425-1560
612-851-9940
E-mail: eebanews@aol.com
Web site: www.eeba.org

Energy Efficiency and Renewable
Energy Clearinghouse
Department of Energy
PO Box 3048
Merrifield, VA 22116
800-363-3732
Network Web site:
www.eren.doe.gov
Energy clearinghouse Web site:
erecbbs.nciinc.com
E-mail: doe.erec@nciinc.com
Web site: www.eren.coe.gov

Energy Information
Administration
Web site: www.eia.doe.gov

Wisconsin Energy Bureau
101 E. Wilson Street, 6th Floor
PO Box 7868
Madison, WI 53707
608-266-8234
Web site: www.doa.state.wi.uis/
deir/boe.htm

Solar Energy

International Solar Energy Society
The American Solar Energy
Society (Federal Energy
Management Program)
2400 Central Avenue, GI
Boulder, CO 80301
303-443-3130
Web site: sni.net/solar

Passive Solar Industries Council
1511 K Street NW, Suite 600
Washington, DC 20005
202-371-0357
Web site: www.psic.org

Solar Energy Industries
Association
122 C Street NW, 4th Floor
Washington, DC 20001
202-383-2600
Web site: www.seia.org

Engineers

American Academy of
Environmental Engineers
130 Holiday Court, #100
Annapolis, MD 21401
410-266-3311
301-261-8958
E-mail: aaee@ea.net
Web site: www.enviro-engrs.org

American Association of
Engineering Societies
1111 19th Street, Suite 608
Washington, DC 20036
202-296-2237
Web site: www.aaes.org/aaes

American Consulting Engineers
Council
1015 15th Street NW, Suite 802
Washington, DC 20005
202-347-7474
Web site: www.acec.org

American Engineers Association
PO Box 820473
Fort Worth, TX 76182
817-656-2324
Web site: www.aea.org

American Institute of Engineers
4666 San Pablo Dam Road, Suite 8
El Sobrante, CA 94803
510-223-8911
E-mail:aie@members-aie.org
Web site: www.members-aie.org

American Society of Civil
Engineers
1015 15th Street NW, Suite 600
Washington, DC 20005
800-548-2723
Web site: www.asce.org

American Society of Plumbing
Engineers
3617 Thousand Oaks Boulevard,
#210
Westlake Village, CA 91362
805-495-7120
E-mail: aspehq@aol.com
Web site: www.aspe.org

Applied Technology Council
555 Twin Dolphin Drive,
Suite 550
Redwood City, CA 94065
415-595-1542
Web site: www.atcouncil.org

Engineers Council
24310 Calvert Street
Woodland Hills, CA 91367
818-992-8292
E-mail: higg@ix.netcom.com
Web site:
www.engineerscouncil.org

Engineering Information Inc.
E-mail: ei@einet.ei.org

IEEE Engineering Management
Society
c/o Institute of Electrical and
Electronics Engineers
345 E. 47th Street
New York, NY 10017
212-705-7900
Web site: www.ieee.org

National Institute for Certification
in Engineering Technologies
1420 King Street
Alexandria, VA 22314-2794
888-476-4238
Web site: www.nicet.org

National Society of Professional
  Engineers
1420 King Street
Alexandria, VA 22314
703-684-2800
E-mail:
  customer.service@nspe.org
Web site: www.nspe.org

Engineering/Audio

Audio Engineering Society, Inc.
60 E. 42nd Street
New York, NY 10165
212-661-8528
Web site: www.aes.org

Government Agencies

Federal Housing Administration
U.S. Department of Housing and
  Urban Development
451 7th Street, SW,
Washington, DC 20410
800-245-2691
Web site: www.hud.com

Federal National Mortgage
  Association (Fannie Mae)
1900 Wisconsin Avenue NW
Washington, DC 20016
202-752-7000
Web site: www.fanniemae.com

U.S. Department of the Interior
National Park Service/
  Preservation Assistance
  Division
*Standards for Rehabilitation and
  Guidelines for Rehabilitating
  Historic Buildings*
1849 C Street NW
Washington, DC 20240
202-565-1180
Web site: www2.cr.nps.gov

U.S. Department of Veterans
  Affairs
1810 Vermont Avenue NW
Washington, DC 20420
202-273-5400
Web site: www.va.gov

Historic Preservation

Advisory Council on Historic
 Preservation
1100 Pennsylvania Avenue NW,
 Suite 809
Washington, DC 20004
202-606-8503
Web site: www.achp.gov

Historic Preservation
National Trust for Historic
 Preservation
1785 Massachusetts Avenue, NW
Washington, DC 20036
202-673-4000
Web site: www.nspe.org

Home Offices

National Association of Home
 Based Businesses, Inc.
10541 Mill Run Circle, Suite 400
Owings Mills, MD 21117
410-363-3698
Web site: www.usahome
 business.com

Horticulture/Greenhouses

American Horticultural Society
PO Box 0105
Mt. Vernon, VA 22121
703-768-5700
E-mail: gardenahs@aol.com

American Society of Horticultural
 Science
600 Cameron Street
Alexandria, VA 22314
703-836-4606
Web site: www.ashs.org

Hobby Greenhouse Association
8 Glen Terrace
Bedford, MA 01730
617-275-0377
E-mail: jhale@world.stb.com
Web site:
 www.hortsoft.com/hga.html

Horticultural Research Institute
1250 I Street NW, Suite 500
Washington , DC 20005
202-789-2900
Web site: www.anla.org

Professional Plant Growers
 Association
PO Box 27517
Lansing, MI 48909
800-647-7742
Web site: www.bpint.org

Housewares

National Housewares
  Manufacturers Association
6400 Shafer Court, Suite 650
Rosemont, IL 60018
847-292-4200
Web site: www.housewares.org

Inspections

American Society of Home
  Inspectors
85 W. Algonquin Road
Arlington Heights, IL 60005
800-743-2744
Palatine, IL 60095
Web site: www.ashi.com

Association of Construction
  Inspectors
8383 E. Evans Road
Scottsdale, AZ 85260
602-998-8021
E-mail: aci@iami.org
Web site: www.iami.org/aci.iam

The Housing Inspection
  Foundation/The Association
  of Home Inspectors
8383 E. Evans Road
Scottsdale, AZ 85260
602-998-4422
E-mail: hif@iami.org
Web site: www.iami.org

National Association of Home
  Inspectors
4248 Park Glen Road
Minneapolis, MN 55416
800-448-3942
Web site: www.nahi.org

Insurance

American Insurance Association
1130 Connecticut Avenue NW,
  Suite 1000
Washington, DC 20036
202-828-7100
202-828-7183
Web site: www.aiadc.org

American Insurance Services
  Group
85 Street John Street
New York, NY 10038
212-669-0400
Web site: www.aisg.org

Associated Risk Managers
  International
816 Congress Avenue, Suite 990
Austin, TX 78701
512-479-6886
Web site: www.arminet.com

Insurance Information Institute
110 William Street
New York, NY 10038
212-669-9200
800-942-4242 (hotline)
E-mail: iiilibrary@aol.com
Web site: www.iii.org

Insurance Institute of America
720 Providence Road
Malvern, PA 19355
800-644-2101
E-mail: cserv@cpcuiia.org

Insurance Institute for Property
  Loss Reduction
73 Tremont Street, Suite 510
Boston, MA 02108
617-722-0200
Web site: www.iiplr.org

Mortgage Insurance Companies of
  America
727 15th Street NW, 12th Floor
Washington, DC 20005
202-393-5566
Web site: www.digitalrelease.com

National Association of
  Catastrophe Adjusters
PO Box 821864
North Richland Hills, TX 76182
817-498-3466
E-mail: nacatadj@aol.com
Web site:
  www.metrongroup.com/naca

National Association of
  Independent Insurance
  Adjusters
300 W. Washington, Suite 805
Chicago, IL 60606
312-853-0808
E-mail: naiiachgo@aol.com

National Association of Insurance
  Brokers
1300 I Street NW, Suite 900 E
Washington, DC 20005
202-628-6700
E-mail: jmoore@naib.org

National Association of Mutual
  Insurance Companies
3601 Vincennes Road
PO Box 68700
Indianapolis, IN 46268
800-33-NAMIC
Web site: www.namic.org

National Association of
  Professional Insurance Agents
400 N. Washington Street
Alexandria, VA 22314
703-836-9340
E-mail: piaweb@planet.org
Web site: www.pianet.com

National Association of Surety
  Bond Producers
5225 Wisconsin Avenue NW,
  Suite 600
Washington DC 20015
202-686-3700
Web site: www.nasbp.org

Risk and Insurance Management
  Society
655 3rd Avenue, 2nd floor
New York, NY 10017
212-286-9292
Web site: www.rims.org

Society of Actuaries
475 N. Martingale Road, Suite 800
Schaumburg, IL 60173
847-706-3500
Web site: www.soa.org

Surety Information Office
5225 Wisconsin Avenue NW,
  Suite 600
Washington, DC 20015
202-686-7463
Web site: www.sio.org

Insurance/Title Groups

American Land Title Association
1828 L Street NW
Washington, DC 20036
800-787-AITA (2482)
Web site: www.alta.org

Title One Home Improvement
   Lenders Association
1625 Massachusetts Avenue NW,
   Suite 601
Washington, DC 20036
202-939-1770
Web site: www.titleone.org

Interior Design

American Center for Design
233 E. Ontario Street, Suite 500
Chicago, IL 60611
312-787-2018
Web site: www.ac4d.org

American Furniture
   Manufacturers Association
PO Box HP-7
High Point, NC 27261
910-884-5000
Web site: www.afmahp.org

American Society of Interior
   Design
608 Massachusetts Avenue NE
Washington, DC 20002
202-546-3480
800-775-2743
Web site: www.interiors.org

Interior Design Society
PO Box 2396
High Point, NC 27261
800-888-9590
Web site:
   www.interiordesign society.org

International Interior Design
   Association
341 Merchandise Mart, Suite 341
Chicago, IL 60654
888-799-IIDA (4432)
Web site: www.iida.com

National Decorating Products
   Association
403 Axminister Drive
St. Louis, MO 63026
800-737-0107
Web site: www.pdra.org

National Home Furnishings
   Association
PO Box 2596
High Point, NC 27260
800-888-9590
Web site:
   www.homefurnish.com/NHFA

Floor Coverings

Carpet Cushion Council
(Affiliated with the Independent
Textile Testing Service, Inc.)
PO Box 546
Riverside, CT 06878
203-637-1312
Web site: www.ittslab.com

Carpet and Rug Institute
310 Holiday Avenue
PO Box 2048
Dalton, GA 30722
800-882-8846
Web site: www.carpet-rug.com

Contractors Co-Op Council
7077 Orangewood Avenue,
Suite 120
Garden Grove, CA 92641
714-898-0583
E-mail: contractorscoop
@worldnet.att.net

Dalton Floor Covering Market
Association
415 E. Walnut Avenue, Suite 204
Dalton, GA 30721
800-288-4101
Web site: www.carpets.org

Floor Covering Installation
Contractors Association
PO Box 948
Dalton, GA 30722
706-226-5488
Web site: www.fcica.com

National Association of Floor
Covering Distributors
401 N. Michigan Avenue,
Suite 2200
Chicago, IL 60611
312-644-6610
Web site: www.nafcd.org

Oriental Rug Importers
Association
100 Park Plaza Drive
Secaucus, NJ 07094
201-866-5054
201-866-6169 (Fax)

Resilient Floor Covering Institute
966 Hungerford Drive, Suite 12-B
Rockville, MD 20850
301-340-8580
Web site: www.buildernet.com

Window Coverings

Window Covering Manufacturers
Association
355 Lexington Avenue, 17th Floor
New York, NY 10017
212-661-4261
E-mail: assoc.mgmt@aol.com

Job Cost Estimating

HomeTech Information Systems
5161 River Road
Bethesda, MD 20816
800-638-8292
Web site:
www.hometechonline.com

R. S. Means Company, Inc.
100 Construction Plaza
PO Box 800
Kingston, MA 20816
800-334-3509
Web site: www.rsmeans.com

Landscape Associations and Nurseries

American Nursery and Landscape
Association
1250 I Street NW
Suite 500
Washington, DC 20005
202-789-2900
Web site: www.anla.org

The American Society of
Landscape Architects
636 Eye Street NW
Washington, DC 20001
202-898-2444
Web site: www.asla.org/asla

Associated Landscape Contractors
of America
150 Elden Street, Suite 270
Herndon, VA 20170
703-736-9666
800-395-ALCA (2522)
Web site: www.alca.org

Associated Professional
Landscape Designers
11 South LaSalle Street,
Suite 1400
Chicago, IL 60603
312-201-0101
Web site: www.apld.com

Council of Tree and Landscape
Appraisers
15245 Shady Grove Road,
Suite 130
Rockville, MD 20850
301-947-0487
E-mail: msp@mgmtsol.com

Landscape Communications
1560 Brookhollow Drive,
Suite 222
Santa Ana, CA 92705
714-979-IRLA (4752)
Web site: www.landscape
online.com

Landscape Architecture
Foundation
4401 Connecticut Avenue NW,
5th Floor
Washington, DC 20009
202-686-0068
Web site: www.alsa.org/alsa

Landscape Contractors
Association
9053 Shady Grove Court
Gaithersburg, MD 20877
301-948-0810
E-mail: lca@mgmtsol.com

Lawn and Garden Marketing &
  Distribution Association
1900 Arch Street
Philadelphia, PA 19103
215-564-3484
E-mail: assnhqt@netaxs.com

The Lawn Institute
1501 Johnson Ferry Road NE,
  Suite 200
Marietta, GA 30062
770-977-5492
Web site: www.lawninstitute.com

National Gardening Association
180 Flynn Avenue
Burlington, VT 05401
802-863-1308
Web site: www.garden.org

National Landscape Association
1250 I Street NW, Suite 500
Washington, DC 20005
202-789-2900
Web site: www.anla.org

Professional Lawn Care
  Association of America
1000 Johnson Ferry Road NE,
  Suite C-135
Marietta, GA 30068
800-458-3466
Web site: www.plcaa.org

Trees

American Association of
  Botanical Gardens & Arboreta
786 Church Road
Wayne, PA 19087
610-688-1120
E-mail: aabga@aol.com
Web site:
  www.aabga.mobot.org/aabga

American Society of Consulting
  Arborists
15245 Shady Grove Road,
  Suite 130
Rockville, MD 20850
301-947-0483
E-mail: asca@mgmtsol.com

Forests/American Forestry
  Association
1516 P Street NW
PO Box 2002
Washington, DC 20005
800-368-5748
Web site: www.amfor.org

International Society of
  Arboriculture
PO Box GG
Savoy, IL 51874
217-355-9411
Web site: www.ag.uiuc.edu

National Arborist Association
Route 101 PO Box 1094
Amherst, NH 03031
603-673-3311
Web site: www.natlarb.com

Landscape/Irrigation

American Association (Society) of
   Irrigation Consultants
PO Box 426
Byron, CA 94514
510-516-1124
Web site: www.asic.org/asic

Irrigation Association
8260 Willow Oaks Corporate
   Drive, Suite 120
Fairfax, VA 22031
703-573-3551
Web site: www.irrigation.org

Lath and Plaster

Minnesota Lath and Plaster
   Bureau/International Institute of
   Lath and Plaster (Other bureaus
   in Los Angeles, San Francisco,
   Seattle, Chicago, St. Louis,
   Denver, South Carolina, Dallas,
   and Georgia)
820 Transfer Road
St. Paul, MN 55114
612-645-0208
612-645-0209 (Fax)

Real Estate

American Homeowners
   Foundation
6776 Little Falls Road
Arlington, VA 22213
800-489-7776
E-mail: amerhome@aol.com

Institute of Real Estate
   Management
430 N. Michigan Avenue
Chicago, IL 60611
800-837-0706
Web site: www.irem.org

National Association of Master
   Appraisers
303 W. Cypress Street
PO Box 12617
San Antonio, TX 78212
800-229-6262
Web site:
   www.appraisalfoundation.org

National Association of Real
   Estate Brokers
1629 K Street NW, Suite 602
Washington, DC 20006
202-785-4477
Web site: www.nareb.org

National Association of Real
   Estate Companies
PO Box 958
Columbia, MD 21044
410-992-6476
Web site: www.narec.inter.net

National Association of
   REALTORS®
430 N. Michigan Avenue
Chicago, IL 60611
312-329-8200
Web site: www.realtor.com

National Association of Real
   Estate Appraisers
8383 E. Evans Road
Scottsdale, AZ 85260
602-948-8000
E-mail: narea@iami.org
Web site: iami.org.narea.html

National Realty Committee
1420 New York Avenue NW,
   Suite 1100
Washington, DC 20005
202-639-8400
E-mail: e-mail@nrc.org

Real Estate Brokerage Managers
   Council
430 N. Michigan Avenue
Chicago, IL 60611
800-621-8738
Web site: www.crb.com

REALTORS® Land Institute
430 N. Michigan Avenue
Chicago, IL 60611
312-329-8440
Web site: www.rliland.com

Security

Central Station Alarm Association
7101 Wisconsin Avenue,
   Suite 901
Bethesda, MD 20814
301-907-0045
Web site: www.csaaul.org

International Security
   Management Association
66 Charles Street, Suite 280
Boston, MA 02114
319-381-4008
E-mail: isma3@aol.com

National Alarm Association
   of America
PO Box 3409
Dayton, OH 45401
800-283-6285
Web site: www.naaa.org

National Burglar and Fire Alarm
   Association
7101 Wisconsin Avenue,
   Suite 901
Bethesda, MD 20814
301-907-3202
Web site: www.nbfaa.com

Site Planning

American Congress on Surveying
  and Mapping
5410 Grosvenor Lane, Suite 100
Bethesda, MD 20814
301-493-0200
Web site: www.acsm-hdqtrs.
  org/acsm/

International Erosion Control
  Association
1355 S. Lincoln
PO Box 774904
Steamboat Springs, CO 80477
800-455-4322
Web site: www.ieca.org

International Institute of Site
  Planning
715 G Street SE
Washington, DC 20003
202-546-2322
E-mail: coffin.coffin@erols.com

Space Planners

Residential Space Planners
  International
20 Ardmore Drive
Minneapolis, MN 55422
800-548-0945

Trade Commissions

Italian Trade Commission
1801 Avenue of the Stars,
  Suite 700
Los Angeles, CA 90067
213-879-0950
E-mail: itc@westnet.com
Web site: www.socma.com

Universal Design

The Center for Universal Design
North Carolina State University
    School of Design
PO Box 8613
Raleigh, NC 27695
919-515-3082
Web site: www.design.ncsu.edu

The Eastern Paralyzed Veterans
    Association (Free booklet
    Planning for Access)
Architecture Department
75-20 Astoria Boulevard
Jackson Heights, NY 11370
800-444-0102 (Fax)

The Granite State Independent
    Living Foundation
PO Box 7268
Concord, NH 03301
603-228-9680
Web site:
    www.mv.com/ipusers/gsilf

Water

American Ground Water Trust
16 Centre Street
Concord, NH 03301
800-423-7748
E-mail: agwthq@aol.com
Web site: www.agwt.org

National Ground Water
    Association
601 Dempsey Road
Westerville, OH 43081
800-551-7379
Web site: www.ngwa.org

National Rural Water Association
PO Box 1428
Duncan, OK 73534
405-252-0629
Web site: www.nrwa.org

Water Quality Association
4151 Naperville Road
Lisle, IL 60532
630-505-0160
Web site: www.wqa.org

Resources

American Seed Trade Association
703-823-8963
Web site: www.amseed.com

Building and Home Improvement
    Products Network
E-mail: build@build.com
Web site: www.build.com

Building and Remodeling News
201-327-1600
Web site: www.buildand
   remodel.com/tiptrick.htm

Building Products Database
E-mail: info@connel.com
Web site: www.connel.com/bpd

Thomas Regional Directory
   Company, Inc. (Resource guide)
Five Penn Plaza
New York, NY 10001
212-629-2100

The Council of Better Business
   Bureaus, Inc.
4200 Wilson Boulevard
Arlington, VA 22203
703-276-0100
Web site: www.bbb.org

Design Works, Inc.
   (For 3-D home kit models)
11 Hitching Post Road
Amherst, MA 01002
413-549-4763

Shop-at-Home
PO Box 221050
Denver, Colorado 80222
800-315-1995

World Energy Council 1998
   Congress
Web site: www.wec98congress.org

Entertainment

General Electric
Appliance Park 6, Room 129
Louisville, KY 40225
800-626-2000

Sony Electronics, Inc. (radio, TV)
12451 Gateway Boulevard
Ft. Myers, FL 33913
800-222-7669

Guides

Ceramic Tile Trade Magazines
Tile & Decorative Surfaces
Published monthly by Tile &
   Decorative Surfaces
   Publishing Inc.
818-704-5555
818-704-6500 (Fax)

FEMA Map Service Center
Baltimore, MD
800-358-9616
(Call to order maps of a particular
   area of the country or even a
   particular county that show
   typography, flood plains,
   climate, etc. Cost: 50 cents
   per map.)

International Tile & Stone
  Exposition
404-747-9400 (For details
  and location)

Materials and Methods Standards
  Association (Produces bulletins
  on materials and methods of
  installation for ceramic tile and
  dimensional stone products)
616-842-7844

National Contractor's Association
  Reference Manual
601-939-2071

Remodeling Magazine
Remodeling Reprints
One Thomas Circle NW, Suite 600
Washington, DC 20005

Tile Letter
National Tile Contractors
  Association
PO Box 13629
Jackson, MS 39236
601-939-2071

Instructional Videos

Investing in a Dream:
  A Guide to Getting the
  Home You Really Want
800-365-ARCH (2724)

Setting Tile by Michael Byrne
Tauton Press
800-283-7252

U-Tile-It Yourself Video Series
Produced by Lam Productions
619-273-0572

More Useful Web Sites and Online Resources

American Home Improvement
  Network
www.improvemnet.com
  (Trends in home improvement)

Benjamin Moore
www.benjaminmoore.com
  (Offers tips on making changes
  to a room that the homeowner
  can do.)

CE On-Line (*Construction
  Equipment* magazine)
www.coneq.com

Designing with Tile (Van Nostrand
  Reinhold) by Carolyn Coyle
(Order through Tile Heritage
  Foundation)
707-431-8453

Do-It-Yourself: Home Portfolio
www.homeportfolio.com (100,000
  resources)

Edison Electric Institute
www.eei.org

Everpure (water free of impurities)
www.everpure.com

Geotechnics America, Inc. (soil
   improvement contractor)
422 Seaboard Drive
Matthews, NC 28105
704-821-9017
Web site: www.geotechnics.com

HouseNet Web site
www.housenet.com (Remodeling
   tips and suggestions of what you
   should and should not do
   yourself.)

Home Equity: A Consumer's
   Guide to Loans and Lines
HSH Associations
Department HEQ
1200 Route 23
Butler, NJ 07405

ITS/ETLHVAC Group
www.etl-havac.com

The Northeast Sustainable Energy
   Associaton
www.nesea.org

Remodeling
www.dreamremodeling.com

Setting Tile by Michael Byrne
   (with companion videos)
Tauton Press
800-283-7252

3D Home Architect (Program you
   can download from Web site:
   www.askjeeves.com)

United States Healthy House
   Institute
www.hhinst.com

To Get the Lowest Interest Rates Possible:

www.hsh.com
www.bankrate.com
www.cardtrak.com

Bibliography

American Institute of Architects. "Home Delivery." New York: 1-22.

"Annual Inquiry and Complaint Summary." Council of Better Business Bureaus Information Series, Arlington, Virginia (1996).

"Attics." Information Technology Specialists, Inc. (January 25, 1998).

Barrett, Amy and Kathleen Morris. "The Rage to Refinance." *Business Week* (December 1, 1997): 36.

Blankenbaker, E. Keith *Modern Plumbing.* Tinley Park, Illinois: Goodheart-Willcox Co., 1997.

Bolt, Steve. *Roofing the Right Way.* New York: McGraw-Hill, 1997.

Bowman, Daria Price and Maureen LaMarca. *Pleasures of the Porch.* New York: Rizzoli, 1997.

Brown, Sheri. "Moving Checklist." from the Web site indyrealtor.com (1998).

Buchholz, Barbara B. *For Your Home: Bathrooms.* New York: Friedman/Fairfax Publishing, 1996.

Buchholz, Barbara B. and Margaret Crane, "Home Is Where the Office Is." *St. Louis Magazine* (November 1997): 68-72.

"Builders Survey of Construction Costs." Economics Department of the National Association of Home Builders paper, Washington, D.C., (November 1995).

Calloway, Stephen, general editor. *The Elements of Style.* New York: Simon & Schuster, 1996.

Campbell, Richard B. "Planting Instructions." *Flowers of Tomorrow,* Parma, Idaho, Web site.

———. "Landscaping Options for the Homeowner." Campbell's Nurseries and Garden Centers paper, Lincoln, Nebraska.

Cauldwell, Rex. *Wiring a House.* Newtown, Connecticut: The Taunton Press, 1996.

"Characteristics of New Single Family Homes." National Association of Home Builders survey, Washington, D.C. (1971–1996).

"Citizen's Guide to the Board of the Zoning Adjustment Variance Process," Board of Zoning and Adjustment in St. Louis County (1998).

Communities magazine, the Fellowship for Intentional Community, Rt. 1, Box 155-B, Rutledge, MO, 63563 (800-995-8342).

Communities Directory, published by Fellowship for Intentional Community, Rt. 1, Box 155-B, Rutledge, Missouri 63563 (800-995-8342).

Coy, Peter. "Home Sweet Office." *Business Week* (April 6, 1998): 30.

Crane, Margaret. "Stellar Cellars." *St. Louis Homes and Lifestyles* (November/December 1996): 49–57.

Craze, Richard. *Practical Feng Shui.* New York: Lorenz Books, 1997.

Davidson, James. *The Complete Home Lighting Book.* Woodstock, New York: The Overlook Press, 1997.

"Discover the Pleasure of Gardening." American Nursery and Landscape Association (formerly American Association of Nurserymen) Newsletter (1997).

"Discover the Pleasure of Gardening." American Nursery and Landscape Association Newsletter (1997–98).

Encyclopedia of Associations. Detroit: Gale Research, 1998.

Ferguson, Myron E. *Build It Right.* Salem, Oregon: Home User Press, 1997.

Greenberg, Martin, editor. "101 Great Money-Making Tips." *Money* magazine, Time, Inc. (1995): 34, 48–52.

Hale, Janice L., publications director. "Build a Hobby Greenhouse," paper produced for the Hobby Greenhouse Association, Bedford, Massachusetts: (1996).

———. *Directory of Manufacturers.* Hobby Greenhouse Association (1998).

———. "Which Greenhouse Configuration Is for You?" Hobby Greenhouse Association paper (1996).

———. "You and Your Residential Greenhouse." Hobby Greenhouse Association paper (October 24, 1996).

Harvey, David A. "ISDN Routers." *Home Office Computing.* Buffalo, New York: (March 1998): 83–90.

Holmes, Kendall, senior editor, "Step by Step." *Remodeling* magazine (March 1994).

"Hot Housing Market Gives Workers Edge." *USA Today* (February 9, 1998): 1B.

"Home Plan Ideas." *Better Homes and Gardens Special Interest Publications* (Spring 1998): 1–160.

"Home Buyers Go Big." *USA Today* (December 8, 1997): 1B.

House Beautiful Home Building Magazine. Hearst Special Publication (Spring 1998): 1–112.

Hube, Karen. "Weary of Private Mortgage Insurance? 'Piggyback' Loan Offers an Alternative." *The Wall Street Journal* (January 29, 1998): C1.

——. "In the Wild West of Subprime Lending, Borrowers Have to Dodge Many Bullets." *The Wall Street Journal* (March 18, 1998): C1.

Jeswald, Peter. *Homework: Ten Steps to Foolproof Planning Before Building.* Berkeley, California: Ten Speed Press, 1995.

Kaufman, Donald and Taffy Dahl. *Color.* New York: Clarkson Potter, 1992.

Keating, Bob. "Your Dog and Backyard Landscaping." InSync Design & Publishing (Internet 1998).

"Landscape Architect." Michigan Occupational Information System Web site (1998).

Lieberman, Dan and Paul Hoffman. *Renovating Your Home for Maximum Profit.* Prima Publishing and Communications, Rocklin, California, 1994.

Madden, Chris Cassan. *Kitchens.* New York: Clarson Potter, 1993.

Maney, Susan, editor. National Association of the Remodeling Industry, Inc., *The Master Plan: For Professional Home Remodeling.* Hachette Filipacchi Magazines, Inc., publishers of *Women's Day* Special Interest Publications, Inc., New York: 1–90.

McNichols, Janet. "Homeowners Seek to Tell Contractor Their Troubles, But He Doesn't Show." *St. Louis Post-Dispatch* (Feb. 2, 1998): W1.

Miller, Judith. *The Style SourceBook.* New York: Stewart, Tabori & Chang, 1998.

Molloy, William J. *The Complete Home Buyer's Bible.* New York: John Wiley & Sons, Inc., 1996.

Moriarty, Ann Marie, senior editor. "The ABCs of Remodeling." *Remodeling* magazine (1991).

"Mover Quotes." Microsurf Internet Services, Inc. (1997).

"Moving Tips." Bekins Movers (1998).

"Packing Tips" and "Boxes and Moving Supplies." Ryder Moving Services Web site (1998).

Paxton, Albert S. *The 1998 National Repair & Remodeling Estimator.* Carlsbad, California: Craftsman Book Co., 1998.

Pearson, David. *The Natural House Catalog.* New York: Fireside Book, 1996.

Petit, Jack. "Realtors: Trees a Plus." Urban Forests (August/September 1994): 7.

Pollen, Michael. *A Place of My Own.* New York: Delta, 1997.

Pruitt, Eric. "Types of Mortgage Loans." REMAX Northern Palm Beaches Web site by Electronic Brochures Inc. (1998).

"Radon Realities." *Better Homes and Gardens* (May 1995): 99.

Ramsey, Dan. *The Complete Idiot's Guide to Smart Moving.* New York: Alpha Books, Prentice Hall, 1998.

Ramsey, Dan and Century 21® editors. *Guide to Remodeling Your Home: The Basics of Planning, Financing, and Implementing Your Project.* Chicago: Real Estate Education Company, 1997.

"Residential Landscape Design." Alabama Cooperative Extension System Web site (1998).

"Residential Room Additions." St. Louis County Department of Public Works brochure.

Rewiski, Renee, editor, "Refrigerator Issues." *Building and Remodeling News* (November 1995).

———. "Oven Issues" (November 1995).

———. "Cooktop Issues" (November 1995).

———. "Venting a Hood" (November 1995).

———. "Installing Kitchen Cabinets" (November 1995).

———. "Fitting Kitchen Cabinets" (November 1995).

Scutella, Richard. *How to Plan, Contract, and Build Your Own Home.* New York: McGraw Hill, 1991.

"The Secretary of the Interior's Standards for Rehabilitation and Guidelines for Rehabilitating Historic Buildings." U.S. Department of the Interior, National Park Service, Preservation Assistance Division (Revised 1983).

Shaw, Lisa, editor. *Everything You Always Wanted to Know about Moving to the Country.* Grafton, New Hampshire: Move to the Country Catalog.

———. *Moving to the Country Once & For All.* Grafton, New Hampshire: Move to the Country Catalog.

Snow, Jane Moss and National Association of Home Builders. "Dreams to Beams: A Guide to Building the Home You've Always Wanted." National Association of Home Builders (1988).

Stevens, David. *The Outdoor Room.* New York: Random House, 1994.

"Style, Women Want Flexible Living Space" and "Low Interest Rates Light Up Home Sales." *USA Today* (January 20, 1998): 8D, 1B.

"Tips for Consumers: Mortgage Choices." Council of Better Business Bureaus brochure (1997).

"Tips for Moving to a New Home." AMJ Campbell Van Lines brochure (1998).

"The Ultimate in Wine Cellars." Bacchus Wine Storage Web site (March 1, 1998).

Weeks, Kay D. "Preservation Briefs." U.S. Department of the Interior, National Park Service, Preservation Assistance Division/Technical Preservation Services manual.

Weimer, Jan. *Kitchen Redos, Revamps, Remodels, and Replacements.* New York: William Morrow and Co., Inc., 1997.

Wenz, Philip S. *Adding to a House.* Newtown, Connecticut: Taunton Press, 1995.

West, Bob. "Looks Aren't Everything." *Lawn & Landscape* magazine (March 1997): 103–105.

Wilthide, Elizabeth. *Floors.* New York: Stewart, Tabori & Chang, 1997.

Index